Airline
Transport Pilot
ORAL
EXAM
GUIDE

MICHAEL D. HAYES

SIXTH EDITION

COMPREHENSIVE PREPARATION
FOR THE FAA CHECKRIDE

AVIATION SUPPLIES & ACADEMICS, INC.
NEWCASTLE, WASHINGTON

Airline Transport Pilot Oral Exam Guide
Sixth Edition
by Michael D. Hayes

Aviation Supplies & Academics, Inc.
7005 132nd Place SE
Newcastle, Washington 98059
asa@asa2fly.com | 425-235-1500 | asa2fly.com

ASA-OEG-ATP6

ISBN   978-1-64425-311-3

Additional formats available:
eBook EPUB   ISBN 978-1-64425-312-0
eBook PDF   ISBN 978-1-64425-313-7

Printed in the United States of America
2027   2026   2025   2024   2023   9   8   7   6   5   4   3   2   1

Library of Congress Cataloging-in-Publication Data

Names: Hayes, Michael D., author.
Title: Airline transport pilot oral exam guide : comprehensive preparation for the FAA checkride /
    Michael D. Hayes.
Other titles: Oral exam guide : comprehensive preparation for the FAA checkride
Description: Sixth edition. | Newcastle, Washington : Aviation Supplies & Academics, Inc., 2023. |
    "ASA-OEG-ATP6"—Title page verso
Identifiers: LCCN 2023026926 (print) | LCCN 2023026927 (ebook) | ISBN 9781644253113
    (trade paperback) | ISBN 9781644253120 (epub) | ISBN 9781644253137 (pdf)
Subjects: LCSH: Airplanes—Piloting—Examination—Study guides. | Airplanes—Piloting—
    Examinations, questions, etc. | Air pilots—Licenses—United States.
Classification: LCC TL710 .H36 2023 (print) | LCC TL710 (ebook) | DDC 629.132/5216076—dc23/
    eng/20230629
LC record available at https://lccn.loc.gov/2023026926
LC ebook record available at https://lccn.loc.gov/2023026927

This guide is dedicated to the many talented students, pilots and flight instructors I have had the opportunity to work with over the years. Also, special thanks to Mark Hayes and many others who supplied the patience, encouragement, and understanding necessary to complete the project.

—M.D.H.

Contents

Introduction ix

1 **Operation of Systems** 1
   A. Landing Gear 2
   B. Powerplant 5
   C. Propellers 13
   D. Fuel System 15
   E. Oil System 19
   F. Hydraulic System 21
   G. Electrical System 23
   H. Pneumatic and Environmental Systems 28
   I. Avionics and Communications 37
   J. Ice Protection 50
   K. Crewmember and Passenger Equipment 52
   L. Flight Controls 55
   M. Pitot-Static System 58
   N. Fire and Smoke Detection, Protection, and Suppression ... 59
   O. Envelope Protection 63
   P. Minimum Equipment List and Configuration Deviation List 65

2 **Performance and Limitations** 71
   A. Takeoff and Climb 72
   B. Cruise 84
   C. Descent and Landing 86
   D. Limitations 91
   E. Deicing and Anti-Icing Procedures 96
   F. Weight and Balance 100

Contents

3 **Weather Information** **107**
   A. Weather Sources...108
   B. Weather Products..109
     Observations 110
     Analysis 114
     Forecasts 116
   C. Meteorology 125
     Atmospheric Composition and Stability.......................125
     Wind..128
     Temperature...131
     Moisture/Precipitation 132
     *Weather System Formation, Including Air Masses
       and Fronts* 134
     Clouds 136
     Turbulence..138
     Jetstream 139
     Clear Air Turbulence...140
     Thunderstorms and Microbursts 142
     Icing and Freezing Level Information............................145
     Fog and Mist 150
     Frost 152
     Obstructions to Visibility.......................................154
   D. Flight Deck Weather and Aeronautical Information 156
   E. Low-Visibility Operations...159
   F. Flight Risk Assessment Tools 161

4 **High Altitude Aerodynamics** **163**
   A. High Altitude Operations 164
   B. Stall Prevention and Recovery Training 176
   C. Upset Prevention and Recovery Training 185

5 **Air Carrier Operations**.. **195**
   A. Turbine Engine Operations 196
   B. Automation...199
   C. Navigation and Flightpath Warning Systems..........................203
   D. High Altitude Emergencies 209

E. Crew Communications...215

F. Checklist Philosophy..219

G. Operational Control..224

H. Ground Operations...226

I. Leadership and Professionalism...229

J. Crew Resource Management 233

K. Safety Culture..238

L. Operations Specifications..243

6 **Human Factors** **247**

A. Flight Physiology 248

B. Fitness for Flight 261

C. ADM Using CRM..264

7 **The Code of Federal Regulations** **273**

A. 14 CFR Part 1..274

B. 14 CFR Part 61..275

C. 14 CFR Part 91..284

D. 14 CFR Part 111 303

General..303

Access to and Evaluation of Records 305

Reporting of Records..307

Pilot Access and Responsibilities...309

PRD Web Resources...311

E. 14 CFR Part 117..311

F. 14 CFR Part 121...315

G. 14 CFR Part 135...330

H. 49 CFR Part 830 (NTSB)..341

Appendix 1 FAA ATP Qualifications Job Aid................................345

Appendix 2 Applicant's Practical Test Checklist...........................349

Introduction

The *Airline Transport Pilot Oral Exam Guide* is a comprehensive guide designed for pilots who are involved in training for the Airline Transport Pilot Certificate. This book will also prove beneficial for those pilots transitioning to turbine aircraft or who have been accepted and are preparing for entry into an initial training course at an airline ground school or ATP Certification Training Program (ATP CTP). It's also a great tool for pilots wanting to maintain and/or refresh their knowledge.

The *Airline Transport Pilot and Type Rating for Airplane Airman Certification Standards* (FAA-S-ACS-11) specifies the areas of operation and tasks in which knowledge must be demonstrated by the applicant before issuance of an ATP Certificate with an Airplane category Multiengine class rating or an ATP Certificate issued with a type rating. This book contains questions and answers pertaining to those areas, as well as references to source material where additional detailed information can be found.

Questions and answers are organized into seven chapters. The first two chapters cover aircraft systems and performance and limitations. The next four chapters include information on weather, high altitude aerodynamics, air carrier operations, and human factors. The last chapter provides a review of the Federal Aviation Regulations (14 CFR Parts 1, 61, 91, 111, 117, 121, and 135, and 49 CFR Part 830). At the end of this guide are two appendixes. Appendix A contains the FAA's ATP Airplane Multiengine Applicant Qualifications Job Aid, which provides the specific requirements for the ATP practical test. Appendix B contains an ATP Practical Test Checklist to be used when making final preparations for the checkride.

This book may be supplemented with other comprehensive study materials as noted in parentheses after each question; for example: (FAA-H-8083-28). The abbreviations for these materials and their titles are listed below. If no reference is given after a question, the answer for that question was researched from interviews with airline pilots, Part 121/135 operators, and examiners. Be sure to use the latest references when reviewing for the test. Also, check the ASA website at **asa2fly.com/oegatp** for the most recent updates to this book due to changes in FAA procedures and regulations as well as for Reader Resources containing additional relevant information and updates.

14 CFR Part 1	*Definitions and Abbreviations*
14 CFR Part 23	*Airworthiness Standards: Normal Category Airplanes*
14 CFR Part 25	*Airworthiness Standards: Transport Category Airplanes*
14 CFR Part 61	*Certification: Pilots, Flight Instructors, and Ground Instructors*
14 CFR Part 91	*General Operating and Flight Rules*
14 CFR Part 111	*Pilot Records Database*
14 CFR Part 117	*Flight and Duty Limitations and Rest Requirements: Flightcrew Members*
14 CFR Part 119	*Certification: Air Carriers and Commercial Operators*
14 CFR Part 121	*Operating Requirements: Domestic, Flag, and Supplemental Operations*
14 CFR Part 125	*Certification and Operations: Airplanes Having a Seating Capacity of 20 or More Passengers or a Maximum Payload Capacity of 6,000 Pounds or More; and Rules Governing Persons on Board Such Aircraft*
14 CFR Part 135	*Operating Requirements: Commuter and On Demand Operations and Rules Governing Persons On Board Such Aircraft*
AC 00-33	*Nickel-Cadmium Battery Operational, Maintenance and Overhaul Practices*
AC 00-63	*Use of Cockpit Displays of Digital Weather and Aeronautical Information*
AC 20-147	*Turbojet, Turboprop, Turboshaft, and Turbofan Engine Induction System Icing and Ice Ingestion*
AC 20-186	*Airworthiness and Operational Approval of Cockpit Voice Recorder Systems*

AC 23-18	*Installation of Terrain Awareness and Warning System (TAWS) Approved for Part 23 Airplanes*
AC 25.1329	*Approval of Flight Guidance Systems*
AC 25-23	*Airworthiness Criteria for the Installation Approval of a Terrain Awareness and Warning System (TAWS) for Part 25 Airplanes*
AC 25-31	*Takeoff Performance Data for Operations on Contaminated Runways*
AC 60-22	*Aeronautical Decision Making*
AC 61-83	*Nationally Scheduled, FAA-Approved, Industry-Conducted Flight Instructor Refresher Course*
AC 61-98	*Currency Requirements and Guidance for the Flight Review and Instrument Proficiency Check*
AC 61-107	*Aircraft Operations at Altitudes Above 25,000 Feet MSL or Mach Numbers Greater Than .75*
AC 61-138	*Airline Transport Pilot Certification Training Program*
AC 61-139	*Institution of Higher Education's Application for Authority to Certify its Graduates for an Airline Transport Pilot Certificate with Reduced Aeronautical Experience*
AC 90-107	*Guidance for Localizer Performance with Vertical Guidance and Localizer Performance without Vertical Guidance Approach Operations in the U.S.*
AC 90-114	*Automatic Dependent Surveillance–Broadcast Operations*
AC 90-117	*Data Link Communications*
AC 91.21-1	*Use of Portable Electronic Devices Aboard Aircraft*
AC 91-70	*Oceanic and Remote Continental Airspace Operations*
AC 91-73	*Parts 91 and 135 Single Pilot, Flight School Procedures During Taxi Operations*
AC 91-74	*Pilot Guide: Flight in Icing Conditions*
AC 91-79	*Mitigating the Risks of a Runway Overrun Upon Landing*

AC 91-85	*Authorization of Aircraft and Operators for Flight in Reduced Vertical Separation Minimum (RVSM) Airspace*
AC 117-2	*Fatigue Education and Awareness Training Program*
AC 117-3	*Fitness for Duty*
AC 120-27	*Aircraft Weight and Balance Control*
AC 120-29	*Criteria for Approval of Category I and Category II Weather Minima for Approach*
AC 120-35	*Flightcrew Member Line Operational Simulations: Line-Oriented Flight Training, Special Purpose Operational Training, Line Operational Evaluation*
AC 120-48	*Communication and Coordination Between Flightcrew Members and Flight Attendants*
AC 120-49	*Parts 121 and 135 Certification*
AC 120-51	*Crew Resource Management Training*
AC 120-54	*Advanced Qualification Program*
AC 120-57	*Surface Movement Guidance and Control System*
AC 120-58	*Pilot Guide—Large Aircraft Ground Deicing*
AC 120-60	*Ground Deicing and Anti-icing Program*
AC 120-62	*Takeoff Safety Training Aid*
AC 120-68	*Pilot Records Database and Pilot Records Improvement Act*
AC 120-71	*Standard Operating Procedures and Pilot Monitoring Duties for Flight Deck Crewmembers*
AC 120-74	*Parts 91, 121, 125, and 135 Flightcrew Procedures During Taxi Operations*
AC 120-76	*Authorization for Use of Electronic Flight Bags*
AC 120-80	*Firefighting of General and High-Energy In-Flight Fires*
AC 120-82	*Flight Operational Quality Assurance*
AC 120-85	*Carriage of Cargo*
AC 120-90	*Line Operations Safety Audits*
AC 120-92	*Safety Management Systems for Aviation Service Providers*

AC 120-100	*Basics of Aviation Fatigue*
AC 120-101	*Part 121 Air Carrier Operational Control*
AC 120-103	*Fatigue Risk Management Systems for Aviation Safety*
AC 120-109	*Stall Prevention and Recovery Training*
AC 120-111	*Upset Prevention and Recovery Training*
AC 120-118	*Criteria for Approval/Authorization of All Weather Operations (AWO) for Takeoff, Landing, and Rollout*
AC 121-42	*Leadership and Command Training for Pilots in Command*
AC 121-43	*Mentoring Training for Pilots in Command*
AC 150/5300-19	*Airport Data and Information Program*
aes.faa.gov	*FAA Automated Exemption System (AES)*
AFM	*Airplane Flight Manual*
AIM	*Aeronautical Information Manual*
AURTA	*Airplane Upset Recovery Training Aid*
CAMI	*Civil Aerospace Medical Institute*
CAMI OK-06-033	*Basic Survival Skills for Aviation*
CAMI OK-21-0375	*Oxygen Equipment Use in General Aviation Operations*
CDC/NHANES	*CDC/National Health and Nutrition Examination Survey*
drs.faa.gov	*Dynamic Regulatory System—Order 8900.1*
FAA FITS	*FAA/Industry Training Standards: Personal and Weather Risk Assessment Guide*
FAA	*Flight Deck Automation Final Report*
FAA-H-8083-1	*Aircraft Weight and Balance Handbook*
FAA-H-8083-2	*Risk Management Handbook*
FAA-H-8083-3	*Airplane Flying Handbook*
FAA-H-8083-9	*Aviation Instructor's Handbook*
FAA-H-8083-15	*Instrument Flying Handbook*
FAA-H-8083-16	*Instrument Procedures Handbook*
FAA-H-8083-25	*Pilot's Handbook of Aeronautical Knowledge*

FAA-H-8083-28   *Aviation Weather Handbook*

FAA-H-8083-30   *Aviation Maintenance Technician Handbook—General*

FAA-H-8083-31   *Aviation Maintenance Technician Handbook—Airframe*

FAA-H-8083-32   *Aviation Maintenance Technician Handbook—Powerplant*

FAA InFO 07015   *Flight Risk Assessment Tool*

FAA InFO 14006   *Prohibition on Personal Use of Electronic Devices on the Flight Deck*

FAA InFO 23003   *Terrain Awareness and Warning Systems (TAWS) Nuisance Alerts*

FAA-S-ACS-11   *Airline Transport Pilot and Type Rating for Airplane Airman Certification Standards*

FCOM   *CRJ Regional Jet Flight Crew Operating Manual*

NASA AIT   *NASA Aircraft Icing Training (online courses)*

P/CG   *Pilot/Controller Glossary*

PRD Pilot User Guide   *Pilot Records Database (PRD) Pilot User Guide*

SAFO 09013   *Fighting Fires Caused by Lithium Type Batteries in Portable Electronic Devices*

SAFO 13002   *Manual Flight Operations*

SAFO 11004   *Runway Incursion Prevention Actions*

SAFO 17001   *Pilot and Flightcrew Awareness of Class B Airspace Boundaries*

SAFO 19001   *Landing Performance Assessments at Time of Arrival*

SAIB CE-11-17   *Instruments (Maneuvering Speed)*

Most of these documents are available on the FAA's website (www.faa.gov). Additionally, many of the publications are reprinted by ASA (asa2fly.com) and are available from aviation retailers worldwide.

A review of the information and references in this guide should provide the necessary preparation for the FAA Airline Transport Pilot Certification Practical Test.

Operation of Systems

Some of the following questions reference the systems of a Bombardier CRJ regional jet. For accuracy, you should review your aircraft's airplane flight manual (AFM) or flight crew operating manual (FCOM). Be capable of explaining the diagrams and schematics of the various systems in your aircraft.

A. Landing Gear

1. Describe the landing gear system components of a typical transport category jet. (AFM)

a. The aircraft's landing gear is a retractable tricycle type, with two main landing gear assemblies mounted on the wing roots and a steerable nose landing gear assembly mounted on the forward fuselage.

b. Each landing gear assembly has two wheels and a shock strut to absorb and dissipate the shock loads upon landing.

c. The main landing gear assemblies are equipped with steel multi-disc brakes.

d. Landing gear extension and retraction is electrically activated by the landing gear selector lever and controlled by a proximity sensing electronic unit (PSEU).

e. Sensors for the PSEU are located on the landing gear and landing gear doors, and the PSEU displays the landing gear position on the engine indicating and crew alerting system (EICAS) display.

f. The landing gear is hydraulically actuated by hydraulic system 3 in normal operation, and there is an alternate independent means of extending the landing gear if the normal system fails.

g. A tail bumper consisting of a shock absorber, a skid assembly, and a strike indicator protects the aircraft's tail structure from tail strikes caused by over-rotation during takeoff.

2. Describe the operational sequence of a typical hydraulic landing gear system.

a. *Extension:*

  i. A selector lever in the cockpit electrically commands the gear to extend.

  ii. A solenoid valve directs hydraulic pressure to the extension side of system.

    iii. Sequencing valves hold the landing gear in place until the landing gear doors have opened.

    iv. With gear doors open, hydraulic pressure causes uplocks to be released and hydraulic pressure is applied to the actuators to extend the gear.

    v. Once extended, downlocks are positioned hydraulically.

    vi. Landing gear position switches provide indicating system with information on gear position.

    vii. Sequencing valves direct hydraulic pressure to close the landing gear doors.

  b. *Retraction:*

    i. A selector lever in the cockpit electrically commands the gear to retract.

    ii. Landing gear position switches provide indicating system with information on gear position (in-transit).

    iii. A solenoid valve directs hydraulic pressure to the retraction side of system.

    iv. Sequencing valves prevent the landing gear from retracting until the landing gear doors have opened.

    v. With gear doors now open, hydraulic pressure is applied to the actuators to retract the gear.

    vi. Wheel rotation is stopped by hydraulic pressure routed to the brake system.

    vii. Landing gear uplocks are positioned.

    viii. Landing gear position switches provide indicating system with information on gear position (up and locked).

    ix. Sequencing valves direct hydraulic pressure to close the landing gear doors.

3. How does a landing gear safety switch function?
(FAA-H-8083-31)

Also known as a ground proximity switch or landing gear squat switch, this switch is usually mounted in a bracket on one of the main gear shock struts and mechanically actuated via the landing gear torque links. The torque links spread apart or move together as the shock strut piston extends or retracts in its cylinder. When the strut is compressed (aircraft on the ground), the torque links are close together, causing the adjusting links to open the safety switch. During takeoff, as the weight of the aircraft leaves the struts, the struts and torque links extend causing the adjusting links to close the safety switch. A ground is completed when the safety switch closes and the solenoid then energizes, unlocking the selector valve so that the gear handle can be positioned to raise the gear. Squat switches also provide signals to other various aircraft systems indicating whether the aircraft is in the air or on the ground such as pressurization, nose wheel steering, thrust reversers, APU, etc.

4. What is a brake anti-skid system? (FAA-H-8083-31)

A system in high-performance aircraft braking systems that provides anti-skid protection and subsequent maximum braking efficiency. Anti-skid system sensors monitor and compare wheel rotation speed to the expected value on a dry runway. Once the system detects a rotational value less than normal, a skid control valve removes some of the hydraulic pressure to the wheel, permitting the wheel to rotate a little faster and stop its sliding. The more intense the skid is, the more braking pressure is removed. The skid detection and control of each wheel is completely independent of the others. The wheel skid intensity is measured by the amount of wheel slow down.

5. What other functions are provided by an anti-skid system? (FAA-H-8083-31)

a. *Touchdown protection*—This circuit prevents the brakes from being applied during the landing approach, even if the brake pedals are depressed. This prevents the wheels from being locked when they contact the runway.

b. *Locked wheel protection* recognizes if a wheel is not rotating. When this occurs, the anti-skid control valve is signaled to fully open, allowing a wheel to recover from a deep skid.

6. Describe a typical large aircraft nose-wheel steering system. (FAA-H-8083-31)

Control of steering is accomplished from the flight deck through the use of a small wheel, tiller, or joystick typically mounted on the left side wall. Mechanical, electrical, or hydraulic connections transmit the controller input movement to a steering control unit (metering or control valve) which directs hydraulic fluid under pressure to one or two actuators designed with various linkages to rotate the lower strut. An accumulator and relief valve, or similar pressurizing assembly, keeps fluid in the actuators and system under pressure at all times which permits the steering actuating cylinders to also act as shimmy dampers. A follow-up mechanism consists of various gears, cables, rods, drums, and/or bell-crank that returns the metering valve to a neutral position once the steering angle has been reached.

7. What is the most common method of providing shock absorption during landing? (FAA-H-8083-31)

A typical pneumatic/hydraulic shock strut uses compressed air or nitrogen combined with hydraulic fluid to absorb and dissipate shock loads. It is sometimes referred to as an air/oil or oleo strut. A shock strut is constructed of two telescoping cylinders or tubes that are closed on the external ends. The upper cylinder is fixed to the aircraft and does not move. The lower cylinder is called the piston and is free to slide in and out of the upper cylinder. Two chambers are formed, with the lower chamber filled with hydraulic fluid and the upper chamber filled with compressed air or nitrogen. An orifice located between the two cylinders provides a passage for the fluid from the bottom chamber to enter the top cylinder chamber when the strut is compressed.

B. Powerplant

1. Describe the major components of a gas turbine engine. (FAA-H-8083-32)

A typical gas turbine engine consists of:

a. An air inlet.

b. Compressor section.

c. Combustion section.

d. Turbine section.

e. Exhaust section.

f. Accessory section.

g. The systems necessary for starting, lubrication, fuel supply, and auxiliary purposes, such as anti-icing, cooling, and pressurization.

2. Turbine engines are classified according to the type of compressors they use. What are the three types of compressors found in turbine engines? (FAA-H-8083-25)

Centrifugal flow, axial flow, and centrifugal-axial flow.

3. Describe a centrifugal-flow compressor. (FAA-H-8083-32)

This compressor has an impeller surrounded by a ring of diffuser vanes. The impeller is driven at high speed by a turbine. Air is drawn into the air inlet and directed to the center of the impeller. The air is then forced centrifugally outward into a diffuser, where the pressure of the air is increased. The pressurized air is then supplied to the combustion section.

4. What is the main function of the diffuser section of a turbine engine? (FAA-H-8083-32)

The diffuser is the divergent section of the engine after the compressor and before the combustion section. It has the all-important function of reducing high-velocity compressor discharge air to a slower velocity at increased pressure. This prepares the air for entry into the flame burning area of the combustion so that the flame of combustion can burn continuously.

5. Describe an axial-flow compressor. (FAA-H-8083-32)

The axial-flow compressor consists of two main elements, a rotor and a stator. The rotor, turning at high speeds, has blades fixed on a spindle that takes in air at the compressor inlet and impels it rearward through a series of stages, paralleling the longitudinal axis of the engine. The action of the rotor increases the compression of the air at each stage, accelerating it rearward through several stages. With this increased velocity, energy is transferred from the compressor to the air in the form of velocity energy. The stator blades act as diffusers at each stage, partially converting high velocity to pressure. Each consecutive pair of rotor and stator blades constitutes a pressure stage; the greater the number of stages, the higher the compression ratio. Most present-day engines utilize up to 16 stages.

6. Explain the function of stator vanes. (FAA-H-8083-32)

The function of the stator vanes is to receive air from the air inlet duct or from each preceding stage and increase the pressure of the air and deliver it to the next stage at the correct velocity and pressure. They also control the direction of air to each rotor stage to obtain the maximum possible compressor blade efficiency.

7. Explain the operation of a centrifugal-axial flow compressor. (FAA-H-8083-3)

The centrifugal-axial flow design uses both kinds of compressors to achieve the desired compression. A typical free power turbine engine (like a Pratt & Whitney PT-6) has two independent counter-rotating turbines. One turbine drives the compressor, while the other drives the propeller through a reduction gearbox. The compressor in the basic engine consists of three axial flow compressor stages combined with a single centrifugal compressor stage. The axial and centrifugal stages are assembled on the same shaft and operate as a single unit.

8. What are the four types of gas turbine engines? (FAA-H-8083-25)

a. *Turbojet*—consists of a compressor, combustion chamber, turbine section, and exhaust section. The compressor section passes inlet air at a high rate of speed to the combustion chamber, which contains the fuel inlet and igniter for combustion. The expanding air drives a turbine, which is connected by a shaft to the compressor, sustaining engine operation. The accelerated exhaust gases from the engine provide thrust. Turbojet engines are limited in range and endurance. They are also slow to respond to throttle applications at slow compressor speeds.

b. *Turbofan*—developed to combine best features of the turbojet and the turboprop. Turbofan engines create additional thrust by diverting secondary airflow around the combustion chamber. The turbofan bypass air generates increased thrust, cools the engine, and aids in exhaust noise suppression and provides turbojet-type cruise speed and lower fuel consumption. The inlet air that passes through a turbofan engine is usually divided into two separate streams of air. One stream passes through the engine core, while a second stream bypasses the engine core. A turbofan's bypass ratio refers to the ratio of the mass airflow that passes through the fan divided by the mass airflow that passes through the engine core.

c. *Turboprop*—is a turbine engine that drives a propeller through a reduction gear. Exhaust gases drive a power turbine connected by a shaft that drives the reduction gear assembly. Reduction gearing is necessary in turboprop engines because optimum propeller performance is achieved at much slower speeds than the engine's operating RPM. Turboprop engines are most efficient at speeds between 250 and 400 mph and altitudes between 18,000 and 30,000 feet. They also perform well at the slow airspeeds required for takeoff and landing and are fuel efficient. The minimum specific fuel consumption of the turboprop engine is normally available in the altitude range of 25,000 feet to the tropopause.

d. *Turboshaft*—delivers power to a shaft that drives something other than a propeller. The biggest difference between a turbojet and turboshaft engine is that on a turboshaft engine, most of the energy produced by the expanding gases is used to drive a turbine rather than produce thrust. Many helicopters use a turboshaft gas turbine engine. In addition, turboshaft engines are widely used as auxiliary power units on large aircraft.

9. Explain the term *engine pressure ratio* (EPR). (FAA-H-8083-25)

EPR is the ratio of turbine discharge to compressor inlet pressure. Pressure measurements are recorded by probes installed in the engine inlet and at the exhaust. Once collected, the data is sent to a differential pressure transducer, which is indicated on a flight deck EPR gauge. An EPR gauge is used to indicate the power output of a turbojet/turbofan engine.

10. Define the terms EGT, TIT, ITT, and TOT. (FAA-H-8083-3, FAA-H-8083-25)

Exhaust gas temperature (EGT)—the temperature of the exhaust gases as they enter the tail pipe, after passing through the turbine.

Turbine inlet temperature (TIT)—the temperature of the gases from the combustion section of the engine as they enter the first stage of the turbine.

Interstage turbine temperature (ITT)—the temperature of the gases between the high-pressure and low-pressure turbine wheels.

Turbine outlet temperature (TOT)—like EGT, turbine outlet temperature is taken aft of the turbine wheel(s).

11. What information is provided by the N_1 and N_2 indicators? (FAA-H-8083-25)

N_1 *indicator*—represents the rotational speed of the low-pressure compressor and is presented on the indicator as a percentage of design RPM. After start, the speed of the low-pressure compressor is governed by the N1 turbine wheel. The N1 turbine wheel is connected to the low-pressure compressor through a concentric shaft.

N_2 *indicator*—represents the rotational speed of the high-pressure compressor and is presented on the indicator as a percentage of design RPM. The high-pressure compressor is governed by the N_2 turbine wheel. The N_2 turbine wheel is connected to the high-pressure compressor through a concentric shaft.

12. What is a limiting factor of a gas turbine engine? (FAA-H-8083-25)

A limiting factor in a gas turbine engine is the temperature of the turbine section. The temperature of a turbine section must be monitored closely to prevent overheating the turbine blades and other exhaust section components. One common method of monitoring the temperature of a turbine section is with an exhaust gas temperature (EGT) gauge.

13. Where are the highest temperatures located in a turbine engine? (FAA-H-8083-25)

The highest temperature in any turbine engine occurs at the turbine inlet. TIT is therefore usually the limiting factor in turbine engine operation.

14. Explain the factors that would affect the thrust output of a turbine engine. (FAA-H-8083-25)

Turbine engine thrust varies directly with air density. As air density decreases with altitude, so does thrust. Additionally, because air density decreases with an increase in temperature, increased temperature also results in decreased thrust. Turbine engines will experience a negligible loss of thrust due to high relative humidity.

15. Gas turbine engines are started by rotating the high-pressure compressor. What are the three types of starters used for rotating the compressor? (FAA-H-8083-32)

The basic types of starters that are in current use for gas turbine engines are direct current (DC) electric motor, starter/generators, and the air turbine type of starter.

16. How does an air turbine starter accomplish turning the high-pressure compressor? (FAA-H-8083-32)

The typical air turbine starter consists of an axial flow turbine that turns a drive coupling through a reduction gear train and a starter clutch mechanism. The air to operate the air turbine starter is supplied from either a ground-operated air cart, the APU, or a cross-bleed start from an engine already operating.

17. Explain the start sequence of a gas turbine engine. (FAA-H-8083-3)

a. To start a gas turbine engine, the compressor section is normally rotated by an electric starter.

b. As compressor RPM increases, air flowing through the inlet is compressed to a high pressure, delivered to the combustion section, and ignited.

c. In gas turbine engines, not all of the compressed air is used to support combustion. Some of the compressed air bypasses the burner section within the engine to provide internal cooling.

d. The fuel/air mixture in the combustion chamber burns in a continuous combustion process and produces a very high temperature, typically around 4,000 degrees Fahrenheit (°F). When this hot air mixes with bypass air, the temperature of the mixed air mass drops to 1,600–2,400°F.

e. The mixture of hot air and gases expands and passes through the turbine blades, forcing the turbine section to rotate which in turn drives the compressor by means of a direct shaft, a concentric shaft, or a combination of both.

f. After powering the turbine section, the combustion gases and bypass air flow out of the engine through the exhaust.

g. Once the hot gases from the burner section provide sufficient power to maintain engine operation through the turbine, the starter is de-energized, and the starting sequence ends.

h. Combustion continues until the engine is shut down by cutting off the fuel supply.

18. What are igniters? (FAA-H-8083-32)

The typical gas turbine engine is equipped with igniters that provide a high heat intensity spark used to ignite the fuel-air mixture. A typical ignition system includes two exciter units, two transformers, two intermediate ignition leads, and two high-tension leads. As a safety factor, the ignition system is actually a dual system, designed to fire two igniter plugs. This type of ignition system provides a high degree of reliability under widely varying conditions of altitude, atmospheric pressure, temperature, fuel vaporization, and input voltage.

19. What is the function of the accessory section on a gas turbine engine? (FAA-H-8083-32)

To provide space for the mounting of accessories necessary for operation and control of the engine. Generally, it also includes accessories concerned with the aircraft, such as electric generators and hydraulic pumps. Secondary functions include acting as an oil reservoir and/or oil sump and housing the accessory drive gears and reduction gears.

20. What are the basic components of a turboprop engine? (FAA-H-8083-32)

The typical turboprop engine can be broken down into assemblies as follows:

a. The power section assembly with the major components of gas turbine engines (compressor, combustion chamber, turbine, and exhaust sections).

(continued)

b. The reduction gear or gearbox assembly—those sections peculiar to turboprop configurations.

c. The torquemeter assembly, which transmits the torque from the engine to the gearbox of the reduction section.

d. The accessory drive housing assembly.

21. What information is provided by a torquemeter in a turboprop aircraft? (FAA-H-8083-25)

Turboprop and turboshaft engines are designed to produce torque for driving a propeller and power output is measured by a torquemeter. The torquemeter measures power applied to the shaft and is calibrated in percentage units, foot-pounds, or psi.

22. Explain the operation of a jet engine thrust reverser. (FAA-H-8083-3)

A thrust reverser is a device fitted in the engine exhaust system that effectively reverses the flow of the exhaust gases. The flow does not reverse through 180°; however, the final path of the exhaust gases is about 45° from straight ahead. This, together with the losses in the reverse flow paths, results in a net efficiency of about 50 percent. It produces even less reverse thrust if the engine RPM is less than maximum in reverse.

23. What are the two types of thrust reversers on jet engines? (FAA-H-8083-3)

a. *Target reverser*—simple clamshell doors that swivel from the stowed position at the engine tailpipe to block all of the outflow and redirect some component of the thrust forward.

b. *Cascade reverser*—normally found on turbofan engines and are often designed to reverse only the fan air portion. Blocking doors in the shroud obstructs forward fan thrust and redirects it through cascade vanes for some reverse component. Cascades are generally less effective than target reversers, particularly those that reverse only fan air, because they do not affect the engine core, which continues to produce forward thrust.

24. After landing, is reverse thrust application more effective at high speeds or low speeds? (FAA-H-8083-3)

Reverse thrust is more effective at high speed than at low speed. For maximum reverse thrust efficiency, the pilot should use it as soon as is prudent after touchdown. Specific procedures for reverse thrust operation for a particular airplane/engine combination are contained in the FAA-approved AFM for that airplane.

25. How is inadvertent deployment of thrust reversers prevented while in flight? (FAA-H-8083-3)

The systems normally contain several lock systems: one to keep reversers from operating in the air, another to prevent operation with the thrust levers out of the idle detent, and/or an auto-stow circuit to command reverser stowage any time thrust reverser deployment would be inappropriate, such as during takeoff and while airborne.

C. Propellers

1. What is a propeller governor? (FAA-H-8083-32)

A governor is an engine RPM-sensing device and high-pressure oil pump. In a constant-speed propeller system, the governor responds to a change in engine RPM by directing oil under pressure to the propeller hydraulic cylinder or by releasing oil from the hydraulic cylinder. The change in oil volume in the hydraulic cylinder changes the blade angle and maintains the propeller system RPM. The governor is set for a specific RPM via the cockpit propeller control, which compresses or releases the governor speeder spring.

2. Explain the "beta range" of operation on a turboprop engine. (FAA-H-8083-3)

The beta range of operation consists of power lever positions from flight idle to maximum reverse. Beginning at power lever positions just aft of flight idle, propeller blade pitch angles become progressively flatter with aft movement of the power lever until they go beyond maximum flat pitch and into negative pitch, resulting in reverse thrust. In a fixed-shaft/constant-speed engine, the engine speed remains largely unchanged as the propeller blade angles achieve their negative values.

3. **Explain the term *reverse pitch*.** (FAA-H-8083-3)

In the reverse pitch position, the engine/propeller turns in the same direction as in the normal (forward) pitch position, but the propeller blade angle is positioned to the other side of flat pitch. In reverse pitch, air is pushed away from the airplane rather than being drawn over it, resulting in braking action rather than forward thrust of the airplane. It is used for backing away from obstacles when taxiing, controlling taxi speed, or to aid in bringing the airplane to a stop during the landing roll.

4. **How are thrust reverser systems designed to prevent inadvertent or un-commanded deployment during flight?** (FAA-H-8083-3)

Thrust reverser systems normally contain several lock systems: one to keep reversers from operating in the air, another to prevent operation with the thrust levers out of the idle detent, and/or an auto-stow circuit to command reverser stowage any time thrust reverser deployment would be inappropriate, such as during takeoff and while airborne.

5. **Describe a typical autofeather system.** (FAA-H-8083-32)

An autofeather system is used normally only during takeoff, approach, and landing. It is used to feather the propeller automatically if power is lost from either engine. The system uses a solenoid valve to dump oil pressure from the propeller cylinder (which allows the prop to feather) if two torque switches sense low torque from the engine. This system has a test-off-arm switch that is used to arm the system.

6. **Explain the difference between a propeller synchronizer (prop sync) and a propeller synchrophaser.** (FAA-H-8083-3)

Propeller synchronizer—Once the propeller RPMs are coarsely matched by the pilot and the system is engaged, the prop sync adjusts the RPM of the slave engine to precisely match the RPM of the master engine and then maintains that relationship.

Propeller synchrophaser—This is a variation of a propeller synchronizer that not only matches RPM but actually compares and adjusts the positions of the individual blades of the propellers in their arcs. There can be significant propeller noise and vibration reductions with a propeller synchrophaser.

7. Explain the purpose of a reduction gearbox on a turboprop aircraft. (FAA-H-8083-32)

The function of the reduction gear assembly is to reduce the high RPM from the engine to a propeller RPM that can be maintained without exceeding the maximum propeller tip speed (speed of sound). Most reduction gear assemblies use a planetary gear reduction. Additional power takeoffs are available for the propeller governor, oil pump, and other accessories. A propeller brake is often incorporated into the gearbox. The propeller brake is designed to prevent the propeller from windmilling when it is feathered in flight and to decrease the time for the propeller to come to a complete stop after engine shutdown.

D. Fuel System

1. Describe the five main subsystems of the fuel system on a large transport category jet aircraft. (FAA-H-8083-31)

Jet transport fuel subsystems are as follows:

a. *Storage*—integral fuel tanks, center wing section or fuselage tanks, long-range auxiliary tanks, and surge tanks.

b. *Vent*—vent tubing and channels connect all tanks to vent space in the surge tanks (if present) or vent overboard; various check valves, float valves, and multiple vent locations.

c. *Distribution*—pressure fueling components, defueling components, transfer system, and fuel jettison or dump system.

d. *Feed*—considered the heart of the fuel system since it delivers fuel to the engines; in-tank fuel boost pumps, usually two per tank, pump fuel under pressure through a shutoff valve to each engine; boost pump bypasses allow fuel flow should a pump fail.

e. *Indicating*—fuel quantity gauges/displays; true fuel flow indicators for each engine; fuel temperature gauges, fuel filter bypass warning lights; low fuel pressure warning lights.

2. Describe the different types of fuel pumps found on turboprop aircraft. (FAA-H-8083-32)

   a. *High-pressure pump*—usually engine-driven gear type pump; provides majority of fuel to engine.

   b. *Low-pressure pump*—usually engine-driven or motive-flow type jet pump; supplies main engine-driven pump with fuel.

   c. *Electric boost pumps*—used for engine start, fuel crossfeed, main jet pump failure, and pressure defuel.

   d. *Ejector/jet pumps*—motive-flow type pumps; used to keep collector tanks at operational levels as well as provide constant fuel flow to the main pumps.

3. What is a fuel control unit? (FAA-H-8083-32)

A fuel control unit is a device used on gas turbine engines to first determine and then meter the appropriate amount of fuel required by the engine for a given set of conditions. These conditions include such variables as power lever position, engine RPM, temperature, and pressure. Gas turbine engine fuel controls can be divided into three basic groups: hydromechanical, hydromechanical/electronic, and full authority digital engine (or electronics) control (FADEC). The hydromechanical/electronic fuel control is a hybrid of the two types of fuel control but can function solely as a hydromechanical control. The third type, FADEC, uses electronic sensors for its inputs and controls fuel flow with electronic outputs. The FADEC-type control gives the electronic controller (computer) complete control.

4. What are the two methods used to prevent ice crystals from forming in the fuel? (FAA-H-8083-32)

   a. An engine oil-to-fuel heat exchanger is located in the system prior to the engine driven fuel pump. Heat from the engine oil maintains the fuel at the correct temperature.

   b. Fuel-air heat exchangers that use hot bleed air to maintain fuel at the correct temperature.

5. What is a collector tank? (AFM)

A collector tank is essentially a fuel tank within a fuel tank. It is an integral part of the inboard tank at the lowest point (closest to fuselage). The tank ensures a constant fuel level and continuous supply of fuel to the engine during normal maneuvering.

6. What is an ejector pump? (FAA-H-8083-31)

A form of jet pump used to pick up a liquid and move it to another location. Ejectors are used to ensure that the compartment in which the boost pumps are mounted is kept full of fuel. Part of the fuel from the boost pump flowing through the ejector produces a low pressure that pulls fuel from the main tank and forces it into the boost pump sump area.

7. What is motive flow? (AFM)

A flow created by the suction of a low-pressure area created by a Venturi.

8. How are the fuel tanks vented on a transport category jet? (FAA-H-8083-31)

Transport category fuel systems require venting similar to reciprocating engine aircraft fuel systems. A series of vent tubing and channels exists that connects all tanks to vent space in the surge tanks (if present) or vent overboard. Venting must be configured to ensure the fuel is vented regardless of the attitude of the aircraft or the quantity of fuel on board. This sometimes requires the installation of various check valves, float valves, and multiple vent locations in the same tank.

9. Give a brief explanation of how fuel is transferred from tank to tank in a transport category aircraft. (FAA-H-8083-31)

The fuel transfer system is a series of plumbing and valves that permits movement of fuel from one tank to another on board the aircraft. In-tank fuel boost pumps move the fuel into a manifold and, by opening the fuel valve (or refueling valve) for the desired tank, the fuel is transferred. Not all jet transports have such fuel transfer capability. Through the use of a fuel feed manifold and crossfeed valves, some aircraft simply allow engines to be run off fuel from any tank as a means for managing fuel location.

10. Why are fuel heaters required in turbine engine aircraft?
(FAA-H-8083-32)

Gas turbine engine fuel systems are very susceptible to the formation of ice in the fuel filters. When the fuel in the aircraft fuel tanks cools to 32°F (0°C) or below, residual water in the fuel tends to freeze, forming ice crystals. When these ice crystals in the fuel become trapped in the filter, they block fuel flow to the engine, which causes a very serious problem. To prevent this problem, the fuel is kept at a temperature above freezing. Warmer fuel also can improve combustion, so some means of regulating the fuel temperature is needed.

11. Describe how fuel is heated in jet aircraft.
(FAA-H-8083-32)

One method of regulating fuel temperature is to use a fuel heater which operates as a heat exchanger to warm the fuel. The heater can use engine bleed air or engine lubricating oil as a source of heat. The bleed air type is called an air-to-liquid exchanger and the oil type is known as a liquid-to-liquid heat exchanger.

12. What are the three types of turbine engine fuel?
(FAA-H-8083-31)

Three basic turbine engine fuel types are available worldwide, although some countries have their own unique fuels. The three basic types of turbine engine fuel are:

Jet A—the most common turbine engine fuel in the U.S.; fractionally distilled in the kerosene range; low volatility and low vapor pressure; flashpoint ranges between 110°F and 150°F; freeze point is −40°F.

Jet A1—the most popular, globally; fractionally distilled in the kerosene range; low volatility and low vapor pressure; flashpoint ranges between 110°F and 150°F; freeze point is −52.6°F.

Jet B —is a wide-cut fuel that is basically a blend of kerosene and gasoline; volatility and vapor pressure fall between Jet A and AVGAS; primarily available in Alaska and Canada due to its low freezing point of −58°F.

Note: Most engine operations manuals permit the use of either Jet A or Jet A-1.

13. How is Jet A turbine fuel identified? (FAA-H-8083-25)

Jet A turbine fuel has a distinctive kerosene smell and is colorless or straw colored. In addition to the smell and color of the fuel, a color-coding system extends to decals and various airport fuel handling equipment. Turbine fuels are identified by white letters on a black background.

14. How are larger aircraft fueled and, if necessary, defueled? (FAA-H-8083-31)

A transport category aircraft fuel distribution subsystem consists of the pressure fueling components, defueling components, transfer system, and fuel jettison or dump system. Single-point pressure fueling at a fueling station accessible by ramp refueling trucks allows all aircraft fuel tanks to be filled with one connection of the fuel hose. Leading and trailing edge wing locations are common for these stations.

Occasionally, defueling the aircraft is required for an inspection or repair. The same fueling station is used, and the hose from the fuel truck is connected to same receptacle used to fuel the aircraft. To allow fuel to exit the aircraft, a defueling valve is opened. Fuel can be pumped out of the aircraft using the boost pumps located in the tanks that need to be emptied, or the pump in the refueling truck can be used to draw the fuel out of the tanks.

E. Oil System

1. What are the components of a turbine lubrication system? (FAA-H-8083-32)

Oil tank, oil pump, oil filters, oil pressure regulating valve, oil pressure relief valve, oil jets, breather systems (vents), check valves, thermostatic bypass valves, air oil coolers, fuel oil coolers, de-oiler, and magnetic chip detectors.

2. What type of instrumentation is provided for display of the lubrication system status? (FAA-H-8083-32)

Gauge connection provisions are incorporated in the oil system for oil pressure, oil quantity, low oil pressure, oil filter differential pressure switch, and oil temperature. For aircraft equipped with engine indicating and crew alerting system (EICAS) computers, an electronic sensor is installed to send a signal to the FADEC control unit and through the EICAS computers, and on to the displays in the flight deck.

3. What are the two basic types of turbine engine lubrication systems? (FAA-H-8083-32)

Both wet- and dry-sump lubrication systems are used in gas turbine engines. Most turbojet engines are of the axial-flow configuration, and use a dry-sump lubrication system. However, some turbine engines are equipped with a combination dry and wet type of lubrication system.

4. What is the main difference between wet- and dry-sump lubrication systems? (FAA-H-8083-32)

Wet-sump engines store the lubricating oil in the engine proper, while dry-sump engines use an external tank that is usually mounted on the engine (or somewhere in the aircraft structure near the engine).

5. How is the oil cooled in a turbine engine? (FAA-H-8083-32)

To ensure proper temperature, oil is routed through either an air-cooled or fuel-cooled oil cooler. With an oil-to-fuel heat exchanger, not only is heat removed from the oil but the fuel is kept at proper temperature, thus eliminating the potential for ice formation within the fuel.

6. What is the most critical lubrication point in a gas turbine engine? (FAA-H-8083-32)

The exhaust turbine bearing is the most critical lubricating point in a turbine engine because of the high temperature normally present. In some engines, air cooling is used in addition to the oil cooling the bearing, which supports the turbine.

F. Hydraulic System

1. Hydraulic systems in aircraft provide power for the operation of what components? (FAA-H-8083-31)

The operation of landing gear, flaps, flight control surfaces, and brakes is largely accomplished with hydraulic power systems.

2. A typical hydraulic system consists of what basic components? (FAA-H-8083-31)

To achieve the necessary redundancy and reliability, the system may consist of several subsystems. Each subsystem has:

a. Main engine driven pumps.
b. Electric hydraulic pumps.
c. Hydraulic reservoirs.
d. Valves—shutoff, check, and drain.
e. Various filters, sensors, switches, and accumulators.

3. What is a hydraulic accumulator? (FAA-H-8083-31)

A hydraulic accumulator is a hydraulic component that consists of two compartments separated by a movable component, such as a piston, diaphragm, or bladder. One compartment is filled with compressed air or nitrogen, and the other is filled with hydraulic fluid and is connected into the system pressure manifold. An accumulator allows an incompressible fluid to be stored under pressure by the force produced by a compressible fluid. Its primary purposes are to act as a shock absorber in the system and to provide a source of additional hydraulic power when heavy demands are placed on the system.

4. What is a hydraulic actuator? (FAA-H-8083-31)

An actuating cylinder transforms energy in the form of fluid pressure into mechanical force, or action, to perform work. There are two major types: single-action actuators, which produce powered movement in one direction only; and double-action (two ports) actuating cylinders, capable of producing powered movement in two directions.

5. What is pump cavitation? (FAA-H-8083-31)

This occurs when air in the hydraulic lines enters the hydraulic pump, causing the pump to be unable to move hydraulic fluid. The pump eventually overheats and fails since it depends on fluid movement for cooling. This condition can occur for several reasons, such as the hydraulic reservoir fluid level being too low, or foaming of the hydraulic fluid.

6. What is the purpose of hydraulic fuses? (FAA-H-8083-31)

Hydraulic fuses are hydromechanical flow-control valves installed in aircraft hydraulic lines, which are designed to prevent excessive or complete loss of all hydraulic fluid in the event of a ruptured hydraulic line.

7. What are the three types of aircraft hydraulic fluid? (FAA-H-8083-31)

a. *Mineral-based fluids*—used in many systems, especially where the fire hazard is low. These fluids are completely interchangeable, have and odor similar to penetrating oil, and are dyed red. MIL-H-5606 is the oldest, used since the 1940s. MIL-H-6083 is rust-inhibited version of MIL-H-5606.

b. *Polyalphaolefins*—is a fire-resistant hydrogenated polyalphaolefin-based fluid developed in the 1960s to overcome the flammability characteristics of MIL-H-5606; its one disadvantage is the high viscosity at low temperature and is generally limited to −40°F. Small aircraft predominantly use MIL-H-5606, but some have switched to MIL-H-83282 if they can accommodate the high viscosity at low temperature.

c. *Phosphate-ester-based fluid (Skydrol)*—used in most commercial transport category aircraft and are extremely fire-resistant. Airframe manufacturers have named the new generations of hydraulic fluid as type IV or Type V based on their performance.

8. **Explain the two main functions of a hydraulic system pressure regulator.** (FAA-H-8083-31)

The regulator is located in the hydraulic system so that pump output can only get into the system pressure circuit by passing through the regulator. The pressure regulator is used to:

a. Manage the output of the pump to maintain system operating pressure within a predetermined range.

b. Permit the pump to turn without resistance (termed unloading the pump) at times when pressure in the system is within normal operating range.

G. Electrical System

1. **Describe some of the advantages and disadvantages of NiCad batteries.** (AC 00-33)

Nickel-cadmium (NiCad) batteries are used frequently in turboprop aircraft.

Advantages:
a. Long service life and excellent reliability.
b. Can maintain sustained voltage until almost completely discharged.
c. Deliver large amounts of current.
d. Short recharge time after heavy use.

Disadvantages:
a. Relatively expensive.
b. Temperature sensitive.
c. Thermal runaway problem.
d. Battery memory can prevent battery from fully recharging.

2. **What is thermal runaway?** (AC 00-33)

Thermal runaway is an uncontrollable rise in battery temperature that will ultimately destroy the battery. This condition can occur when a NiCad battery is operated at above normal temperatures and is subjected to high charging currents associated with constant voltage charging. As the temperature of the battery increases, the effective internal resistance decreases and higher current is drawn from the constant voltage charging source. The higher current increases the battery temperature, which in turn results in even higher charging currents and temperatures.

3. Describe lead-acid batteries. (FAA-H-8083-30)

A common type of battery used in small aircraft as well as some turbine aircraft. The cells of the battery are connected in series. In discharging, the chemical energy stored in the battery is changed to electrical energy; in charging, the electrical energy supplied to the battery is changed to chemical energy and stored. Each cell of a lead acid battery normally develops 2 volts. The most common lead acid batteries are 12 or 24 volt and are rated in amp hours. An amp-hour equals 1 amp delivered for 1 hour.

4. What is a generator? (FAA-H-8083-30)

Any device that converts mechanical energy into electrical energy by electromagnetic induction. Alternating current (AC) and direct current (DC) generators are the most common types; both operate by inducing an AC voltage in coils varying the amount and direction of the magnetic flux cutting through the coils.

5. Describe the function of a starter-generator unit. (FAA-H-8083-32)

Many gas turbine aircraft are equipped with starter-generator systems that use a combination starter-generator, which operates as a starter motor to drive the engine during starting and then as a generator to supply the electrical system power after the engine has reached a self-sustaining speed.

6. Describe generator control units (GCUs). (FAA-H-8083-30)

GCUs are multifunction electrical components that provide electrical system control and protective functions such as:

a. Voltage regulation.
b. Over-voltage protection.
c. Load paralleling between generators.
d. Automatic cancellation of start cycle.
e. Reverse polarity protection.

7. **What are inverters?** (FAA-H-8083-30)

   Inverters are used in some aircraft systems to convert a portion
   of the aircraft's DC power to AC power, which is used mainly for
   instruments, radio, radar, lighting, and other accessories. There
   are two types of inverters, rotary and static, designed to supply
   current at a frequency of 400 cycles per second. Some are designed
   to provide more than one voltage; for example, 26 volt AC in one
   winding and 115 volts in another.

8. **Why do most large aircraft use AC power rather than DC
   power?** (FAA-H-8083-30)

   Alternating current has largely replaced direct current in
   commercial power systems for a number of reasons:

   a. It can be transmitted over long distances more readily and more
      economically than direct current, since AC voltages can be
      increased or decreased by means of transformers.

   b. Space and weight can be saved, since AC devices, especially
      motors, are smaller and simpler than DC devices.

   c. In most AC motors, no brushes are required so commutation
      trouble at high altitude is eliminated.

   d. Circuit breakers operate satisfactorily under load at high
      altitudes in an AC system, whereas arcing is so excessive in DC
      systems that circuit breakers must be replaced frequently.

   e. Most airplanes using a 24-volt DC system have special
      equipment that requires a certain amount of 400-cycle AC
      current, making it necessary to convert with inverters.

9. **What is an electrical bus bar?** (FAA-H-8083-25)

   A common electrical system component that interfaces power from
   a common source, such as a generator, to a variety of electrical
   components connected to the bus. Most transport category
   aircraft use multiple bus systems, allowing for a certain degree of
   redundancy in the event of a failure of any one component.

10. **What are electrical bus ties?** (FAA-H-8083-3)

    A bus tie is an electrical switch that connects (or disconnects)
    different electrical buses. Bus ties provide a means of isolating a
    powered bus from one that has failed. They can also redirect power
    to buses that have lost their primary power source.

11. What is a rectifier? (FAA-H-8083-30)

A rectifier is a device that transforms AC into DC by limiting or regulating the direction of current flow. Rectifiers provide a simple and efficient method of obtaining high voltage DC at low amperage. They can also be an excellent source of high amperage at low voltage, depending on the type of rectifier used.

Remember: AC to DC = Rectifier
          DC to AC = Inverter

12. What is a diode? (FAA-H-8083-30)

A two-element electrical device that allows current to travel in one direction only. Sometimes thought of as an electronic check valve.

13. What is a hot battery bus? (FAA-H-8083-31)

The hot battery bus is an electrical bus that directly connects to the aircraft battery. The bus is always hot with a charged battery in the aircraft. It powers basics like the entry door light and clock. It also powers critical flight safety items like fire extinguishers, fuel shut offs, and fuel pumps. In a massive system failure, the hot battery bus is the last bus to fail.

14. Describe the function of a transformer and a transformer rectifier unit. (FAA-H-8083-30, FAA-H-8083-31)

A transformer changes electrical energy of a given voltage into electrical energy at a different voltage level. A transformer rectifier unit (TRU) is a component used to reduce the AC voltage and change it into DC for charging the battery and for operating DC equipment in an aircraft.

15. What is a relay? (FAA-H-8083-30)

A relay is an electrical component that uses a small amount of current flowing through a coil to produce a magnetic pull to close a set of contacts through which a large amount of current can flow. The core in a relay coil is fixed.

16. What is a solenoid? (FAA-H-8083-30)

An electromagnetically operated switch with a moveable core. Used to operate a variety of devices including switches, valves, and electromechanical devices.

17. What are several types of circuit protection devices?
(FAA-H-8083-30)

   a. *Circuit breaker*—Designed to break the circuit and stop the
   current flow when the current exceeds a predetermined value.

   b. *Fuse*—A strip of metal that will melt when current in excess of
   its carefully determined capacity flows through it. Installed in
   a circuit so that all the current in that circuit passes through it;
   usually made of an alloy of tin and bismuth.

   c. *Current limiter*—A fuse made of copper used primarily to
   sectionalize an aircraft circuit.

**18. Define the following electrical system troubleshooting
terms: *short circuit, open circuit.* (FAA-H-8083-30)**

A short circuit is a low-resistance path. It can be across the power
source or between the sides of a circuit. It usually creates high
current flow, which will burn out or cause damage to the circuit
conductor or components.

An open circuit is one that is not complete or continuous.

**19. Define the following terms: *volts, current, amps,
resistance, ohms.* (FAA-H-8083-30)**

Volts—the unit of measure for electrical potential or electromotive
force (voltage).

Current—the rate at which the charge is flowing.

Amps—the unit of measure of current or the rate of electron flow in
an electrical conductor.

Resistance—the opposition a device or material offers to the flow
or current.

Ohms—the standard unit used to measure resistance.

Note: A useful water pipe analogy to help understand these terms
is: voltage is equivalent to water pressure, current is equivalent to
flow rate, and resistance is equivalent to pipe size.

20. What is a ram air turbine (RAT), and what is it used for? (FAA-H-8083-31)

The RAT is installed in the aircraft to provide electrical and hydraulic power in the event that the primary sources of aircraft power are lost. Ram air is used to turn the blades of a turbine that, in turn, operates a hydraulic pump and generator. The turbine and pump assembly is generally installed on the inner surface of a door installed in the fuselage. The door is hinged, allowing the assembly to be extended into the slipstream by pulling a manual release in the flight deck. In some aircraft, the RAT automatically deploys when the main hydraulic pressure system fails and/or electrical system malfunction occurs.

H. Pneumatic and Environmental Systems

1. What are some of the common components found in most pneumatic systems? (FAA-H-8083-31)

a. *Relief valves*—Used in pneumatic systems to prevent damage. They act as pressure-limiting units and prevent excessive pressures from bursting lines and blowing out seals.

b. *Control valves*—Controls the direction and amount of flow.

c. *Check valves*—A one-direction flow control valve.

d. *Restrictors*—A type of control valve which reduces the rate of airflow and the speed of operation of an actuating unit.

e. *Filters*—Protect pneumatic systems against dirt.

2. What is bleed air? (FAA-H-8083-32)

Bleed air is taken from any of the various pressure stages of a compressor. The exact location of the bleed ports is, of course, dependent on the pressure or temperature required for a particular job. The ports are small openings in the compressor case adjacent to the particular stage from which the air is to be bled; thus, varying degrees of pressure or heat are available simply by tapping into the appropriate stage (i.e., P 2.5 or P 3.0 air). Air is often bled from the final or highest pressure stage, since at this point, pressure and air temperature are at a maximum. At times it may be necessary to cool this high pressure air. If it is used for cabin pressurization or other purposes where excess heat would be uncomfortable or detrimental, the air is sent through a refrigeration unit.

3. Which systems use bleed air? (FAA-H-8083-32)

Bleed air is utilized in a wide variety of ways depending on the aircraft. Some of the most common applications are:

a. Cabin pressurization, heating, and cooling.

b. Deicing and anti-icing equipment.

c. Pneumatic starting of engines.

d. Auxiliary drive units (ADU).

4. What are several operational considerations when flying an aircraft equipped with a bleed air system?

The available amount of power produced by an engine is reduced with the use of bleed air, since air pressure and heat are extracted from the compressors prior to combustion.

Restrictions are imposed concerning the use of bleed air during takeoffs and maximum performance situations, such as go-arounds. When use of bleed air during takeoff is necessary (i.e., operation of deice or anti-ice equipment in icing conditions), correction factors are applied restricting takeoff speeds and weights.

Leaks that develop in the bleed air ducting can result in onboard fires due to the extremely high operating temperatures. Bleed air systems use a system of sensors located along the various ducts to alert pilots of bleed air leaks or over-temperature conditions.

5. What is an APU and what is it used for? (FAA-H-8083-32)

An auxiliary power unit is a gas turbine powered engine used to provide a supplementary source of pneumatic and electrical power to the aircraft, usually located in the aft fuselage and isolated from the rest of the airplane by a firewall. An APU can be used simultaneously with or independently from the other airplane power sources, and are normally used to operate aircraft systems while on the ground. However, they may also be used in-flight as a source of backup electrical power for the main generators, as well as pneumatic power for in-flight pressurization and air conditioning systems.

6. What are the two most common air-cooling systems utilized in turbine-powered aircraft? (FAA-H-8083-31)

Air-cycle machine and vapor-cycle machine.

7. What is an air-cycle machine (ACM)? (FAA-H-8083-31)

A type of cooling system used mainly in larger turbine-powered aircraft, consisting of an expansion turbine (cooling turbine), an air-to-air heat exchanger, and valves that control airflow through the system. The expansion turbine incorporates an impeller and a turbine on a common shaft. High-pressure air from the compressor is routed through the turbine section; as the air passes through the turbine, it rotates the turbine and the impeller. After the compressed air performs the work of turning the turbine, it undergoes a pressure and temperature drop. It is this temperature drop that produces the cold air used for air conditioning.

8. Discuss the operational cycle of a typical ACM. (FAA-H-8083-31)

Bleed air is fed to a primary heat exchanger where it is cooled by ground air (driven by cooling fans) or ram air (in-flight). Heat exchangers are similar in design to radiators. The cooled bleed air is then routed to a turbine-driven compressor.

The compressor compresses the cooled air resulting in an increase in temperature. The compressed air is then routed to a secondary heat exchanger where the air is again cooled. A water separator removes water vapor, which is then used to provide additional cooling for the heat exchanger.

The compressed, dry air is then routed to drive a turbine where it is also expanded and, therefore, cooled again (near 0°C at this point). Depending on the temperature selected, cold air is mixed with hot air in a mixing chamber and then supplied to the cabin/cockpit areas by recirculation fans.

The air cycle system is often called the air conditioning package or "pack." It is usually located in the lower half of the fuselage or in the tail section of turbine-powered aircraft.

9. What is a vapor-cycle machine (VCM)? (FAA-H-8083-31)

A type of cooling system used mostly in smaller aircraft, or aircraft with a limited supply of bleed air (smaller engines). VCMs are similar in principle to the kitchen refrigerator or air conditioner in a car. They use similar components and operating principles, and in most cases depend upon an electrical system for power. This system usually has a greater cooling capacity than an air-cycle system, and in addition, can usually be used for cooling on the ground when the engines are not operating. These systems are also used on several large transport category type of aircraft.

10. What are the major components of a vapor-cycle machine? (FAA-H-8083-31)

The compressor, condenser, evaporator, and expansion valve. Other minor items may include the condenser fan, receiver (refrigerated gas storage), dryer, surge valve, and temperature controls. These items are interconnected by appropriate tubing to form a closed loop in which the refrigerated gas is circulated during operation.

11. Explain the operational cycle of a typical VCM. (FAA-H-8083-31)

a. *Compressor*—Increases the pressure of refrigerated gas when in vapor form. This high pressure raises the condensation temperature of the gas and produces the force necessary to circulate the gas through the system. The compressor is driven either by an electric motor or air-turbine drive mechanism.

b. *Condenser*—Refrigerated gas is pumped to the condenser for the next step in the cycle. At the condenser, the gas goes through a heat exchanger where outside (ambient) air removes heat from it. When heat is removed from the high-pressure gas, its state changes and it condenses to a liquid, releasing the heat the gas picked up from the cabin air.

c. *Receiver*—From the condenser, the liquid gas flows to the receiver which acts as a reservoir for the liquid refrigerant. The fluid level in the receiver varies with system demands. During peak cooling periods, there will be less liquid than when the load is light. The prime function of the receiver is to ensure that the thermostatic expansion valve is not starved for refrigerant under heavy cooling load conditions.

d. *Evaporator*—Some vapor-cycle systems use an evaporator or subcooler to reduce the temperature of the liquid refrigerant after it leaves the receiver. By cooling the refrigerant, premature vaporization (flash-off) can be prevented. Maximum cooling takes place when the refrigerant changes from a liquid to a gaseous state. Air routed past the evaporator is cooled and recirculated to the cabin/cockpit areas.

12. Describe the operation of a heat exchanger.
(FAA-H-8083-31)

A heat exchanger is a device used to exchange heat from one medium to another. Radiators, condensers, and evaporators are all examples of heat exchangers. Heat always moves from the object or medium having the greatest level of heat energy to a medium or object having a lower level.

13. What are the three basic components of an aircraft oxygen system? (CAMI OK-21-0375)

Most oxygen systems (portable or installed) consist of three components:

a. A storage system (containers).
b. A delivery system.
c. Mask or nasal cannula.

14. What are several types of oxygen systems in use?
(FAA-H-8083-25, FAA-H-8083-31)

Systems are often characterized by the type of regulator used to dispense the oxygen:

a. Diluter-demand.
b. Pressure-demand.
c. Continuous-flow.
d. Electrical pulse demand.

15. Explain how a diluter-demand oxygen system operates.
(FAA-H-8083-25)

Diluter-demand oxygen systems supply oxygen only when the user inhales through the mask. An automix lever allows the regulators to automatically mix cabin air and oxygen or supply 100 percent oxygen, depending on the altitude. The demand mask provides a tight seal over the face to prevent dilution with outside air and can be used safely up to 40,000 feet.

16. What type of oxygen system is used to provide oxygen to the crew in a transport category aircraft?
(FAA-H-8083-31)

The pressure-demand flow system is widely used as a crew system, especially on the larger transport aircraft. Many aircraft have a combination of both pressure-demand and continuous flow systems that may be augmented by portable equipment.

17. How does a pressure-demand oxygen system operate?
(FAA-H-8083-25, FAA-H-8083-31)

When oxygen is delivered only as the user inhales, or on demand, it is known as a demand-flow system. During the hold and exhalation periods of breathing, the oxygen supply is stopped and the duration of the oxygen supply is prolonged, as none is wasted. Pressure demand oxygen systems are similar to diluter demand oxygen equipment, except that oxygen is supplied to the mask under pressure at cabin altitudes above 34,000 feet. Pressure demand regulators create airtight and oxygen-tight seals, but they also provide a positive pressure application of oxygen to the mask face piece that allows the user's lungs to be pressurized with oxygen; this makes them safe at altitudes above 40,000 feet.

18. What type of oxygen system is commonly used on transport category aircraft to provide oxygen to the passengers in the event of a pressurization failure?
(FAA-H-803-31)

A fully integrated supplementary oxygen system is used as backup on pressurized aircraft in case of pressurization failure. This system uses solid chemical oxygen generators stored in the overhead PSU attached to hoses and masks for every passenger on board the aircraft. When a depressurization occurs, or the flight crew activates a switch, a compartment door opens and the masks and hoses fall out in front of the passengers. The action of pulling the mask down to a usable position actuates an electric current, or ignition hammer, that ignites the oxygen candle and initiates the flow of oxygen. Typically, 10 to 20 minutes of oxygen is available for each user. This is calculated to be enough time for the aircraft to descend to a safe altitude for unassisted breathing.

19. At what cabin altitudes do oxygen system regulators provide a flow of oxygen? (FAA-H-8083-25)

Most regulators approved for use up to 40,000 feet are designed to provide zero percent cylinder oxygen and 100 percent cabin air at cabin altitudes of 8,000 feet or less, with the ratio changing to 100 percent oxygen and zero percent cabin air at approximately 34,000 feet cabin altitude. Most regulators approved up to 45,000 feet are designed to provide 40 percent cylinder oxygen and 60 percent cabin air at lower altitudes, with the ratio changing to 100 percent at the higher altitude.

20. How does a continuous-flow oxygen system operate? (FAA-H-8083-25)

Continuous flow oxygen systems are usually provided for passengers. The passenger mask typically has a reservoir bag that collects oxygen from the continuous flow oxygen system during the time when the mask user is exhaling. The oxygen collected in the bag allows a higher inspiratory flow rate during the inhalation cycle, which reduces the amount of air dilution. Ambient air is added to the supplied oxygen during inhalation after the reservoir bag oxygen supply is depleted. The exhaled air is released to the cabin.

21. What are several functions that must be accomplished by a cabin pressurization system? (FAA-H-8083-31)

It must be capable of maintaining a cabin pressure altitude of approximately 8,000 feet at the aircraft's maximum designed cruising altitude. The system must also be designed to prevent rapid changes of cabin altitude that may be uncomfortable or injurious to passengers and crew. The pressurization system should permit a reasonably fast exchange of air from inside to outside the cabin, in order to eliminate odors and remove stale air.

22. What areas are pressurized in most turbine-powered aircraft? (FAA-H-8083-25)

In the typical pressurization system, the cabin, flight compartment, and baggage compartments are incorporated into a sealed unit capable of containing air under a pressure higher than outside atmospheric pressure.

23. Describe in general terms how the cabin pressurization system functions. (FAA-H-8083-25)

In a typical pressurization system, the cabin, flight compartment, and baggage compartments are incorporated into a sealed unit capable of containing air under a pressure higher than outside atmospheric pressure. On aircraft powered by turbine engines, bleed air from the engine compressor section is used to pressurize the cabin. Superchargers may be used on older-model turbine-powered aircraft to pump air into the sealed fuselage. Piston-powered aircraft may use air supplied from each engine turbocharger through a sonic venturi (flow limiter). Air is released from the fuselage by a device called an outflow valve. By regulating the air exit, the outflow valve allows for a constant inflow of air to the pressurized area.

24. What is a pressurization controller? (FAA-H-8083-31)

The pressurization controller is the source of control signals for the pressurization system. The controller automatically (or manually) controls the outflow valves to maintain the desired pressurization level, and provides several adjustment knobs to obtain the desired type of pressurized condition.

25. Describe the various pressurization controller indicators. (FAA-H-8083-25)

a. *Cabin differential pressure gauge*—Indicates the difference between inside and outside pressure. This gauge should be monitored to ensure the cabin is not approaching the maximum allowable differential pressure.

b. *Cabin altimeter*—Indicates cabin pressure altitude. Provides a check on system performance; in some cases the cabin altimeter indicator may be incorporated into the cabin differential pressure gauge indicator, thus eliminating the need for two separate gauges.

c. *Cabin rate-of-climb or descent*—Indicates cabin rate-of-climb.

26. What are outflow valves? (FAA-H-8083-31)

The principal control of the pressurization system is the outflow valve. Cabin pressure is maintained by manually or automatically regulating the amount of cabin air vented overboard by the outflow valve(s), which is placed in a pressurized portion of the fuselage, usually underneath the lower compartments. The flow through an outflow valve is determined by the degree of valve opening, ordinarily controlled by an automatic system that can be set by the flight crewmembers.

27. Discuss the operation of outflow valves on the ground and in the air. (FAA-H-8083-31)

In many aircraft, the outflow valve(s) will be held fully open on the ground by a landing gear operated switch. During flight, as altitude is gained, the valve(s) close(s) gradually to make a greater restriction to the outflow of cabin air. The cabin rate-of-climb or descent is determined by the rate of closing or opening of the outflow valve(s). During cruising flight the cabin altitude is directly related to the degree of outflow valve opening.

28. Define *cabin differential pressure.* (FAA-H-8083-31)

Cabin differential pressure is the ratio between inside and outside air pressures and is a measure of the internal stress on the fuselage skin. If the differential pressure becomes too great, structural damage to the fuselage may occur.

29. What is the purpose of a negative pressure-relief valve? (FAA-H-8083-31)

All pressurized aircraft require some form of a negative pressure-relief valve. This valve may also be incorporated into the outflow valve or may be an individual unit. A common form of negative pressure-relief valve is a simple hinged flap on the rear wall (pressure dome) of the cabin. This valve opens when outside air pressure is greater than cabin pressure. During pressurized flight, the internal cabin pressure holds the flap closed and the negative pressure-relief valve prevents cabin altitude from accidentally going higher than the aircraft altitude.

30. What is a dump valve? (FAA-H-8083-31)

Also known as a safety-relief or manual depressurization valve. A manually operated valve for controlling pressurization when all other means of control have failed. Permits rapid depressurization during fires or an emergency descent.

31. What are positive pressure-relief valves?
(FAA-H-8083-31)

Also known as an automatic cabin-pressure relief valve, these
are used on all pressurized aircraft. May actually be built into the
outflow valve or may be an entirely separate unit. The pressure-
relief valve automatically opens when the cabin differential
pressure reaches a preset value.

32. How is the pressurization system controlled on aircraft equipped with digital aircraft monitoring systems?
(FAA-H-8083-31)

The system is almost completely automatic. Increased use of
automatic redundancy and advanced operating logic simplifies
operation of the pressurization system. In aircraft equipped with
an EICAS or electronic centralized aircraft monitor (ECAM), the
pressurization panel may contain no gauges. Pressurization system
information is provided on the environmental control system
(ECS) page of the monitoring system. The cabin pressurization
panel remains in the cockpit primarily for manual control.

I. Avionics and Communications

1. Give a brief description of an autopilot system.
(AC 25.1329)

The autopilot function provides automatic control of the airplane,
typically in pitch, roll, and yaw. The term includes the sensors,
computers, power supplies, servo-motors/actuators and associated
wiring, necessary for its function. It includes any indications and
controllers necessary for the pilot to manage and supervise the
system. Any part of the autopilot system that remains connected
to the primary flight controls when the autopilot is not in use is
regarded as a part of the primary flight controls.

2. What is the function of a flight director (FD)?
(AC 25.1329)

An FD is a visual cue or set of cues that are used during manual
control of the airplane as command information to direct the pilot
how to maneuver the airplane, usually in pitch, roll and/or yaw, to
track a desired flight path. The FD, displayed on the pilot's primary

head-down attitude indicator (ADI) or head up display (HUD), is a component of the FGS and is integrated with airborne attitude, air data, and NAV systems.

3. Describe an electronic flight instrument system (EFIS). (FAA-H-8083-31)

An EFIS is a number of cathode-ray tube (CRT) or flat-panel display screens in cockpit instrumentation to replace individual mechanical gauges. It uses dedicated signal generators that receive flight, navigation, and powerplant information to drive independent displays. Through a display controller, the pilot can select the various mode or screen features to be displayed. Modern EFIS usually consists of a primary flight display (PFD), a multifunction display (MFD), and an engine indicating and crew alerting system (EICAS) display.

4. What is a flight management system (FMS)? (FAA-H-8083-31)

An FMS is an onboard computer system which integrates inputs from various subsystems to assist the pilot in controlling the airplane's lateral and vertical paths. The main component of an FMS is the flight management computer (FMC) which communicates with the EICAS or ECAM, the ADC, the thrust management computer that controls the autothrottle functions, the EFIS symbol generators, the automatic flight control system, the inertial reference system, collision avoidance systems, and all of the radio navigational aids via data busses.

5. How does a pilot input commands to the fight management system (FMS)? (FAA-H-8083-31)

The interface to the system is a control display unit (CDU) that is normally located forward on the center pedestal in the cockpit. The typical FMS uses two CDUs that operate independently as the pilot's unit and the copilot's unit. Each unit contains a full alphanumeric keypad, a CRT or LCD display/work screen, status and condition annunciators, and specialized function keys. In normal operation, the pilot and copilot divide the workload, with the pilot's CDU set to supervise and interface with operational parameters and the copilot's CDU handling navigational chores.

6. What is an electronic flight bag (EFB)? (AC 120-76)

An EFB is any device, or combination of devices, actively displaying EFB applications. An EFB hosts applications that generally replace conventional paper products and tools traditionally carried in the pilot's flight bag. EFB applications include natural extensions of traditional flight bag contents, such as replacing paper copies of weather information with access to near-real-time information. EFBs are either portable or installed equipment.

7. Briefly describe the two EFB classifications. (AC 120-76)

Portable EFBs—Portable components supporting EFB applications are considered portable electronic devices (PEDs). For a PED to be considered an EFB, the PED must actively display Types A and/or B software application(s). (For example, when a PED is displaying personal email, the PED is not considered an EFB; when the same PED is authorized and actively displaying a Type B aeronautical chart application, it is then considered an EFB.)

Installed EFBs—Installed equipment indicates equipment or EFB components that are installation-approved under the aircraft type design. EFB equipment components supporting EFB applications are considered to be installed when they are incorporated into aircraft type design under 14 CFR Part 21 or as a proper alteration under 14 CFR Part 43 (§43.3).

8. Describe two EFB application types. (AC 120-76)

EFB applications are categorized as Type A or B, and they can be hosted on either portable or installed components.

Type A applications:

a. Have a failure condition classification that is considered to have no safety effect.

b. Include items such as flightcrew member-required rest logs, pilot flight and duty-time logs, minimum equipment lists (MEL), and configuration deviation lists (CDL).

c. Do not substitute for or replace any paper, system, or equipment required by airworthiness or operational regulations.

(continued)

d. Do not require specific authorization for use (i.e., although the Type A EFB application is part of the operator's EFB program, Type A EFB applications are not identified or controlled in the operations specifications [ops specs] or management specifications [MSpecs]).

Type B applications:

a. Have a failure condition classification considered minor.

b. Include items such as electronic aeronautical charts, electronic checklists, weather and aeronautical information, weight and balance calculations, and performance calculations for takeoff, en route, approach and landing, missed approach, go-around, etc.

c. May substitute or replace paper products of information required for dispatch or to be carried in the aircraft.

d. May not substitute for or replace any installed equipment required by airworthiness or operating regulations.

e. Require specific authorization for operational authorization for use (i.e., each Type B EFB application must be authorized by the FAA in the ops specs or MSpecs).

9. What are examples of portable EFB components that support EFB functionality? (AC 120-76)

EFB mount, display, external Global Positioning System (GPS), cables/cords/adapters, and portable wireless transmitters.

10. Who has the responsibility of verifying that any EFB depicted information is current and up to date? (AC 120-76)

It is the responsibility of the pilot-in-command (PIC) to verify EFB depictions of an en route, terminal area, approach, airport map, or sectional is current and up-to-date. Operators should establish revision control procedures so that flight crews and others can ensure that the contents of the database are current and complete.

11. Do regulations allow the use of portable electronic devices (PEDs) onboard an aircraft? (AC 120-76, AC 91.21-1)

PEDs are typically consumer commercial off-the-shelf (COTS) electronic devices functionally capable of communications, data processing, and/or utility. The use of any PED in an aircraft is subject to compliance with PED regulations (§91.21, §121.306, §125.204, and §135.144) and must be evaluated by the user/operator prior to use to ensure the PED will not interfere in any way with the operation of aircraft. The definition of a PED is intended to encompass transmitting portable electronic devices (T-PEDs). Compliance with PED regulations is further explained in AC 91.21-1, Use of Portable Electronic Devices Aboard Aircraft.

12. Describe how an onboard weather radar system functions. (FAA-H-8083-31)

An onboard weather radar uses an adjustable aircraft mounted radar antenna to detect, in real time, weather phenomena near the aircraft. Radio waves used in weather radar systems are in the super high frequency (SHF) range and are transmitted forward of the aircraft from a directional antenna usually located behind a non-metallic nose cone. Pulses of approximately 1 microsecond in length are transmitted and a duplexer in the radar transceiver switches the antenna to receive for about 2,500 microseconds after the pulse is transmitted to receive and process any returns. This cycle repeats and the receiver circuitry builds a two dimensional image of precipitation for display. Gain adjustments control the range of the radar. A control panel facilitates this and other adjustments.

13. How are the radar returns depicted on the flight deck? (FAA-H-8083-31)

The on-board weather radar receiver is set up to depict heavy returns as red, medium return as yellow and light returns as green on a display in the flight deck. Magenta is reserved to depict intense or extreme precipitation. Most modern aircraft integrate the weather radar display into the navigation display(s).

14. Describe an inertial navigation system (INS).
(FAA-H-8083-15)

An INS is a computer-based navigation system that tracks the movement of an aircraft via signals produced by onboard accelerometers. The initial location of the aircraft is entered into the computer, and all subsequent movement of the aircraft is sensed and used to keep the position updated. An INS does not require any inputs from outside signals.

15. Is the United States GPS system part of the Global Navigation Satellite System (GNSS)? (FAA-H-8083-16)

Yes. GNSS is an umbrella term adopted by the International Civil Aviation Organization (ICAO) to encompass any independent satellite navigation system used by a pilot to perform onboard position determinations from the satellite data. The four global GNSS systems are GPS (United States), GLONASS (Russia), Galileo (European Union), and BeiDou (China).

16. Explain the term *Satellite-Based Augmentation System* (SBAS). (AC 90-107)

SBAS is a wide area coverage augmentation system. The user receives GPS constellation augmentation information from a geostationary satellite-based transmitter. SBAS complements the core GPS satellite constellation by increasing navigation accuracy, integrity, continuity and availability provided within a service area. The U.S. SBAS is known as the Wide Area Augmentation System (WAAS).

17. The U.S. version of the Ground-Based Augmentation System (GBAS) is referred to as the Local Area Augmentation System (LAAS). What is GBAS? (FAA-H-8083-16)

GBAS is a ground-based augmentation to GPS that focuses its service on the airport area (approximately a 20–30 mile radius) for precision approach, DPs, and terminal area operations. It broadcasts its correction message via a VHF radio data link from a ground-based transmitter. GBAS yields the extremely high accuracy, availability, and integrity necessary for Category I, II, and III precision approaches and provides the ability for flexible, curved approach paths. GBAS requires FAA-approved avionics installed in the aircraft.

Note: The worldwide community has adopted GBAS as the official term for this type of navigation system. The FAA is also adopting the term GBAS to be consistent with the international community.

18. Describe the Automatic Dependent Surveillance – Broadcast (ADS-B) system. (AIM 4-5-7)

The ADS-B system is composed of aircraft avionics and ground-based infrastructure. Onboard avionics determine the position of the aircraft by using the GNSS and transmit position information, along with additional information about the aircraft, to ground stations for use by ATC and other ADS-B services. This information is automatically transmitted at a rate of approximately once per second. ADS-B is:

Automatic—The system automatically broadcasts aircraft position with no external interrogation required.

Dependent—The system depends on GPS for position information.

Surveillance—The system provides surveillance information to ATC.

Broadcast—The system is always broadcasting.

19. What are the two types of ADS-B equipment? (AC 90-114)

ADS-B Out—automatically broadcasts aircraft's GPS position, altitude, velocity, and other information out to ATC ground based surveillance stations as well as directly to other aircraft. It is required in all airspace where transponders are required.

ADS-B In—equipment that handles the receipt, processing, and display of ADS-B transmissions. ADS-B In capability is necessary to receive ADS-B traffic and broadcast services, including Flight Information Service–Broadcast (FIS-B) and Traffic Information Services–Broadcast (TIS-B).

20. Explain why, in the United States, ADS-B equipped aircraft exchange information on one of two frequencies. (AIM 4-5-7)

1090 MHz frequency—Associated with Mode A, C, and S transponder operations. 1090 MHz transponders with integrated ADS-B functionality extend the transponder message sets with additional information known as an "extended squitter," and are referred to as 1090ES. ADS-B with 1090ES is required by all aircraft operated in the United States above 18,000 feet (Class A airspace).

978 MHz frequency—ADS-B equipment operating on 978 MHz is known as the Universal Access Transceiver (UAT). UATs have the ability to both transmit and receive information. The transmission of ADS-B information from an aircraft is known as ADS-B Out and the receipt of ADS-B information by an aircraft is known as ADS-B In.

Note: In general, operators flying at 18,000 feet and above (Class A airspace) are required to have 1090ES equipment. Those that do not fly above 18,000 feet may use either UAT or 1090ES equipment.

21. Briefly describe Traffic Information Service–Broadcast (TIS-B). (AIM 4-5-6, AIM 4-5-8, AC 90-114)

TIS-B is the broadcast of ATC derived traffic information to ADS-B equipped (1090ES or UAT) aircraft from ground radio stations. The source of this traffic information is derived from ground-based air traffic surveillance sensors. TIS-B service is available throughout the NAS where there is both adequate surveillance coverage from ground sensors and adequate broadcast coverage from ADS-B ground radio stations.

Note: Traffic Information Services-B (TIS-B) is not related to Traffic Information Service (TIS). TIS is only available at specific terminal Mode S radar sites. Though similar in some ways, TIS is not related to TIS-B. *See* AIM 4-5-6.

22. Explain the limitations a pilot should be aware of when using TIS-B. (AIM 4-5-8, AC 90-114)

a. TIS-B is not intended to be used as a collision avoidance system and does not relieve the pilot's responsibility to "see and avoid" other aircraft, in accordance with 14CFR §91.113b.

b. A pilot may receive an intermittent TIS-B target of themselves, typically when maneuvering (e.g., climbing turns) due to the radar not tracking the aircraft as quickly as ADS-B.

c. The ADS-B-to-radar association process within the ground system may at times have difficulty correlating an ADS-B report with corresponding radar returns from the same aircraft. When this happens the pilot may see duplicate traffic symbols (i.e., "TIS-B shadows") on the cockpit display.

d. Updates of TIS-B traffic reports will occur less often than ADS-B traffic updates. TIS-B position updates will occur approximately once every 3 to 13 seconds depending on the type of radar system in use within the coverage area. In comparison, the update rate for ADS-B is nominally once per second.

e. The TIS-B system only uplinks data pertaining to transponder-equipped aircraft. Aircraft without a transponder will not be displayed as TIS-B traffic.

23. Describe the Traffic Alert Collision Avoidance System (TCAS). (FAA-H-8083-15)

TCAS is an airborne system developed by the FAA that operates independently from the ground-based ATC system. TCAS was designed to increase flight deck awareness of nearby aircraft and to serve as a last line of defense against midair collisions.

There are two levels of TCAS systems:

TCAS I—Developed to accommodate GA and regional airlines. This system issues traffic advisories (TAs) and relative bearing and altitude information of potentially conflicting traffic to assist pilots in visual acquisition of nearby aircraft and collision avoidance.

TCAS II—A more sophisticated system which provides the same information of TCAS I. It also analyzes the projected flightpath of approaching aircraft and issues resolution advisories (RAs) to the pilot to resolve potential midair collisions. Additionally, if communicating with another TCAS II equipped aircraft, the two systems coordinate RAs to their respective flight crews.

24. Briefly describe the terrain awareness and warning system (TAWS). (FAA-H-8083-15)

A TAWS uses GPS positioning and a database of terrain and obstructions to provide true predictability of the upcoming terrain and obstacles. The warnings it provides pilots are both aural and visual, instructing the pilot to take specific action. Because TAWS relies on GPS and a database of terrain/obstacle information, predictability is based upon aircraft location and projected location. The system is time based and therefore compensates for the performance of the aircraft and its speed.

25. What are the three principle alerting functions a Class A TAWS system will provide indications of? (AC 25-23)

a. Forward-looking terrain-avoidance (FLTA), which includes:
   - Reduced required terrain clearance.
   - Imminent terrain impact.
b. Premature descent alert (PDA).
c. Basic GPWS functions, which include:
   - Excessive rates of descent.
   - Excessive closure rate to terrain.
   - Negative climb rate or altitude loss after takeoff.
   - Flight into terrain when not in landing configuration.
   - Excessive downward deviation from and ILS glideslope.
   - Descent of the airplane to 500 feet above the terrain or nearest runway elevation (voice callout).

26. What are the three principle alerting functions a Class B TAWS system will provide indications of? (AC 25-23)

a. FLTA, which includes:
   - Reduced required terrain clearance.
   - Imminent terrain impact.
b. PDA.
c. Basic GPWS functions, which include:
   - Excessive rates of descent.
   - Negative climb rate or altitude loss after take-off.
   - Descent of the airplane to 500 feet above the terrain or nearest runway elevation (voice callout).

27. Can a terrain awareness and warning system (TAWS-B) be used for navigation? (AC 25-23)

The limitations section of the aircraft's AFM or AFM Supplement will state that navigation must not be predicated upon the use of TAWS. A terrain display is intended to serve as a situational awareness tool only. It may not provide the accuracy and/or fidelity on which to solely base decisions and plan maneuvers to avoid terrain or obstacles.

28. What are high frequency (HF) radio communications used for in aviation? (AC 91-70)

High radio frequencies between 3 and 30 MHz are used for air-to-ground voice communication in overseas operations. HF radios have been in use for almost a century over oceanic and remote continental areas. HF communications are dependent on transmitted signals striking the ionosphere and reflecting back to antennae at ground stations.

29. Explain why HF communications are utilized in aircraft communications. (FAA-H-8083-28)

HF communications at low to mid-latitudes are used by aircraft during transoceanic flights and routes where line-of-sight VHF communication is not an option. HF enables a skip mode to send a signal around the curvature of the Earth. HF communications on the dayside can be adversely affected when a solar flare occurs and its photons rapidly alter the electron density of the lower altitudes of the ionosphere, causing fading, noise, or a total blackout. Usually these disruptions are short-lived (tens of minutes to a few hours), so the outage ends fairly quickly.

30. What is controller-pilot data link communication (CPDLC)? (AC 90-117)

CPDLC is a means of communication between controller and pilot. Messages from an aircraft to the Air Traffic Service Unit (ATSU) may follow a standard format or may be free text. Messages from a controller normally follow a standard format and usually require a response from the pilot.

31. What is Automatic Dependent Surveillance – Contract (ADS-C)? (AC 90-117)

ADS-C is an automated surveillance information system that sends position and other flight reports to the ATSU. After initial log-on/ notification, a link is established between the ground system and the aircraft. Without pilot input, the oceanic ATSU/Aeronautical Operational Control (AOC) can establish a "contract" with the aircraft to receive reports of aircraft identification, position, altitude, Mach number, vertical rate, true track, magnetic heading, ground speed, navigation waypoints, and meteorological data.

32. How are CPDLC and ADS-C used in aircraft communications? (AC 91-70)

CPDLC eliminates the often challenging HF voice communications that were the only communication link with oceanic and remote continental airspace air traffic controllers for decades. With CPDLC, you and the controller transfer ATC clearance requests and instructions digitally, reducing the likelihood of miscommunication. ADS-C is also widely used in oceanic and remote continental airspace and, in combination with CPDLC, has become required equipment to be assigned the most efficient routes across the NAT organized track system (OTS), where ATC allows minimum separation between aircraft.

33. At some airports, pilots can receive their pre-departure clearance (PDC) and digital automatic terminal information service (D-ATIS) information over the aircraft communications addressing and reporting system (ACARS). What is ACARS? (AC 90-117)

ACARS is a digital data link system for transmitting short, relatively simple messages between aircraft and ground stations via VHF, HF, or satellite. The aircraft portion of ACARS consists of an avionics computer called an ACARS management unit (MU) and a CDU. On the ground, the ACARS system is made up of a network of radio transceivers to receive (or transmit) data link messages and route them to various airlines on the network.

34. Where is high frequency data link (HFDL) communications used primarily? (AC 90-117)

HF provides an effective means of voice communication over long distance in oceanic and remote continental airspace. HF communication is no longer restricted to voice and provides another means of sending and receiving digital communication. HFDL augments existing VHF and satellite communications (SATCOM) (i.e., CPDLC and ADS-C) data link communication systems. A subnetwork of 15 HFDL ground stations extends worldwide communication coverage beyond that of VHF data link communication subnetworks.

35. Describe the function of an emergency locator transmitter (ELT). Do the regulations require ELTs to be installed on air carrier aircraft? (FAA-H-8083-31, 14 CFR 91.207)

An ELT is an independent battery powered transmitter activated by the excessive G-forces experienced during a crash. An ELT transmits a digital signal every 50 seconds on a frequency of 406.025 MHz at 5 watts for at least 24 hours. The signal is received anywhere in the world by satellites in the COSPAS-SARSAT satellite system. Aircraft engaged in scheduled flights by scheduled air carriers are not required to have ELT equipment.

Note: Modern ELTs may also transmit a signal on 121.5 MHz. However, ELTs transmitting on 121.5 have gradually been phased out in favor of the 406 MHz standard, and transmissions on 121.5 MHz are no longer received and relayed via satellite.

36. What information is recorded by the cockpit voice recorder (CVR) system? (AC 20-186)

A CVR system records the aural environment of the cockpit and communications to, from, and between flight crewmembers, and in some cases required data link messages to assist investigations of accidents and incidents. The objective is met by complying with the current requirements in 14 CFR Parts 23, 25, 27, 29, 91, 121, 125, 129, and 135.

37. For what period of time is the CVR required to operate?
(14 CFR 121.359, 135.151)

The CVR system must be operated continuously from the use of
the checklist before the flight to completion of the final checklist at
the end of the flight.

J. Ice Protection

**1. What are several methods to prevent or control ice
formation on aircraft?** (FAA-H-8083-31)

a. *Thermal*—heating surfaces using hot air.

b. *Electrical*—heating by electrical elements.

c. *Pneumatic*—breaking up ice formations, usually by inflatable
   boots.

d. *Chemical application*—glycol-based fluid.

2. Explain how deice boots function. (FAA-H-8083-31)

Pneumatic deicing systems use rubber deicers, called boots or
shoes, attached to the leading edge of the wing and stabilizers.
The deicers are composed of a series of inflatable tubes, which
during operation are inflated with pressurized air and deflated in
an alternating cycle. This inflation and deflation causes the ice to
crack and break off. The ice is then carried away by the airstream.
Deicer tubes are inflated by an engine-driven air pump (vacuum
pump), or by air bled from gas turbine engine compressors. The
inflation sequence is controlled by either a centrally-located
distributor valve, or by solenoid-operated valves located adjacent
to the deicer air inlets.

3. Explain how leading edge anti-ice systems function.
(FAA-H-8083-31)

Thermal systems used for the purpose of preventing the formation
of ice use heated air ducted span-wise along the inside of the
leading edge of the airfoil and distributed around its inner surface.
There are several methods used to provide heated air. These
include bleeding hot air from the turbine compressor, engine
exhaust heat exchangers, and ram air heated by a combustion
heater. Some aircraft systems include an automatic temperature
control, in which temperature is maintained within a predetermined

range by mixing heated air with cold air. A system of valves is provided in some installations to enable certain parts of the anti-icing system to be shut off. In the event of an engine failure, these valves also permit supplying the entire anti-icing system with heated air from one or more of the remaining engines.

4. What system is used for propeller anti-icing? (FAA-H-8083-32)

Most turboprop aircraft utilize a "hot prop" system which consists of an electrical energy source, a resistance heating element, system controls, and necessary wiring. The heating elements are mounted internally or externally on the propeller spinner and blades. Electrical power from the aircraft system is transferred to the propeller hub through electrical leads, which terminate in slip rings and brushes. Flexible connectors are used to transfer power from the hub to the blade elements. Icing control is accomplished by converting electrical energy to heat energy in the heating element. An automatic timer is used to control the sequence and operation of heating current in the blade elements.

5. What methods are used to prevent ice from forming in the engine air inlet? (AFM)

An engine inlet anti-ice system prevents ice from forming in the induction system via methods such as high-pressure bleed air, and electrically-heated elements. In some aircraft, hot exhaust air may be utilized. These systems are mounted on the engine nacelle air inlet lip, as well as in the forward area of the inertial separator (S-shaped duct). Some systems have a timer that automatically activates and deactivates the system, while other systems are operational from engine start to engine shut down.

6. What is an inertial separator? (AFM)

An S-shaped duct in the induction system of a turboprop engine that separates incoming air from suspended particles of ice, dirt, birds, etc., by forcing the incoming air to turn before entering the engine. Since foreign objects are solid they tend to continue in a straight line and most are separated by inertia at these bend points.

7. **What aircraft surfaces may be provided with icing protection? What type of protection?** (FAA-H-8083-31)

   a. *Leading edges of the wings*—thermal pneumatic, thermal electric, chemical, and pneumatic (deice).

   b. *Leading edges of vertical and horizontal stabilizers*—thermal pneumatic, thermal electric, and pneumatic (deice).

   c. *Windshield and windows*—thermal pneumatic, thermal electric, and chemical.

   d. *Heater and engine air inlets*—thermal pneumatic and thermal electric.

   e. *Pitot and static air data sensors*—thermal electric.

   f. *Propeller blade leading edge and spinner*—thermal electric and chemical.

   g. *Carburetor(s)*—thermal pneumatic and chemical.

   h. *Lavatory drains and portable water lines*—thermal electric.

K. Crewmember and Passenger Equipment

1. **Briefly describe the various types of oxygen masks provided for flight crewmembers and passengers.** (CAMI OK-21-0375)

   Nasal cannulas—Continuous-flow devices that offer the advantage of personal comfort. They are restricted by FAA regulations to 18,000 feet service altitude because of the risk of reducing oxygen-blood saturation levels if one breathes through the mouth or talks too much.

   Oral-nasal re-breather—The simplest in operation, least expensive, and the most common. It has an external plastic bag that inflates every time you exhale. The purpose of the bag is to store exhaled air so that it may be mixed with 100 oxygen from the system. These masks supply adequate oxygen to keep the user physiologically safe up to 25,000 feet.

   Quick-don mask—Must demonstrate the ability to be donned with one hand in 5 seconds or less, while accommodating prescription glasses. Quick-don masks are typically suspended or stored to permit quick and unimpeded access by cockpit crew. These masks are typically rated to altitudes up to 40,000 feet.

Airline drop-down units (Dixie cup)—A phase-sequential continuous-flow mask that looks similar to a general aviation re-breather but is functionally different. A phase sequential mask allows the user to go to higher altitudes by using a series of one-way ports that allow a mixture of 100 percent oxygen and cabin air into the mask. Exhalation is vented to the atmosphere; as a result, the bag does not inflate. This mask can be safely used at emergency altitudes up to 40,000 feet.

2. Describe protective breathing equipment (PBE). (14 CFR 121.337)

PBE is used in the event of smoke and fire and protects the entire head and shoulders of the person wearing it. It contains an oxygen generator which makes it a totally self-contained unit. It is required by 14 CFR Part 121 regulations.

3. What are several examples of the types of emergency equipment a flight crew is required to verify is onboard and available for use prior to flight? (drs.faa.gov)

Emergency equipment includes fire extinguishers, smoke detectors, PBE, portable oxygen bottles, first aid kits, emergency medical kits, a crash axe, megaphones, flotation devices, liferafts, and flashlights.

4. The regulations require flight crewmembers to brief the passengers on the location of what types of survival equipment? (drs.faa.gov)

When applicable, crewmembers must brief the passengers on the following:

a. *Fire extinguishers*—Location and use of fire extinguishers.

b. *Flotation equipment*—For flights that involve extended overwater operation, type, location, and use of required flotation equipment.

c. *Life rafts and slide rafts*—Must instruct passengers on life raft and slide/raft retrieval from stowage and their preparation for use.

(continued)

d. *Oxygen equipment*—For flights above 12,000 feet MSL, crewmembers must brief passengers on the normal and emergency use of oxygen.

e. *Pyrotechnic signaling device*—For each life raft.

5. All flight crewmembers must be familiar with the type, location, and purpose of each item of emergency equipment on board an aircraft. Give several examples of this equipment. (drs.faa.gov)

Fire and oxygen bottles, first aid kits, life rafts, life preservers, crash axes, and emergency exits/lights. Also, familiarity with items of egress equipment such as slides, slide rafts, escape straps or handles, hatches, ladders, or movable stairs should be included.

6. What are some of the responsibilities of the airline flight crewmembers in the event an emergency evacuation of the aircraft becomes necessary? (drs.faa.gov)

a. Recognize and act promptly in situations requiring an aircraft emergency evacuation.

b. Use good judgment when there is a need to terminate aircraft evacuations.

c. Communicate and coordinate throughout the evacuation process, until the evacuation is completed or terminated.

d. Recognize when evacuation equipment is inoperative or faulty, prevent the use of such equipment, and divert egressing passengers to usable exits.

e. Appropriate actions on aircraft equipped with APUs that have a tendency to "torch."

f. Manage passenger safety following unwarranted evacuations, especially after passengers have egressed from the aircraft and are on the ramp or taxiway.

L. Flight Controls

1. What are examples of primary and secondary/auxiliary flight controls? (FAA-H-8083-25)

Primary—ailerons, elevators, and rudder.

Secondary/Auxiliary—tabs, leading edge flaps, trailing edge flaps, spoilers, and slats.

2. Explain the purpose of trim tabs. (FAA-H-8083-31)

Trim tabs trim the aircraft in flight; that is, they correct any tendency of the aircraft to move toward an undesirable flight attitude. They control aircraft balance so that the aircraft maintains straight-and-level flight without pressure on the control column, control wheel, or rudder pedals. Movement of the tab in one direction causes a deflection of the control surface in the opposite direction. Most of the trim tabs installed on aircraft are mechanically operated from the cockpit through an individual cable system; some aircraft have trim tabs operated by an electrical actuator. Trim tabs are installed on elevators, rudders, and ailerons.

3. What is the function of a servo tab? (FAA-H-8083-31)

Servo tabs are very similar in operation and appearance to the trim tabs. Sometimes referred to as flight tabs, they are used primarily on the large main control surfaces to aid in moving the control surface and holding it in the desired position. Only the servo tab moves in response to movement of the cockpit control. The force of the airflow on the servo tab then moves the primary control surface. Less force is needed to move the main control surface when servo tabs are used.

4. Explain the function of leading edge flaps. (FAA-H-8083-31)

Leading edge flaps are airfoils extended from and retracted into the leading edge of the wing, used principally on large high-speed aircraft. When they are in the "up" (retracted) position, they fair in with the wings and serve as part of the wing trailing edge. When in the "down" (extended) position, the flaps pivot on the hinge points and drop to about a 45° or 50° angle with the wing chord line. This increases the wing camber and changes the airflow, providing greater lift.

5. What is flap asymmetry? (AFM)

Flap asymmetry is when the flap position varies within a pair of flaps.

6. What are ground spoilers? (FAA-H-8083-31)

Ground spoilers are lift-decreasing devices that are extended only after the aircraft is on the ground. They assist in braking action.

7. What are flight spoilers? (FAA-H-8083-31)

Flight spoilers are auxiliary wing flight control surfaces, mounted on the upper surface of each wing that operate in conjunction with the ailerons to provide lateral control. A wing's flight spoiler assists in lateral control by extending whenever the aileron is rotated up. When actuated as speed brakes, the spoiler panels on both wings raise up—the panel on the "up" aileron wing raises more than the panel on the "down" aileron side. This provides speed brake operation and lateral control simultaneously. The purpose of the spoilers is to disturb the smooth airflow across the top of the airfoil, thereby creating an increased amount of drag and a decreased amount of lift on that airfoil.

8. What are speed brakes? (FAA-H-8083-31)

Dedicated speed brake panels similar to flight spoilers in construction can be found on the upper surface of the wings of heavy and high-performance aircraft. They are designed specifically to increase drag and reduce the speed of the aircraft when they are deployed. The speed brake control in the cockpit can deploy all spoiler and speed brake surfaces fully when operated. Often, these surfaces are also rigged to deploy on the ground automatically when engine thrust reversers are activated.

9. What are leading edge slats? (FAA-H-8083-31)

A slat is a movable control surface attached to the leading edge of a wing. When the slat is closed (low angle-of-attack, high airspeed), it forms the leading edge of the wing. When in the open position (high angle-of-attack, low airspeed), the slat is extended forward, creating a slot between the slat and the wing leading edge. This increases the wing camber and changes the airflow, providing greater lift and allowing the aircraft to be controlled at airspeeds below the otherwise normal landing speed.

10. What are slots? (FAA-H-8083-30)

A slot in the leading edge of a wing directs high-energy air from under the wing to the airflow above the wing, accelerating upper airflow. By accelerating the airflow above the wing, airflow separation will be delayed to higher angles of attack. This allows the wing to continue to develop lift at substantially higher angles of attack. Slots are often placed on the part of the wing ahead of the ailerons, so during a wing stall, the inboard part of the wing stalls first and the ailerons remain effective.

11. What are stabilons? (FAA-H-8083-31)

Stabilons are small wing-like horizontal surfaces mounted on the aft fuselage to improve longitudinal stability of airplanes that have an exceptionally wide center of gravity range.

12. What are tailets? (FAA-H-8083-31)

Small vertical fins mounted to the lower sides of the horizontal stabilizer tips, designed to improve directional stability.

13. What are winglets? (FAA-H-8083-31)

Winglets are the near-vertical extension of the wingtip that reduces the aerodynamic drag associated with vortices that develop at the wingtips as the airplane moves through the air. By reducing the induced drag at the tips of the wings, fuel consumption decreases and range is extended.

14. What is a vortex generator? (FAA-H-8083-25)

Vortex generators are used to delay or prevent shock wave-induced boundary layer separation encountered in transonic flight. They are small, low aspect ratio airfoils placed at a 12° to 15° angle of attack (AOA) to the airstream. Usually spaced a few inches apart along the wing ahead of the ailerons or other control surfaces, vortex generators create a vortex that mixes the boundary airflow with the high energy airflow just above the surface. This produces higher surface velocities and increases the energy of the boundary layer. Thus, a stronger shock wave is necessary to produce airflow separation.

15. Explain the purpose of wing fences. (FAA-H-8083-31)

Wing fences are flat, metal, vertical plates fixed to the upper
surface of the wing. They obstruct spanwise airflow along the wing
and prevent the entire wing from stalling at once. They are often
attached on swept-wing aircraft to prevent the spanwise movement
of air at high AOA. Their purpose is to provide better slow-speed
handling and stall characteristics.

**16. Why do some aircraft have both inboard and outboard
ailerons?** (FAA-H-8083-25)

Some jet transports have two sets of ailerons, a pair of outboard
low-speed ailerons and a pair of high-speed inboard ailerons.
During low-speed flight, all lateral control surfaces operate
to provide maximum stability. This includes all four ailerons,
flaps, and spoilers. At high speeds, the flaps are retracted and the
outboard ailerons are locked out of the aileron control system.

M. Pitot-Static System

**1. Briefly describe the main components of the pitot static
system of a transport category aircraft.** (AFM)

The pitot static system provides pitot and static air pressure
to air data computers (two), a cabin pressure control panel
and an integrated standby instrument. The system consists of
two electrically-heated pitot static probes, an alternate pitot
probe, alternate static ports, and an electrically heated total air
temperature probe (TAT). Each of the pitot static probes consists of
a pitot mast and two static ports. Pitot pressure from each probe is
supplied to the same side ADC and static pressure from each probe
is supplied to each ADC. Static pressure from each of the probes
is supplied to each ADC. The alternate pitot probe and static ports
supply pressure to the integrated standby instrument (ISI).

**2. Explain the factors that make pitot-static systems
in transport category aircraft more complex.**
(FAA-H-8083-31)

Jet transport category aircraft operate at high altitude where
the ambient temperature can exceed 50°F below zero. The
compressibility of air is also altered at high speeds and at high
altitudes. Airflow around the fuselage changes, making it difficult
to pick up consistent static pressure inputs.

3. **How do flight crews compensate for factors of air temperature and density to obtain accurate instrument indications?** (FAA-H-8083-31)

While many analog instruments have compensating devices built into them, the use of an air data computer (ADC) is common for these purposes on high-performance aircraft. Moreover, modern aircraft utilize digital air data computers (DADC). The conversion of sensed air pressures into digital values makes them more easily manipulated by the computer to output accurate information that has compensated for the many variables encountered.

4. **What information does an air data computer (ADC) provide?** (FAA-H-8083-15, FAA-H-8083-31)

An ADC receives and processes pitot pressure, static pressure, and temperature to calculate very precise altitude, IAS, TAS, and air temperature. Outputs from the ADC are electric to drive servo motors or for use as inputs in pressurization systems, flight control units, and other systems. Digital ADC (DADC) outputs are distributed to these same systems and the cockpit display (EFIS) using a digital data bus.

N. Fire and Smoke Detection, Protection, and Suppression

1. **What are the subsystems of the fire protection system in most large turbine engine aircraft?** (FAA-H-8083-31)

A fire detection system and a fire extinguishing system.

2. **What are the areas on a transport category aircraft that have a fixed fire detection and/or fire extinguishing system?** (FAA-H-8083-31)

   a. Engines and APU.
   b. Cargo and baggage compartments.
   c. Lavatories on transport aircraft.
   d. Electronic bays.
   e. Wheel wells.
   f. Bleed air ducts.

3. **What are the different types of aircraft fire detection systems in common use?** (FAA-H-8083-31)

Thermal switch system—Heat-sensitive units that complete electrical circuits at a certain temperature. If the temperature rises above a set value in any section of the circuit, the thermal switch will close, completing the light circuit to indicate the presence of a fire or overheat condition.

Thermocouple system—Depends upon rate of temperature rise; compares the rate of temperature rise of an unprotected thermocouple to a protected thermocouple. If the temperature rises rapidly, the thermocouple produces a voltage due to the temperature difference between the two. If both are heated at the same rate, no voltage will result and no warning signal is given.

Continuous-loop detector system—Also called a sensing system, permits more complete coverage of a fire hazard area than any spot-type temperature detectors. Continuous-loop systems are versions of the thermal switch system. They are overheat systems with heat sensitive units that complete electrical circuits at a certain temperature. There is no rate of heat rise sensitivity in a continuous-loop system.

4. **Describe the operation of an engine or APU fire switch.** (FAA-H-8083-31)

The engine and APU fire switches are typically installed on the center overhead panel or center console in the flight deck. When an engine fire switch is activated, the following occurs: the engine stops because the fuel control shuts off, the engine is isolated from the aircraft systems, and the fire extinguishing system is activated. Some aircraft use fire switches that need to be pulled and turned to activate the system, while others use a push-type switch with a guard. To prevent accidental activation of the fire switch, a lock is installed that releases the fire switch only when a fire has been detected. This lock can be manually released by the flight crew if the fire detection system malfunctions.

5. **What are the different types of detectors used in the aircraft fire protection systems of most large turbine-engine aircraft?** (FAA-H-8083-31)

   A complete aircraft fire protection system incorporates several different detection methods, including rate-of-temperature-rise detectors, radiation-sensing detectors, smoke detectors, overheat detectors, carbon monoxide detectors, combustible mixture detectors, optical detectors, and observation of crew or passengers.

6. **What are the two primary types of smoke detectors used on aircraft?** (FAA-H-8083-31)

   Light refraction type—Contains a photoelectric cell that detects light refracted by smoke particles. Smoke particles refract the light to the photoelectric cell and, when it senses enough of this light, it creates an electrical current that sets off a light.

   Ionization type—Detector generates an alarm signal (both horn and indicator) by detecting a change in ion density due to smoke in the cabin. The system is connected to the 28 volt DC electrical power supplied from the aircraft. Alarm output and sensor sensitive checks are performed simply with the test switch on the control panel.

7. **What are the two types of flame detectors?** (FAA-H-8083-31)

   Optical sensors, often referred to as flame detectors, are designed to alarm when they detect the presence of prominent, specific radiation emissions from hydrocarbon flames. The two types of optical sensors available are infrared (IR) and ultraviolet (UV), based on the specific emission wavelengths that they are designed to detect. IR-based optical flame detectors are used primarily on light turboprop aircraft and helicopter engines.

8. **How is smoke detection accomplished in the cargo and baggage compartments?** (FAA-H-8083-31)

   Each compartment is equipped with an optical smoke detector that monitors air in the cargo compartments for smoke. Fans bring air from the cargo compartment into the smoke detector and if smoke is detected, a warning is provided on the flight deck.

9. Cargo and baggage compartments use what type of fire extinguishing systems? (FAA-H-8083-31)

The cargo compartment extinguishing system is activated by the flight crew if the smoke detectors detect smoke in the cargo compartment. Some aircraft are outfitted with two types of fire extinguisher containers. The first system is the dump system that releases the extinguishing agent directly when the cargo fire discharge switch is activated. This action extinguishes the fire. The second system is the metered system. After a time delay, the metered bottles discharge slowly and at a controlled rate through the filter regulator. Halon from the metered bottles replaces the extinguishing agent leakage. This keeps the correct concentration of extinguishing agent in the cargo compartment to keep the fire extinguished for 180 minutes.

10. How are fires in the cabin or flight deck extinguished? (FAA-H-8083-31)

Portable fire extinguishers are used to extinguish fires in the cabin or flight deck. The Halon extinguishers are used on electrical and flammable liquid fires. Some transport aircraft also use water fire extinguisher for use on non-electrical fires.

11. What are the two types of batteries used to power personal electronic devices (PEDs)? (SAFO 09013)

The two types of batteries commonly used to power consumer PEDs brought on aircraft are lithium batteries (disposable) and lithium-ion batteries (rechargeable). Both these types are capable of ignition and subsequent explosion due to overheating. Overheating results in thermal runaway, which can cause the release of either molten burning lithium or a flammable electrolyte. Once one cell in a battery pack goes into thermal runaway, it produces enough heat to cause adjacent cells to go into thermal runaway. The resulting fire can flare repeatedly as each cell ruptures and releases its contents. A battery in thermal runaway can reach temperatures above 1,100°F.

12. **What are the recommended procedures for fighting a lithium battery fire?** (AC 120-80, SAFO 09013)

   a. Relocate passengers away from the device.

   b. Utilize a halon, halon replacement, or water fire extinguisher to prevent the spread of the fire to adjacent battery cells and materials.

   c. Pour water or another nonalcoholic liquid over the cells immediately after knock down or extinguishment of the fire. Only water or other nonalcoholic liquid can provide sufficient cooling to prevent reignition, propagation, or both of the fire to adjacent batteries. Water, though it may react with the tiny amount of lithium metal found in a disposable battery, is most effective at cooling remaining cells, stopping thermal runaway, and preventing additional flareups. Significant cooling is needed to prevent the spread of fire to additional cells in a battery pack.

O. Envelope Protection

1. **Describe an angle of attack (AOA) indicator.** (FAA-H-8083-31)

   An AOA indicating system detects the angular difference between the relative wind and the fuselage. The sensing mechanism and transmitter are usually located on the forward side of the fuselage and contain a heating element to ensure ice-free operation. Signals are sent from the sensor to the cockpit or computer(s) as required. An AOA indicator may be calibrated in actual angle degrees, arbitrary units, percentage of lift used, symbols, or even fast/slow.

   Note: In the past, commercial aircraft were not typically equipped with AOA indicators. More modern aircraft have AOA sensor units installed that send output signals to an ADC where the AOA data is used to create an AOA indication, usually on a primary flight display.

2. Describe several types of flight envelope protection systems installed in transport category aircraft. (drs.faa.gov)

Flight envelope protection varies by aircraft type and, in some instances, by series. They include, but are not limited to:

a. *Fully integrated envelope protection*—employs protection algorithms as part of a larger set of flight control laws found on fly-by-wire aircraft. The system actively limits flight control position downstream of pilot input in order to keep the aircraft from exceeding predetermined envelope limits. The system may have high speed/low speed, bank angle, and load factor protections, in addition to AOA protection.

b. *Deterrent envelope protection*—or force feedback envelope protection, employs protection indirectly by applying force feedback cues, such as force gradients or steps, to the pilot in an effort to deter the pilot flying from continuing a control input that would cause the aircraft to exceed the normal flight envelope.

c. *Stick pusher*—typically employs mechanical means to lower the aircraft's AOA if a predetermined value is exceeded.

3. What is the purpose of stick shaker and stick pusher systems? (FAA-H-8083-3)

Stick pusher—A device that acts to automatically reduce the airplane's AOA before the airplane reaches a dangerous stall condition, or it may aid in recovering the airplane from a stall if an airplane's natural aerodynamic characteristics do so weakly.

Stick shaker—An artificial stall warning device that vibrates the control column when an impending stall is detected. Stick shakers normally activate at around 107 percent of the actual stall speed.

P. Minimum Equipment List and Configuration Deviation List

1. What is a minimum equipment list (MEL)? (drs.faa.gov)

An MEL is an operator-specific, FAA-approved document that includes a list of items that may be inoperative during a flight. The MEL allows an operator to continue a flight (or series of flights), with certain items inoperative, or reposition to a place where repairs can be made. The MEL serves as a reference guide for dispatchers and pilots to determine whether takeoff of an aircraft with inoperative instruments or equipment is authorized under the provisions of applicable regulatory requirements.

2. Explain the content and organization of an MEL. (FAA-H-8083-3)

The MEL includes a "General Section," comprised of definitions, general policies, as well as operational procedures for flight crews and maintenance personnel. Each aircraft component addressed in the MEL is listed in an alphabetical index for quick reference. A table of contents further divides the manual in different chapters, each numbered for its corresponding aircraft system designation (i.e., the electrical system, also designated as system number 24, would be found in chapter 24 of the MEL).

3. After landing at your destination, you discover an equipment item that is no longer functioning normally. Can you defer maintenance of this item if it is not listed in the MEL? (FAA-H-8083-3)

Pilots may defer repair of items on those aircraft systems and components allowed by the approved MEL. Per 14 CFR §91.213(a)(3)(ii), an MEL must provide for the operation of the aircraft with the instruments and equipment in an inoperable condition. If particular items do not allow for safe operation, they do not appear on the MEL and takeoff is not authorized until the item is adequately repaired or replaced (§91.213[a]). In cases where repairs may temporarily be deferred, operation or dispatch of an aircraft whose systems have been impaired is often subject to limitations or other conditional requirements explicitly stated in the MEL. Such conditional requirements may be of an operational nature, a mechanical nature, or both.

4. What is a configuration deviation list (CDL)? (FAA-H-8083-3)

AA configuration deviation list (CDL) is used in the same manner as an MEL, but it differs in that it addresses missing external parts of the aircraft rather than failing internal systems and their constituent parts. These parts typically include elements such as service doors, power receptacle doors, slat track doors, landing gear doors, APU ram air doors, flaps fairings, nose-wheel spray deflectors, position light lens covers, slat segment seals, static dischargers, etc.

5. Which aircraft have configuration deviation lists (CDLs), and where can a CDL be located? (drs.faa.gov)

A CDL is developed for most U.S.-built transport 14 CFR Part 25 aircraft and many 14 CFR Part 23 aircraft by aircraft manufacturers during the initial certification process. However, they are not a required element for aircraft certification. The manufacturer makes the decision to develop or not to develop a CDL. If deemed necessary, the aircraft manufacturer develops a proposed CDL and submits it to the responsible Aircraft Certification Office. For U.S.-manufactured airplanes, once the CDL is FAA-approved, it is either incorporated into the limitations section of the airplane flight manual (AFM) as an appendix or published as a supplement to the AFM.

6. Define the term *deferred maintenance*. (drs.faa.gov)

The operator's approved MEL allows the operator to continue a flight or series of flights with certain inoperative equipment. The continued operation must meet the requirements of the MEL deferral classification and the requirements for the equipment loss.

7. What are (O) and (M) procedures? (drs.faa.gov)

(O) and (M) procedures in the MEL refer to specific operating conditions and limitations, and to specific maintenance procedures used to deactivate inoperative items.

8. What is the difference between (O) and (M) procedures? (drs.faa.gov)

The (O) symbol indicates a specific "operations" procedure that must be accomplished during planning and/or operating when the item is inoperative. These procedures may be required for flight planning purposes, or they may require action by the flight crew. Additionally, MEL items that affect the aircraft weight and balance (W&B) and cargo loading may require procedures for additional personnel, such as those involved with aircraft load control.

The (M) symbol indicates a specific "maintenance" procedure that must be accomplished prior to operation when the item becomes inoperative. (M) procedures should be accomplished by the appropriately qualified maintenance personnel. Depending on the complexity of the procedures, an operator may authorize other personnel (e.g., a flightcrew member) with the appropriate qualifications to perform (M) procedures. Only appropriately qualified maintenance personnel may conduct procedures requiring specialized knowledge or skill or requiring the use of tools or test equipment.

9. What are the four main categories of aircraft inspections performed in an airline continuous maintenance program? (FAA-H-8083-30)

Airlines utilize a continuous maintenance program that includes both routine and detailed inspections. However, the detailed inspections may include different levels of detail. Often referred to as *checks*, the A-check, B-check, C-check, and D-check involve increasing levels of detail. A-checks are the least comprehensive and occur frequently. D-checks are extremely comprehensive, involving major disassembly, removal, overhaul, and inspection of systems and components; D-checks might occur only three to six times during the service life of an aircraft.

10. **What are the time limits allowed for repairs to inoperative systems or components that were deferred?** (drs.faa.gov)

    Category A—Items must be repaired within the time interval specified in the remarks column of the certificate holder's approved MEL.

    Category B—Items must be repaired within 3 consecutive calendar days (72 hours), excluding the day the malfunction was recorded in the aircraft maintenance record/logbook.

    Category C—Items must be repaired within 10 consecutive calendar days (240 hours), excluding the day the malfunction was recorded in the aircraft maintenance record/logbook.

    Category D—Items must be repaired within 120 consecutive calendar days (2,880 hours), excluding the day the malfunction was recorded in the aircraft maintenance log and/or record.

11. **After maintenance has been deferred on an MEL or CDL item, will the systems that are impaired by the deferral result in any aircraft operational limitations or restrictions?** (FAA-H-8083-3)

    In cases where repairs may temporarily be deferred, operation or dispatch of an aircraft whose systems have been impaired is often subject to limitations or other conditional requirements explicitly articulated in the MEL. Such conditional requirements may be of an operational nature, a mechanical nature, or both.

12. **Describe several examples of operational conditions that would apply after deferring a MEL or CDL item.** (FAA-H-8083-3)

    a. Limited use of aircraft systems.

    b. Downgraded IFR landing minima.

    c. Fuel increases due to additional burn, required APU usage, or potential fuel imbalance situations.

    d. Precautionary checks to be performed by the crew prior to departure, or special techniques to be applied while in flight.

    e. Weight penalties affecting takeoff, cruise, or landing performance (runway limit, climb limit, usable landing distance reduction, and VREF, takeoff V-speeds, N_1/EPR adjustments).

13. **What are several examples of flight restrictions that would apply after deferring maintenance on a MEL or CDL item?** (drs.faa.gov)

The operational flight plan must account for any operational limitations, such as aircraft or flight restrictions, imposed by the conditions or limitations of an MEL. Examples of operational limitations include but are not limited to:

a.   Altitude restrictions
b.   Cabin pressure limitations
c.   Temperature limitations
d.   Performance capabilities
e.   Weight restrictions
f.   Fuel penalties and limitations
g.   Navigational limitations
h.   Communication limitations
i.   Weather restrictions (including ice and rain limitations)

14. **What is a nonessential equipment and furnishings (NEF) program?** (drs.faa.gov)

A NEF program allows operators to use the deferral authority granted in the MEL to provide deferral relief for inoperative, damaged, or missing nonessential items located throughout the aircraft (i.e. passenger compartment, flight deck area, service areas, cargo areas, crew rest areas, lavatories, and galley areas; etc.). NEF items are:

a.   Items installed on the aircraft as part of the original type certification (TC), supplemental type certificate (STC), engineering order, or other form of alteration, that have no effect on the safe operation of the aircraft.

b.   Items not required by the applicable certification or operational rules.

c.   Items that, if inoperative, damaged, or missing, have no effect on the aircraft's ability to be operated safely under all operational conditions.

Performance
and Limitations

A. Takeoff and Climb

1. Define the following takeoff performance speeds: V_S, V_{MCG}, V_1, V_{EF}, V_R, V_{LOF}, V_2. (FAA-H-8083-3)

- V_S—Stalling speed or minimum steady flight speed at which the airplane is controllable.

- V_{MCG}—Minimum control speed on the ground. The calibrated airspeed during the takeoff run at which, when the critical engine is suddenly made inoperative, it is possible to maintain control of the airplane using the rudder control alone (without the use of nosewheel steering), as limited by 150 pounds of force, and using the lateral control to the extent of keeping the wings level to enable the takeoff to be safely continued.

- V_1—Critical engine failure speed or takeoff decision speed. It is the speed at which the pilot is to continue the takeoff in the event of an engine failure or other serious emergency. At speeds less than V_1, it is considered safer to stop the aircraft within the accelerate-stop distance. It is also the minimum speed in the takeoff, following a failure of the critical engine at V_{EF}, at which the pilot can continue the takeoff and achieve the required height above the takeoff surface within the takeoff distance.

- V_{EF}—The speed at which the critical engine is assumed to fail during takeoff. This speed is used during aircraft certification.

- V_R—Rotation speed, or the speed at which the rotation of the airplane is initiated to takeoff attitude. This speed cannot be less than V_1 or less than $1.05 \times V_{MCA}$ (minimum control speed in the air). On a single-engine takeoff, it must also allow for the acceleration to V_2 at the 35-foot height at the end of the runway.

- V_{LOF}—Lift-off speed, or the speed at which the airplane first becomes airborne. This is an engineering term used when the airplane is certificated and must meet certain requirements. If it is not listed in the AFM, it is within requirements and does not have to be taken into consideration by the pilot.

- V_2—Takeoff safety speed means a referenced airspeed obtained after lift-off at which the required one-engine-inoperative climb performance can be achieved.

2. Before every takeoff in a transport category aircraft, what performance calculations must be made? (FAA-H-8083-3)

Takeoff data, including V_1, V_R, and V_2 speeds, takeoff power settings, and required field length should be computed prior to each takeoff and recorded on a takeoff data card. This data is based on airplane weight, runway length available, runway gradient, field temperature, field barometric pressure, wind, icing conditions, and runway condition. Both pilots should separately compute the takeoff data and cross-check in the flight deck with the takeoff data card.

3. What are takeoff data cards? (FAA-H-8083-3)

Takeoff data, including V_1, V_R, and V_2 speeds, takeoff power settings, and required field length should be computed prior to each takeoff and recorded on a takeoff data card. This data is based on airplane weight, runway length available, runway gradient, field temperature, field barometric pressure, wind, icing conditions, and runway condition. Both pilots should separately compute the takeoff data and cross-check in the flight deck with the takeoff data card.

4. Depending on the specific rule under which an airplane was certified, what are examples of calculations that must be performed to determine the allowable takeoff weight? (drs.faa.gov)

a. AFM maximum weight limitations (structural)—takeoff, zero fuel, landing.

b. Airport elevation and temperature—departure point, destination, alternate.

c. Runway limit weight—accelerate-stop distance, accelerate-go (one engine inoperative), all-engines takeoff distance.

d. Takeoff climb limit weight—first segment, second segment, transition segment (divided into third and fourth segments under some rules).

e. Takeoff obstacle limit weight.

f. Enroute climb limit and terrain clearance weights—all engines operative, one engine inoperative, two engines inoperative.

(continued)

g. Approach climb limit weight.

h. Landing climb limit weight.

i. Destination landing distance weight.

j. Alternate landing distance weight.

5. How does a flight crew perform all of the calculations necessary to determine takeoff performance before a flight? (FAA-H-8083-16)

Flight crews are provided airport/runway analysis information in tables or computer software. Airport/runway analysis involves the complex, usually computerized, computations of aircraft performance, using extensive airport/obstacle databases and terrain information. This yields maximum allowable takeoff and landing weights for particular aircraft/engine configurations for a specific airport, runway, and range of temperatures. The computations also consider flap settings, various aircraft characteristics, runway conditions, obstacle clearance, and weather conditions. Obstacle data also is available from these service providers for operators who desire to perform their own analysis using the one engine inoperative (OEI) climb performance and flight path data furnished in the AFM or when using an aircraft electronic performance program supplied by the manufacturer or other service provider.

6. Describe the type of events during a takeoff roll that would result in a rejected takeoff (RTO). (FAA-H-8083-3)

Engine failure, fire or smoke, unsuspected equipment on the runway, bird strike, blown tires, direct instructions from the governing ATC authority, or recognition of a significant abnormality (split airspeed indications, activation of a warning horn, etc.).

7. The takeoff data published for any aircraft is based on what conditions? (FAA-H-8083-3)

The FAA-approved takeoff data for any aircraft is based on aircraft performance demonstrated in ideal conditions, using a clean, dry runway, and maximum braking (reverse thrust is not used to compute stopping distance).

8. **What is the significance of high-speed aborts in contributing to takeoff-related commercial aviation accidents worldwide?** (FAA-H-8083-3)

   Ill-advised rejected takeoff decisions by flight crews and improper pilot technique during the execution of a rejected takeoff contribute to a majority of takeoff-related commercial aviation accidents worldwide. Statistically, although only 2 percent of rejected takeoffs are in this category, high-speed aborts above 120 knots account for the vast majority of RTO overrun accidents. A brief moment of indecision may mean the difference between running out of runway and coming to a safe halt after an aborted takeoff.

9. **Describe the various factors that would affect the actual stopping distance required in a rejected takeoff.** (FAA-H-8083-3)

   a. Reduced runway friction (grooved/non-grooved).
   b. Mechanical runway contaminants (rubber, oily residue, debris).
   c. Natural contaminants (standing water, snow, slush, ice, dust).
   d. Wind direction and velocity.
   e. Low air density.
   f. Flaps configuration.
   g. Bleed air configuration.
   h. Underinflated or failing tires.
   i. Penalizing MEL or CDL items.
   j. Deficient wheel brakes or RTO auto-brakes.
   k. Inoperative anti-skid.
   l. Pilot technique and individual proficiency.

10. **Can a pilot assume that aborting a takeoff at the calculated V_1 will always ensure a safe takeoff or RTO maneuver if initiated at that point in time?** (FAA-H-8083-3)

    Taking pilot response times into account, the go/no-go decision should be made before V_1 so that deceleration can begin no later than V_1. If braking has not begun by V_1, the decision to continue the takeoff is made by default. Delaying the RTO maneuver by just one second beyond V_1 increases the speed 4 to 6 knots on average. Knowing that crews require 3 to 7 seconds to identify an impending RTO and execute the maneuver, it stands to reason that a decision should be made prior to V_1 in order to ensure a successful outcome of the rejected takeoff. This prompted the FAA to expand on the regulatory definition of V_1 and to introduce a couple of new terms through the publication of Advisory Circular (AC) 120-62, *Takeoff Safety Training Aid*.

11. Explain why a flight crew would consider using a reduced V_1 speed for takeoff. (FAA-H-8083-3)

The main purpose for using a reduced V_1 is to properly adjust the RTO stopping distance in case of wet or contaminated runways, while adding approximately 2 seconds of time for the crew to respond.

12. Most aircraft manufacturers recommend that operators identify a low-speed regime and a high-speed regime of the takeoff run. Explain. (FAA-H-8083-3)

Low-speed regime (i.e. 80 knots and below)—Pilots should abort takeoff for any malfunction or abnormality (actual or suspected).

High-speed regime (i.e., 100 knots and above)—Takeoff should only be rejected because of catastrophic malfunctions or life-threatening situations.

13. What is a clearway? (AC 120-62)

A cleared area beyond the end of the runway, not less than 500 feet wide, centrally located about the extended center line of the runway, that contains no obstructions and is under the control of the airport authorities.

14. What is a stopway? (AC 120-62)

An area beyond the end of the runway, at least as wide as the runway and centered along the extended center line of the runway, able to support the airplane during a rejected takeoff without causing structural damage to the airplane, and designated by the authorities for use in decelerating the airplane during a rejected takeoff.

15. Define the term *accelerate-go takeoff distance*. (drs.faa.gov)

The accelerate-go (with one engine inoperative) takeoff distance is the total distance required to perform the following actions:

a. With all engines operating, accelerate to V_{EF} speed with the flight crew's recognition of the failure at V_1.

b. With one engine inoperative, continue acceleration to V_R speed at which time the nosegear is raised off the ground.

c. Climb to the specified runway crossing height (RCH) and cross it at V_2 speed.

16. Define the term *accelerate-stop takeoff distance*. (drs.faa.gov)

The total distance required to perform the following actions:

a. With all engines operating at takeoff thrust, accelerate from a standing start to V_{EF} speed, at which the critical engine is assumed to fail.

b. Make the transition from takeoff thrust to idle thrust, extend spoilers or other drag devices, and apply wheel brakes.

c. Decelerate and bring the airplane to a full stop.

17. Define the term *takeoff climb limit weight*. (drs.faa.gov)

The weight at which the airplane can climb at a specified minimum climb gradient or specified minimum climb rate in still air through the segments of the takeoff flight path. Climb performance for turbine-powered transport category and commuter category airplanes is measured in terms of a gradient (percent of height gained divided by distance traveled) in specified climb segments.

18. What are several factors that determine the usable runway length available for takeoff? (drs.faa.gov)

The usable runway length may be shorter or longer than the actual runway length due to stopways, clearways, and obstacle clearance planes.

19. What is the rule concerning required takeoff distances for transport or commuter category aircraft? (drs.faa.gov)

The required takeoff distance is the longest of three takeoff distances: accelerate-stop, accelerate-go, and all-engines. Since the available runway length is a fixed value, allowable takeoff weight for any given runway is determined by the most restrictive of the applicable distances.

20. Define the term *all-engines takeoff distance*. (drs.faa.gov)

All-engines takeoff distance is the total distance required, with all engines at takeoff thrust, to accelerate to V_R or V_2 speed (appropriate to the airplane type) and rotate and climb to a specified RCH.

21. What is the definition of *balanced field length*? (AC 120-62)

The runway length (or runway plus clearway and/or stopway) where, for takeoff weight, the engine-out accelerate-go distance equals the accelerate-stop distance.

22. Define the term *critical field length*. (AC 120-62)

The minimum runway length (or runway plus clearway and/or stopway) required for a specific takeoff weight. This distance may be the longer of the balanced field length, 115 percent of the all engine takeoff distance, or established by other limitations such as maintaining V_1 to be less than or equal to V_R.

23. How does airport elevation affect takeoff performance? (drs.faa.gov)

Airport elevation is accounted for in takeoff computations because the true airspeed (ground speed in no-wind conditions) for a given takeoff increases as air density decreases. As airport elevation increases, the takeoff run required before the airplane reaches V_1, V_{LOF}, and V_2 speeds increases; the stopping distance from V_1 increases; and a greater air distance is traversed from liftoff to the specified RCH because of the increased true airspeed at the indicated V_2 speed.

24. How does air temperature affect takeoff performance?
(drs.faa.gov)

As air temperature increases, airplane performance is adversely affected because of a reduction in air density. Less dense air causes a reduction in attainable takeoff thrust and aerodynamic performance.

25. How does density altitude affect takeoff performance?
(drs.faa.gov)

Takeoff performance is usually depicted in an AFM for various elevations and temperatures. The effect of variations in barometric pressure is not usually computed or required by the regulations. However, some airplanes with specific engine installations must have corrections in allowable weight for lower-than-standard barometric pressure.

26. How does weight affect takeoff performance?
(drs.faa.gov)

Increasing takeoff weight increases the following:

a. V_{LOF} and the ground run distance required to reach the liftoff point.

b. The air distance required to travel from the liftoff point to the specified runway crossing height.

c. The distance required to bring the aircraft to a stop from V_1 speed, and the energy absorbed by the brakes during the stop.

27. How does flap selection affect takeoff performance?
(drs.faa.gov)

The effect of selecting more flap (within the allowable range) reduces V_R, V_{LOF}, and the required ground-run distance to reach liftoff. All of these increase the accelerate-stop distance limit weight, the accelerate-go distance limit weight, and the all-engines operating limit weight. The additional flap extension increases aerodynamic drag and also decreases the climb gradient the airplane can maintain past the end of the runway. In the case of a short runway, it may not be possible to take off without the flaps set at the greatest extension allowed for takeoff. In the case of a long runway, at a high elevation and a high ambient temperature, it may only be possible to climb at the required gradient with the minimum allowable takeoff flap extension.

28. How does runway slope affect takeoff performance?
(drs.faa.gov)

Uphill grades increase the ground run required to reach the points at which V_1, V_R, and V_{LOF} are attained, but they also improve stopping distance. When climbing over an uphill grade runway you'll need more distance to reach the specified RCH. The reverse is true of downhill grades. Gradient corrections are computed for in both runway length and takeoff speeds, and the average runway gradient (determined by dividing the difference in elevation of the two ends of the runway by the runway length) is normally used.

For large variations in runway height (±5 feet), the retarding effect on the uphill segment is proportionally greater than the acceleration gained on the downhill portion. In this case the slope used for computations should be proportionately greater than the average slope.

29. How do wind conditions affect takeoff performance?
(drs.faa.gov)

The effect of wind on the aircraft's climb gradient is significant, with tailwinds decreasing the gradient and headwinds increasing it:

a. *Headwinds*. It is not required, but the distances may be used to compute performance; only half of the reported steady-state wind component (parallel to the runway) may be used.

b. *Tailwinds*. For a downwind takeoff or landing, at least 150% of the reported steady state tailwind component must be used to compute the performance effect. Most airplanes are certified for takeoff with not more than 10 knots of tailwind component, but some have been certified with higher limits. To use these, the operator must not be limited by the AFM and must be authorized by the operations specifications.

c. *Crosswinds*. The maximum gust velocity must be used in the most unfavorable direction for computing the effective crosswind component. Crosswind values in most AFMs are stated as demonstrated values rather than as limits.

30. **How does water and contamination of runways affect takeoff performance?** (drs.faa.gov)

AFM performance data is based on a dry or wet* runway. When a runway is contaminated by water, snow, or ice, charted AFM performance values will not be obtained. The manufacturer's guidance material has appropriate corrections for these conditions to apply to performance calculations.

The wet-to-dry stopping distance ratio on a well-maintained, grooved, wet runway is usually around 1.15 to 1. Where the grooves are not maintained and rubber deposits are heavy, the stopping distance ratio could be as high as 1.9 to 1. On ungrooved runways, the stopping distance ratio is usually about 2 to 1. In the case of a runway with new pavement or where rubber deposits are present, the ratio could be as high as 4 to 1. Some newly surfaced asphalt runway surfaces can be extremely slippery when only slightly wet.

Note: Wet runway accountability was included in 14 CFR Part 25, amendment 25-92.

31. **How do tire speeds and brake limits affect takeoff performance?** (drs.faa.gov)

Allowable takeoff weight may be limited by either tire speed limits or the ability of the brakes to absorb the heat energy generated during the stop. The energy the brakes must absorb during a stop increases by the square of the speed at which the brakes are applied.

Accelerate-stop distances are determined with cold brakes. When brakes are hot, they may not be able to absorb the energy generated, and charted AFM stopping distances may not be achieved. The heat generated by the stop may cause the wheels or tires to fail. Short turnaround times and rejected takeoffs present a potential hazard in terms of heat buildup in tires and in brake assemblies.

32. **V_1 speed is not a fixed value. What are several factors that would affect the V_1 speed for takeoff?** (drs.faa.gov)

    a. Gross weight.
    b. Density altitude.
    c. Flap setting.
    d. Anti-ice.
    e. Runway slope or gradient.
    f. Runway surface (slush on runway, etc.).

33. **Define the term *engine-out climb gradient*.** (drs.faa.gov)

    Turbine-powered transport category and commuter category airplanes climb performance is measured in terms of a gradient (height gained divided by distance traveled expressed as a percent) in specified climb segments. In the event of an engine failure, large, turbine-powered airplanes must be capable of climbing at a specified gradient through each of the defined climb segments of the takeoff flight path.

34. **What are the basic climb segments of the takeoff path of a large turbine-powered airplane?** (drs.faa.gov, 14 CFR 25.111)

    First segment—This segment is included in the takeoff runway required charts, and is measured from the point at which the aircraft becomes airborne until it reaches the 35-foot height at the end of the runway distance required. Speed initially is V_{LO} and must be V_2 at the 35 foot height.

    Second segment—This is the most critical segment of the profile. The second segment is the climb from the 35 foot height to 400 feet above the ground. The climb is done at full takeoff power on the operating engine(s), at V_2 speed, and with the flaps in the takeoff configuration. The required climb gradient in this segment is 2.4 percent for two-engine aircraft, 2.7 percent for three-engine aircraft, and 3.0 percent for four-engine aircraft.

    Third or acceleration segment—During this segment, the airplane is considered to be maintaining the 400 feet above the ground and accelerating from the V_2 speed to the V_{FS} speed before the climb profile is continued. The flaps are raised at the beginning of the acceleration segment and power is maintained at the takeoff setting as long as possible (5 minutes maximum).

Fourth or final segment—This segment is from the 400 to 1,500 foot AGL altitude with power set at maximum continuous. The required climb in this segment is a gradient of 1.2 percent for two-engine airplanes, 1.55 for three-engine airplanes, and 1.7 percent for four-engine airplanes.

35. Define the term *screen height*. (AC 120-62)

Screen height is the height of an imaginary screen which the airplane would just clear at the end of the runway, or runway and clearway, in an unbanked attitude with the landing gear extended. The required screen height for turbine aircraft is 35 feet on a dry runway and 15 feet on a wet runway.

36. What is the most effective means of ensuring that adequate engine-out climb performance is achieved? (drs.faa.gov)

By limiting the takeoff gross weight so that, considering fuel burn, the aircraft will be light enough to ensure the necessary performance. This is usually accomplished by restricting the amount of fuel and/or passengers or cargo that can be carried.

37. What are several examples of performance charts used for takeoff and climb data? (AFM)

a. Minimum takeoff power.

b. Maximum takeoff weight.

c. Takeoff distance.

d. Accelerate-stop.

e. Accelerate-go distance.

f. Net gradient of climb one engine inoperative.

g. Rate-of-climb two engines.

h. Rate-of-climb one engine.

i. Service ceiling one engine inoperative.

j. Time, fuel, distance to cruise/climb.

k. Performance climb-time, fuel, and distance.

B. Cruise

1. Define the term *specific range*. (FAA-H-8083-25)

Specific range refers to the number of nautical air miles of flying distance per pound of fuel burned. Due to the relatively high fuel flows present in most turboprop and jet aircraft, the specific range is usually stated in nautical air miles flown per 100 lbs or 1,000 lbs of fuel burned.

2. How would you obtain specific range? (FAA-H-8083-25)

Specific range can be defined in the following relationship and calculation:

a. NM divided by pounds of fuel;
b. NM per hour divided by pounds of fuel per hour; or
c. Knots divided by fuel flow.

3. How would a maximum range condition be achieved? (FAA-H-8083-25)

The maximum range condition is obtained at maximum lift/drag ratio (L/D_{MAX}). It is important to note that for a given configuration, the L/D_{MAX} occurs at a particular AOA and lift coefficient and is unaffected by weight or altitude.

4. What is lift/drag ratio? (FAA-H-8083-25)

The lift-to-drag ratio (L/D) is the amount of lift generated by a wing or airfoil compared to its drag. Aircraft with higher L/D ratios are more efficient than those with lower L/D ratios.

5. A change in weight will alter which values required to obtain L/D_{MAX}? (FAA-H-8083-25)

A variation in weight will alter the values of airspeed and power necessary to obtain the L/D_{MAX}.

6. During cruise flight, what should a pilot do to maintain L/D_{MAX}? (FAA-H-8083-25)

Variations of speed and power required must be monitored as part of the cruise control procedure to maintain the L/D_{MAX}.

7. How would you obtain specific endurance? (FAA-H-8083-25)

Specific endurance refers to flying time per pound of fuel burned and is determined by taking the flight time and dividing by fuel flow in pounds per hour. The ability of the airplane to convert fuel energy into flying time is an important factor in flying operations.

8. How would a maximum endurance condition be achieved? (FAA-H-8083-25)

At the point of minimum power required, since this condition requires the lowest fuel flow to keep the airplane in steady level flight.

9. What engine inoperative enroute performance is required for turbine-powered transport category airplanes? (drs.faa.gov)

These airplanes must, at all points along the intended route after an engine fails, be able to clear all terrain and obstructions by 1,000 feet that are within 5 SM on either side of the intended track. This requirement must be met at the forecast temperature for the required altitudes at the planned time of the flight.

10. Define the term *driftdown*. (drs.faa.gov)

A procedure by which an airplane—with one or more engines inoperative and the remaining engines at maximum continuous thrust (MCT), while maintaining a specified speed (usually best L/D × 1.01%)—descends to the altitude at which the airplane can maintain altitude and begin to climb. This altitude is defined as driftdown height.

11. What are several examples of performance charts used for enroute/cruise data? (drs.faa.gov)

a. High speed, intermediate, and long range cruise power.
b. One engine inoperative cruise power.
c. Holding time.
d. Endurance and range profile.

12. **In which altitude range is the minimum specific fuel consumption of a turboprop engine normally available?** (drs.faa.gov)

From 25,000 feet to the tropopause (typically 35,000 feet).

C. Descent and Landing

1. **What is the 3 to 1 rule when planning a descent in a high-performance aircraft?** (FAA-H-8083-16)

A general rule of thumb for initial IFR descent planning in jets is the 3 to 1 rule. This means that it takes 3 NM to descend 1,000 feet. If an airplane is at flight level (FL) 310 and the approach gate or initial approach fix is at 6,000 feet, the initial descent requirement equals 25,000 feet (31,000−6,000). Multiplying 25 times 3 equals 75; therefore, begin descent 75 NM from the approach gate, based on a normal jet airplane, idle thrust speed Mach 0.74 to 0.78, and vertical speed of 1,800–2,200 fpm. For a tailwind adjustment, add 2 NM for each 10 knots of tailwind. For a headwind adjustment, subtract 2 NM for each 10 knots of headwind.

Another example of application of the 3 to 1 rule using ground speed. Multiply the altitude to lose by 3 to find the DME distance to start down. Determine your ground speed, divide by 2, and add a 0 to the end of the solution to find the vertical speed required for the descent.

Example: You're at 25,000 feet and need to cross a fix at 10,000 feet. Your ground speed is 440 knots.

$15 \times 3 = 45$ NM

$440 \div 2 = 220$, and add a zero $= 2,200$ fpm

Begin your descent at 45 NM and use 2,200 fpm.

2. **Define the following V-speeds: V_S, V_{S0}, V_{S1}.** (14 CFR Part 1)

V_S—Stalling speed or the minimum steady flight speed at which the airplane is controllable.
V_{S0}—Stalling speed or the minimum steady flight speed in the landing configuration.
V_{S1}—Stalling speed or minimum steady flight speed obtained in a specified configuration.

3. What is the definition of V_{REF}? (FAA-H-8083-3)

Reference landing speed. Turbine aircraft operate at a number of different weights, requiring an adjustment to the airspeed for a given approach and landing. V_{REF} is calculated for each landing and is usually $1.3 \times V_{S0}$. Normally found on take off and landing data (TOLD) cards where V_{REF} has been calculated in advance for a variety of configuration, weight, and temperature combinations.

4. What does the approach climb airspeed guarantee for a transport category jet on approach? (FAA-H-8083-3)

Flying the approach climb speed guarantees adequate performance in a go-around situation with an inoperative engine.

5. Explain what the landing climb speed guarantees. (FAA-H-8083-3, 14 CFR 25.119)

The landing climb speed guarantees adequate performance in arresting the descent and making a go-around from the final stages of landing with the airplane in the full landing configuration and maximum takeoff power available on all engines.

6. What landing distance limitations apply to turbine-powered aircraft? (drs.faa.gov, 14 CFR 121.195, 135.385)

a. Turbojets must be able to land within 60% of the effective runway at both the destination and the alternate airports (allowing for normal enroute fuel and oil consumption).

b. Turboprop airplanes must be able to land within 60% of the effective runway at the destination and 70% at the alternate airport.

c. A flight may be dispatched that cannot meet the 60% runway requirement at the destination if an alternate airport is designated where the flight can land within the distance specified for an alternate airport.

d. When a runway is forecasted to be wet or slippery at the destination, 15% must be added to the required landing runway length. A correction is not applied to the alternate landing runway length for preflight planning.

7. **What are the factors that may impact operational landing distance calculations at time of arrival?** (drs.faa.gov, SAFO 19001)

   a. Runway slope.
   b. Airport elevation.
   c. Wind.
   d. Temperature.
   e. Airplane weight and configuration.
   f. Approach speed at threshold.
   g. Adjustment to landing distance (such as autoland).
   h. Planned use of airplane ground deceleration devices.

8. **Define the term *contaminated runway*.** (P/CG, AC 25-31)

   A runway is considered contaminated whenever standing water, ice, snow, slush, frost in any form, heavy rubber, or other substances are present. For purposes of condition reporting and airplane performance, a runway is considered contaminated when more than 25 percent of the runway surface area (within the reported length and the width being used) is covered by frost, ice, and any depth of snow, slush, or water.

9. **What is the most efficient braking procedure for turboprop aircraft?** (FAA-H-8083-3)

   Reverse-thrust propellers should be applied as soon as possible after touchdown to reduce landing distance to a minimum. Braking should occur as the aircraft slows and wing lift is reduced.

10. **What is the recommended terminology for describing braking action?** (AIM 4-3-8)

    When available, ATC furnishes the quality of braking action received from pilots. The quality of braking action is described by the terms "good," "good to medium," "medium," "medium to poor," "poor," and "nil." When pilots report the quality of braking action by using the terms noted above, they should use descriptions that are easily understood, such as, "braking action poor the first half of the runway," together with the particular type of aircraft.

11. What is a runway condition assessment matrix (RCAM)? (SAFO 16009, AIM 4-3-9)

The RCAM is a new methodology used by airport operators to perform assessments of runway conditions and by pilots to interpret reported runway conditions. The RCAM is presented in a standardized format, based on airplane performance data supplied by airplane manufacturers, for each of the stated contaminant types and depths. The RCAM replaces subjective judgments of runway surface conditions with objective assessments tied directly to contaminant type and depth categories. This methodology communicates actual runway conditions to pilots in terms that directly relate to expected aircraft performance

12. How is runway assessment and condition reported? (AIM 4-3-9)

Aircraft braking coefficient is dependent upon the surface friction between the tires on the aircraft wheels and the pavement surface. Less friction means less aircraft braking coefficient and less aircraft braking response. Runway condition code (RwyCC) values range from 1 (poor) to 6 (dry). For frozen contaminants on runway surfaces, a runway condition code reading of 4 indicates the level when braking deceleration or directional control is between good and medium.

13. Define the term *hydroplaning*. (drs.faa.gov)

Hydroplaning occurs when the tires are lifted off a runway surface by the combination of aircraft speed and a thin film of water present on the runway.

14. What are the three basic types of hydroplaning? (drs.faa.gov)

Dynamic—Occurs when there is standing water on the runway surface. Water about 1/10th of an inch deep acts to lift the tire off the runway. The minimum speed at which dynamic hydroplaning occurs has been determined to be 8.6 times the square root of the tire pressure in pounds per square inch.

Viscous—Occurs as a result of the viscous properties of water. A very thin film of fluid cannot be penetrated by the tire and the tire consequently rolls on top of the film. Viscous hydroplaning

(continued)

can occur at much slower speeds than dynamic hydroplaning but requires a smooth acting surface.

Reverted rubber hydroplaning—Occurs when a pilot, during the landing roll, locks the brakes for an extended period of time while on a wet runway. The friction creates heat, which combined with water creates a steam layer between the aircraft tire and runway surface.

15. What is the best method of speed reduction if hydroplaning is experienced on landing? (drs.faa.gov)

Aerodynamic braking is the most effective means of dealing with a hydroplaning situation. Use of flaps, increased angle of attack, spoilers, reverse thrust, etc., will produce more desirable results than braking.

16. Describe the potential hazards that would increase the risk of a runway overrun. (AC 91-79)

a. Unstabilized approach—Safe landings begin long before touchdown.

b. High airport elevation or high density altitude—Results in a higher true airspeed, ground speed, and corresponding longer landing distance.

c. Effect of excess airspeed over runway threshold—With each 10% increase in landing speed, landing distance increases by 20%.

d. Airplane landing weight—A 10% increase in gross weight at landing results in a 5% increase in landing velocity and a 10% increase in landing distance.

e. Landing beyond the touchdown point—If the airplane does not touch down within the AFM or POH landing distance, it will not be possible to achieve the calculated landing distance.

f. Downhill runway slope—10% increase in landing distance for each percent of downhill grade.

g. Excessive height over the runway threshold—With each 10 feet above standard 50 feet threshold height, add 200 feet to landing distance.

h. Delayed use of deceleration devices—For each second beyond 2 seconds, add 200 feet to landing distance.

i. Landing with a tailwind—For each 10 knots, increase landing distance by 21%.

j. A wet or contaminated runway—A safety margin of 15% should be added to the actual landing distance.

17. When landing on wet or contaminated runways, the FAA encourages flight crews to assess landing performance based on conditions existing at time of arrival, distinct from conditions forecast prior to departure. What conditions should be considered? (AC 91-79, SAFO 19001)

Conditions to be considered may include weather, RwyCC (if provided), field conditions (FICON) report (if provided), the airplane's weight, braking systems to be used, and any other conditions the flight crew deems necessary to conduct a safe landing, such as PIREPS of braking action. Once the actual landing distance is determined at the time of arrival, an additional safety margin of at least 15 percent should be added to the actual landing distance.

D. Limitations

1. Define the following airspeed limitations: V_S, V_1, V_{EF}, V_R, V_{LOF}, V_2, V_B, V_{MCG}, V_{MO}, and M_{MO}. (FAA-H-8083-3)

V_S—Stalling speed or minimum steady flight speed at which the airplane is controllable.

V_1—Critical engine failure speed or takeoff decision speed. It is the speed at which the pilot is to continue the takeoff in the event of an engine failure or other serious emergency. At speeds less than V_1, it is considered safer to stop the aircraft within the accelerate-stop distance. It is also the minimum speed in the takeoff, following a failure of the critical engine at V_{EF}, at which the pilot can continue the takeoff and achieve the required height above the takeoff surface within the takeoff distance.

V_{EF}—Speed used during certification at which the critical engine is assumed to fail.

(continued)

V_R—Rotation speed, or speed at which the rotation of the airplane is initiated to takeoff attitude. This speed cannot be less than V_1 or less than $1.05 \times V_{MCA}$ (minimum control speed in the air). On a single-engine takeoff, it also allows for the acceleration to V_2 at the 35-foot height at the end of the runway.

V_{LOF}—Lift-off speed, or speed at which the airplane first becomes airborne. This is an engineering term used when the airplane is certificated to meet certain requirements. The pilot takes this speed into consideration if the AFM lists it.

V_2—Takeoff safety speed, or a referenced airspeed obtained after lift-off at which the required one-engine-inoperative climb performance can be achieved.

V_B—Design speed for maximum gust intensity.

V_{MCG}—Minimum control speed on the ground, or the calibrated airspeed during the takeoff run at which, if the critical engine suddenly fails, it is possible to maintain directional control using only aerodynamic controls.

V_{MO}—Maximum operating limit speed expressed in terms of knots.

M_{MO}—Maximum operating limit speed expressed as a Mach number (the decimal ratio of true airspeed to the speed of sound).

2. What limitations apply to engine operation? (AFM)

Several limitations should be observed when operating a turbine engine. Exceeding any of these usually requires a maintenance inspection before further operation. Limitations should be observed in each of the different phases of aircraft operation, such as starting, idle, takeoff, maximum continuous power, cruise climb and cruise, maximum reverse, etc. Some examples are:

a. Maximum torque.

b. Maximum observed ITT.

c. Maximum and minimum N_1 and N_2 (low- and high-speed compressor speed).

d. Maximum and minimum prop RPM.

e. Maximum and minimum oil pressure.

f. Maximum and minimum oil temperature.

3. What are some examples of limitations that apply to the propeller?

a. Propeller rotational speed limits (transient, reverse).

b. Propeller rotational overspeed limits (max RPM, time limits).

4. What are some examples of limitations that apply when starting? (AFM)

a. *External power limits*—The external power source (GPU) should be capable of generating sufficient volts and amps for starting.

b. *Starter limits*—Use of the starter is limited in the amount of time it may be continuously operated. Exceeding these times will usually result in overheating and damage to the starter's internal components (e.g., 30 seconds on, 3 minutes off, 30 seconds on, 3 minutes off, 30 seconds on, 30 minutes off).

5. What limitations apply to aircraft generators? (AFM)

a. Maximum sustained generator load limits apply for a specified minimum N_1 value.

b. Minimum N_1 values are specified for a given generator load.

6. Are there any limitations concerning outside air temperatures? (AFM)

Yes—minimum and maximum outside air temperature limits must be observed. Minimum outside air temperatures affect oil temperature for fuel heater operation. A minimum fuel temperature must be maintained to avoid fuel system icing. Maximum outside air temperatures have limitations due to their effect on engine operational temperature limits. Also, maximum temperatures are sometimes specified for avionics in the cockpit.

7. Are there any limitations that apply to the aircraft fuel system? (AFM)

Yes—examples of these are:

a. Use only the recommended fuel; normally Jet A, Jet A-1, Jet B, etc.

b. In the event the recommended fuel is not available, only certain fuels may be used (reference AFM).

(continued)

    c. Limitations to use of emergency engine fuels; such as length of time they can be used between engine overhauls, maximum altitude limitations, inoperative equipment limitations (i.e., auxiliary pumps must be operational).

    d. Maximum allowable fuel imbalance between wing fuel tanks.

    e. Minimum fuel quantities in auxiliary and main tanks.

    f. Minimum fuel system pressures.

8. What is one major limitation that applies to the cabin pressurization system? (FAA-H-8083-31)

Maximum cabin differential pressure—If the differential pressure becomes too great, structural damage to the fuselage may occur. Depending on the particular aircraft, maximum cabin differential pressure values will vary. The design, manufacturing, and selection of structural materials, as well as engine bleed-air capacity (which maintains a constant volume of airflow to the fuselage) all affect it.

9. State the different weight limitations that apply when conducting large aircraft operations. (FAA-H-8083-1)

    a. Maximum ramp weight.

    b. Maximum takeoff weight.

    c. Maximum landing weight.

    d. Maximum zero fuel weight.

    e. Maximum weight in the cargo compartments.

    f. Cabin floor loading.

10. What limitations apply concerning the types of maneuvers an aircraft is approved for? (FAA-H-8083-25)

The category the aircraft was certified under determines the type of maneuvers it is approved for. Normal category aircraft are prohibited from acrobatic maneuvers including spins.

11. What are the maximum limit load factors for aircraft certified in the Normal, Utility, and Acrobatic categories? (14 CFR Part 23, Part 25, FAA-H-8083-25)

Category	Limit Load Factor
Transport	−1.0 to +2.5 (may not be greater than +3.8 depending on design MTOW)
Normal and Commuter	−1.52 to +3.8
Utility	−1.76 to +4.4
Acrobatic	−3.0 to +6.0

12. After takeoff, during the initial climb, you encounter wake turbulence from a B-747 that just departed the same runway. As you maneuver through the turbulence at the aircraft's maneuvering speed, you find it necessary to make a series of sequential, full opposite rudder inputs. Are you in any danger of exceeding the aircraft's structural limits? (AURTA, 14 CFR 25.1583)

At any speed, large aggressive control reversals can lead to loads that can exceed structural design limits. The rudders on modern jet transport airplanes are sized to counter the yawing moment associated with an engine failure at very low takeoff speeds and to ensure yaw control throughout the flight envelope, using up to maximum pedal input. An inappropriate rudder input can produce a large sideslip angle, which will generate a large rolling moment that requires significant lateral control input to stop the airplane from rolling. The rudder should not normally be used to induce roll through sideslip because the transient sideslip can induce very rapid roll rates with significant time delay. The combination of rapid roll rates and time delay can startle the pilot, which in turn can cause the pilot to overreact in the opposite direction. The overreaction can induce abrupt yawing moments and violent out-of-phase roll rates, which can lead to successive cyclic rudder deflections, known as rudder reversals.

13. **When operating an aircraft in turbulence at maneuvering speed, are you guaranteed protection from structural damage to the aircraft?** (SAIB CE-11-17)

No—maneuvering speed is the speed below which you can, in smooth air, move a single flight control one time to its full deflection for one axis of airplane rotation only (pitch, roll or yaw) without risk of damage to the airplane. Speeds up to, but not exceeding, the maneuvering speed allow an aircraft to stall prior to experiencing an increase in load factor that would exceed the limit load of the aircraft. Operating at or below maneuvering speed does not provide structural protection against multiple full control inputs in one axis or full control inputs in more than one axis at the same time.

E. Deicing and Anti-Icing Procedures

1. **Explain the overall effect icing has on aircraft performance.** (AC 120-58)

   a. Ice, snow, or frost formations having a thickness and surface roughness similar to medium or coarse sandpaper on the leading edge and upper surface of a wing can reduce wing lift by as much as 30 percent and increase drag by 40 percent.

   b. The changes in lift and drag significantly increase stall speed, reduce controllability, and alter aircraft flight characteristics.

   c. Thicker or rougher frozen contaminants can have increasing effects on lift, drag, stall speed, stability and control, with the primary influence being surface roughness located on critical portions of an aerodynamic surface.

   d. The adverse effects on the aerodynamic properties of the airfoil may result in sudden departure from the commanded flight path and may not be preceded by any indications or aerodynamic warning to the pilot.

2. **Current regulations in 14 CFR Parts 121 and 135 rely on the clean aircraft concept. Explain this concept.** (AC 120-58)

   14 CFR §121.629, §125.221, and §135.227, and §91.527 prohibit takeoff when snow, ice, or frost is adhering to wings, propellers, control surfaces, engine inlets, and other critical surfaces of the aircraft. This rule is the basis for the clean aircraft concept. It

is imperative that takeoff not be attempted unless the PIC has ascertained, as required by the FAR, that all critical components of the aircraft are free of ice, snow, or frost formations.

3. Explain the difference between ground deicing and ground anti-icing. (AC 120-60)

Ground deicing—A procedure used to remove frost, ice, slush, or snow from the aircraft in order to provide clean surfaces. The procedure can be accomplished using fluids, infrared (IR) energy, mechanical means, or by heating the aircraft. Deicing fluid is usually applied heated to ensure maximum deicing efficiency.

Ground anti-icing—A procedure used to provide protection against the formation of frost or ice and accumulation of snow or slush on clean surfaces of the aircraft for a limited period of time (holdover time (HOT)).

4. How is ice removal and prevention accomplished on the ground? (AC 120-58)

The common practice is to deice and anti-ice an aircraft before takeoff. Various techniques of ground deicing and anti-icing have been developed. The most common of these techniques is to use freezing-point depressant (FPD) fluids in the ground deicing process and to anti-ice with a protective film of FPD fluid to delay the reforming of ice, snow, or frost.

5. Deicing and anti-icing procedures may be performed as a one-step or two-step process. Explain. (AC 120-58)

One-step procedure—Accomplished using a heated or, in some cases, an unheated FPD mixture. In this process, the residual FPD fluid film provides very limited anti-icing protection. The protection can be enhanced by the use of cold fluids or by the use of techniques to cool heated fluid during the deicing process.

Two-step procedure—Involves both deicing and anti-icing. Deicing is accomplished with hot water or a hot mixture of FPD and water. The ambient weather conditions and the type of accumulation to be removed from the aircraft must be considered when determining which deicing fluid to use. The second (anti-icing) step involves applying a mixture of SAE or ISO Type II and water to the critical surfaces of the aircraft.

6. Define the term *holdover time* (HOT). (AC 120-60)

Holdover time is the estimated time that deicing/anti-icing fluid will prevent the formation of frost or ice and the accumulation of snow on the critical surfaces of an aircraft.

7. When does the HOT begin? (AC 120-60)

HOT begins when the final application of deicing/anti-icing fluid commences, and expires when the deicing/anti-icing fluid loses its effectiveness.

8. How do flight crewmembers calculate HOT? (AC 120-60)

Flight crews use HOT tables that provide safe times based on the following criteria at time of application: air temperature, type of precipitation, rate of precipitation, and the type of deicing or anti-icing fluid used.

9. According to an operator's FAA-approved deicing/anti-icing program, what is a pre-takeoff check, and when must it be performed? (AC 120-60)

A check of the aircraft's wings or representative aircraft surfaces for frozen contaminants. This check is conducted within the aircraft's HOT and may be made by observing representative surfaces from the flight deck, cabin, or outside the aircraft, depending on the type of aircraft and operator's FAA-approved program.

10. Explain when a pre-takeoff contamination check is required. (AC 120-60)

It must be made when an aircraft's HOT has been exceeded. It is done to ensure the aircraft's wings, control surfaces, and other critical surfaces, as defined in the certificate holder's program, are free of all frozen contaminants. This check must be completed within 5 minutes before beginning takeoff and from outside the aircraft, unless the certificate holder's FAA-approved program specifies otherwise.

11. Describe the four standard aircraft deicing and anti-icing fluid types: Type I, II, III, and IV. (NASA AIT)

Type I fluids are the thinnest of fluids. As such, they can be used on any aircraft, as they shear/blow off even at low speeds. They also have the shortest holdover times (HOT) or estimated times of protection in active frost or freezing precipitation.

Type II and IV fluids add thickening agents to increase viscosity. The thickeners allow fluid to remain on the aircraft longer to absorb and melt the frost or freezing precipitation. This translates to longer HOTs, but it also means a higher speed is required to shear off the fluid.

Type III fluids are relatively new and have properties in between Type I and Type II/IV fluids. Type III fluids also contain thickening agents and offer longer HOTs than Type I, but they are formulated to shear off at lower speeds. They are designed specifically for small commuter-type aircraft but work as well for larger aircraft.

Note: Holdover times (HOT) are published in a range to account for variations in precipitation intensity: shorter time for heavier intensity, longer time for lighter intensity.

12. After the ground crew has completed deicing/anti-icing the aircraft, they will provide the flight crew with what information? (AC 120-60)

The ground crew will provide the flight crew with the following elements:

a. Fluid type (e.g., Type I, II, III, or IV). Fluid product name optional for each type of fluid if fluid meets product on-wing viscosity requirements.

b. Fluid/water mix ratio by volume of Types II, III, and IV. Reporting the concentration of Type I fluid is not required.

c. Specify in local time (hours and minutes) the beginning of the final fluid application (e.g., 1330).

d. Post-application check accomplished. Specify date (day, written month, year).

Note: Element d. is required for recordkeeping, optional for crew notification. Transmission of elements a. through c. to the flight crew confirms that a post deicing/anti-icing check was completed and the aircraft is clean.

13. Describe the Runway Condition Assessment Matrix (RCAM). (AIM 4-3-9)

RCAM is the tool airport operators will use to report a runway surface assessment when contaminants such as water, ice, snow, slush, and others are present on runways, taxiways, and aprons. Once an assessment has been performed, the RCAM defines the format by which the airport operator reports and determines a Runway Condition Code (RwyCC).

F. Weight and Balance

1. Define the following weights: empty weight, basic empty weight, basic operating weight, fleet operational empty weight, maximum zero fuel weight, maximum ramp weight, maximum takeoff weight, maximum landing weight, maximum taxi weight, and useful load. (FAA-H-8083-1, AC 120-27)

Empty weight—The weight of the airframe, engines, all permanently installed equipment, and unusable fuel. Depending upon the part of the federal regulations under which the aircraft was certificated, either the undrainable oil or full reservoir of oil is included.

Basic empty weight (BEW)—The aircraft empty weight, adjusted for variations in standard items.

Basic operating weight (BOW)—The empty weight of the aircraft plus the weight of the required crew, their baggage and other standard item such as meals and potable water.

Fleet operating empty weight (FOEW)—The average operational empty weight (OEW) used for a fleet or group of aircraft of the same model and configuration.

Maximum zero fuel weight—The maximum authorized weight of an aircraft without fuel. This is the total weight for a particular flight less the fuel. It includes the aircraft and everything that will be carried on the flight except the weight of the fuel.

Maximum ramp weight—The maximum weight approved for ground maneuver. It includes weight of start, taxi, and runup fuel.

Maximum takeoff weight—The maximum weight approved for the start of the takeoff run.

Maximum landing weight—The maximum weight approved for the landing touchdown.

Maximum taxi weight—The maximum allowable aircraft weight for taxiing.

Useful load—The difference between takeoff weight and BEW. It includes payload, usable fuel, and other usable fluids not included as operational items.

2. What is a loading schedule? (AC 120-27)

The loading schedule is a method for calculating and documenting aircraft weight and balance (W&B) prior to taxiing, to ensure the aircraft will remain within all required W&B limitations throughout the flight. It is used to document compliance with the certificated W&B limitations contained in the manufacturer's AFM, type certificate data sheet (TCDS), and weight and balance manual (WBM).

Several types of loading schedules are commonly used, including computer programs as well as "paper" schedules, which can be graphical, such as an alignment ("chase around chart") system, slide rule, or numerical, such as an adjusted weight or index system.

3. How does an operator determine standard passenger and baggage weights for loading an aircraft? (AC 120-27, CDC/NHANES)

There are three methods available to operators to determine passenger and baggage weights:

a. *Standard average weights*—The operator determines standard average passenger weights based on CDC/NHANES information and seasonal clothing variances.

b. *Average weights based on survey results*—Operators conduct surveys and studies to gather data to determine the percentage of male and female passengers and to calculate an average passenger weight.

c. *Actual weights*—Some airlines may weigh passengers, baggage, and cargo to obtain more accurate weights. However, this method can be time-consuming and may not be practical for larger aircraft.

4. If actual weights are not available, what are the standard weights established for fuel, water, and oil? (FAA-H-8083-1)

Type	Pounds per U.S. gallon	
	32°F	59°F
AVGAS (aviation gasoline)	6.14 lbs	6.01 lbs
JET A & A-1	6.75 lbs	6.68 lbs
Water	8.35 lbs	8.33 lbs
Oil	7.50 lbs	7.43 lbs

5. Define the following terms: carry-on bag, checked bags, heavy bags, plane-side loaded bags, cargo, COMAT, HAZMAT. (AC 120-27, drs.faa.gov)

Carry-on bag—A bag allowed to be carried on board by the passenger. It should be of a size and shape that will allow it to be stowed under the passenger seat or in a storage compartment. The operator establishes the exact dimensional limits based on the particular aircraft stowage limits.

Checked bags—Those bags placed in the cargo compartment of the aircraft including bags that are too large to be placed in the aircraft cabin or those bags that are required to be carried in the cargo compartment by regulation, security program, or company policy.

Heavy bags—Any bag that weighs more than 50 pounds but less than 100 pounds. Bags that are 100 pounds or more are considered cargo.

Plane-side loaded bags—Any bag or item that is placed at the door or steps of an aircraft and subsequently placed in the aircraft cargo compartment or cargo bin.

Cargo—Any property carried on an aircraft other than mail, stores, and accompanied or mishandled baggage.

COMAT—Company materials. This is an industry term used by certificate holders to describe nonrevenue materials and supplies owned by the certificate holder that are shipped by the certificate holder in support of its operations.

HAZMAT—Hazardous materials. Materials or substances as defined in 49 CFR §171.8. Hazardous materials are also referred to as dangerous goods (DG).

6. Define the term *mean aerodynamic chord* (MAC). (FAA-H-8083-1, AC 120-27)

MAC is the chord of an imaginary airfoil that has all of the aerodynamic characteristics of the actual airfoil. It can be thought of as the chord drawn through the geographic center of the plan area of the wing. The MAC is established by the manufacturer, which defines its leading edge and its trailing edge in terms of distance (usually inches) from the datum.

7. Define the term *percent of mean aerodynamic chord* (%MAC). (FAA-H-8083-1)

Percent of mean aerodynamic chord (%MAC) is the distance in inches of the CG from LEMAC divided by the MAC. It is a good standard for CG location in airplanes because it permits a standard weight and balance program for different types of airplanes.

8. Define the terms LEMAC and TEMAC. (FAA-H-8083-1)

LEMAC—Leading edge of the mean aerodynamic chord expressed in inches aft of the datum.

TEMAC—Trailing edge of the mean aerodynamic chord expressed in inches aft of the datum.

9. What is the formula for determining %MAC? (FAA-H-8083-1)

$$\text{CG inches \%MAC} = \frac{\text{Distance aft of LEMAC} \times 100}{\text{MAC}}$$

Example:
MAC = TEMAC 206 in – LEMAC 144 in
MAC = 62 in long
Loaded aircraft CG location = 161 in

In order to find the percent MAC, first determine the distance of the CG from LEMAC:

CG – LEMAC = Distance from LEMAC
161 in – 144 in = 17 in

Then use the formula to determine the location of the CG expressed in percent MAC:

$$\text{CG inches \%MAC} = \frac{\text{Distance aft of LEMAC} \times 100}{\text{MAC}}$$

(continued)

$$CG \text{ inches } \%MAC = \frac{17 \text{ in} \times 100}{62 \text{ in}}$$

$$CG \text{ inches } \%MAC = 27.4$$

The CG of the airplane is located at 27.4 percent MAC.

10. Describe a typical weight and balance calculation for a turboprop aircraft.

Weight—Takeoff weight is checked against the maximum allowable takeoff weight for the particular flight, which is usually obtained from airport analysis charts and cannot be exceeded. Landing weight is also checked against the maximum allowable landing weight for the destination, ensuring that it has not been exceeded.

a. Basic operating weight + adult weight + child weight + cargo weight = zero fuel weight

b. Zero fuel weight + fuel on board weight = ramp weight

c. Ramp weight – ground fuel weight = takeoff weight

d. Takeoff weight – enroute fuel weight = landing weight

Balance—Most regional/commuter airlines use a variety of methods to make balance computations quickly, such as quick reference charts, slide-rule-type computers, loading summary charts, etc. The approved random loading rules that establish minimum/ maximum amounts of weight in each of the aircraft compartments also provide the ground/flight crew with a quick and efficient method of loading the aircraft within CG.

11. What is a load manifest? (AC 120-101, 14 CFR 121.665)

A load manifest is an electronic or hardcopy form used by the certificate holder to ensure compliance with the manufacturer's aircraft limitations or approved air carrier flight manual limitations. The form must be prepared and signed for each flight by employees of the certificate holder who have the duty of supervising the loading of aircraft and preparing the load manifest forms or by other qualified persons authorized by the certificate holder.

12. What type of information is required on a load manifest? (drs.faa.gov, 14 CFR 121.693)

A domestic operator must prepare a load manifest that contains the following information:

a. Individual weights of the aircraft, fuel and oil, cargo and baggage, passengers, and crewmembers.

b. Maximum allowable takeoff weight, runway to be used, runway limit, climb limit, en route performance limits, destination landing weight limits, and destination or alternate landing distance limits.

c. Total aircraft takeoff weight (as computed under approved procedures).

d. Documentation that the aircraft is properly loaded with the center of gravity (CG) within approved limits.

e. Passenger names (unless such information is maintained elsewhere by the operator).

13. What is a loading envelope? (AC 120-27)

A loading envelope is a weight and CG envelope used in a loading schedule. Loading the aircraft within the loading envelope will maintain the aircraft weight and CG within the manufacturer's type-certificated limits throughout the flight.

14. What is an aircraft loading schedule? (AC 120-27)

The loading schedule is used to document compliance with the certificated weight and balance limitations contained in the manufacturer's AFM and WBM. The loading schedule is developed by the operator based on its specific loading calculation procedures and provides the operational limits for use with the operator's W&B program.

15. What are some of the problems caused by overloading an aircraft? (FAA-H-8083-1)

a. The aircraft will need a higher takeoff speed, which results in a longer takeoff run.

b. Both the rate and angle of climb will be reduced.

c. The service ceiling will be lowered.

d. The cruising speed will be reduced.

e. The cruising range will be shortened.

f. Maneuverability will be decreased.

g. A longer landing roll will be required because the landing speed will be higher.

h. Excessive loads will be imposed on the structure, especially the landing gear.

16. What effect does a forward center of gravity have on an aircraft's flight characteristics? (FAA-H-8083-25)

Higher stall speed—Stalling angle of attack reached at a higher speed due to increased wing loading.

Slower cruise speed—Increased drag, greater angle of attack required to maintain altitude.

More stable—When angle of attack increased, the airplane tends to reduce angle of attack; longitudinal stability.

Greater back elevator pressure required—Longer takeoff roll, higher approach speeds, and problems with the landing flare.

17. What effect does an aft center of gravity have on an aircraft's flight characteristics? (FAA-H-8083-25)

Lower stall speed—Less wing loading.

Higher cruise speed—Reduced drag, smaller angle of attack required to maintain altitude.

Less stable—Stall and spin recovery more difficult. When angle of attack is increased it tends to result in even more increased angle of attack.

Weather
Information

3

A. Weather Sources

1. What are the two main categories of sources of weather data? (FAA-H-8083-28)

Federal Government—The FAA and National Weather Service (NWS) collect weather observations. The NWS analyzes the observations and produces forecasts and the FAA and NWS disseminate observations, analyses, and forecasts through a variety of systems. The Federal Government is the only approval authority for sources of weather observations (e.g., contract towers and airport operators).

Commercial weather information providers—Repackage proprietary weather products based on NWS information with formatting and layout modification but make no material changes to the weather information. Other commercial providers produce forecasts, analyses, and other proprietary weather products which may substantially differ from the information contained in NWS products. Operators who use products prepared by a commercial weather provider as opposed to using repackaged may require FAA approval.

2. Do flight crews have the flexibility to use weather products not observed and produced by the FAA/NWS? (AIM 7-1-3, FAA-H-8083-16)

Air carriers and operators certificated under the provisions of Part 119 are required to use the aeronautical weather information systems defined in the operations specifications issued to that certificate holder by the FAA. These systems may use basic FAA/NWS weather services, contractor or operator-proprietary weather services, and/or Enhanced Weather Information System (EWINS) when approved in the operations specifications.

3. What are Enhanced Weather Information Systems (EWINS)? (AIM 7-1-3, AC 91-70)

EWINS are systems for gathering, evaluating, and disseminating aviation weather information, and for issuing weather reports and forecasts prepared by properly trained and qualified aviation meteorologists or aircraft dispatchers. Air carriers use EWINS which are proprietary to each carrier. Air carriers require FAA approval to use EWINS.

4. What is Flight Information Services (FIS)? (AC 00-63)

FIS is a service that provides meteorological information (METI) and aeronautical information (AI) to enhance pilot awareness of weather and/or airspace constraints while providing information for decision support tools and improving safety. METI and AI data link services enable flight crews to support the Next Generation Air Transportation System (NextGen) concepts of information sharing and provide flight crews with a common operating picture necessary to support the evolving global air traffic management (ATM) concepts.

B. Weather Products

1. 14 CFR Parts 91, 121, and 135 require certificate holders to use weather reports and forecasts from specified sources. What are examples of approved sources of weather data? (14 CFR 91.1039, 121.101, 135.213, drs.faa.gov)

a. NWS offices (including contract observatories).

b. Flight Service Stations (FSS).

c. Automated Surface Observing System (ASOS).

d. Automated Weather Observing System (AWOS).

e. Supplementary Aviation Weather Reporting System (SAWRS).

f. Limited Aviation Weather Reporting Stations (LAWRS).

g. Non-Federal Observation (NF-OBS) Program.

For operations within the 48 contiguous United States and the District of Columbia, 14 CFR §121.101 requires a certificate holder to use weather reports prepared by the NWS or a source approved by the NWS.

2. **Part 121 regulations require the aircraft dispatcher to provide the PIC with the most current available information before a flight departs and while a flight is en route. Can aeronautical information (AI) received on the flight deck via FIS-B, be used to solely satisfy this regulatory requirement?** (14 CFR 121.601, drs.faa.gov, AC 00-63)

No. Availability of METI and AI in the cockpit does not fulfill the requirement of § 121.601, which requires aircraft dispatchers to provide the PIC with all available current reports or information on airport conditions and irregularities of navigation facilities that may affect the safety of the flight.

3. **When do air carrier flight crews obtain most of their weather information?** (FAA-H-8083-16)

Most of the weather information that flight crews receive is issued to them prior to the start of each flight segment, but the weather used for in-flight planning and execution of an instrument approach is normally obtained en route via government sources, company frequency, or Aircraft Communications Addressing and Reporting System (ACARS).

Observations

1. **What is an aviation routine weather report (METAR)?** (FAA-H-8083-28)

The METAR is the weather observer's interpretation of the weather conditions at a given site and time. There are two types of METARs: an hourly METAR and an aviation selected special weather report (SPECI). This is a special report that can be given at any time to update the METAR for rapidly changing weather conditions, aircraft mishaps, or other critical information.

2. **What are several types of surface weather observing programs?** (FAA-H-8083-28)

Manual surface weather observations—Observations made by a human weather observer who is certified by the FAA.

Automated observations—Derived from instruments and algorithms without human input or oversight. In the United States, there are two main kinds of automated observing systems: the ASOS and the AWOS. Automated observations contain "AUTO" in the report unless they are augmented by a human weather observer.

Augmented observations—At select airports, the automated observing system have input and oversight by human weather observers or tower controllers certified in weather observing. Human observers report weather elements that are beyond the capabilities of the automated system and/or are deemed operationally significant. AUTO is not used in augmented reports.

3. When reading an automated observation, how recent are the observed elements within the report? (FAA-H-8083-28)

In an automated observation, sky condition is an evaluation of sensor data gathered during the 30-minute period ending at the actual time of the observation. All other elements are based on sensor data that is within 10 minutes or less of the actual time of the observation.

4. What is a PIREP (UA), and where can they be found? (FAA-H-8083-28)

A pilot report (PIREP) provides valuable information regarding the conditions as they actually exist in the air, which cannot be gathered from any other source. Pilots can confirm the height of bases and tops of clouds, locations of wind shear and turbulence, and the location of inflight icing. There are two types of PIREPs: routine (UA) and urgent (UUA). PIREPs should be given to the ground facility with which communications are established (i.e., FSS, ARTCC, or terminal ATC). Altitudes are given in MSL, visibilities in SM, and distances in NM.

5. What is an aircraft report (AIREP)? (FAA-H-8083-28)

AIREPs are messages from an aircraft to a ground station. AIREPs are normally comprised of the aircraft's position, time, flight level, estimated time of arrival (ETA) over its next reporting point, destination ETA, fuel remaining, and meteorological information. The majority of routine AIREPs are automated and report wind and temperature at selected intervals along the flight route, derived from onboard sensors and probes. Some aircraft are equipped with sensors and probes to measure humidity/water vapor, turbulence, and icing data. There are two types of AIREPs: routine or position (ARP), and special (ARS).

6. Briefly describe NWS weather radar observations.
(FAA-H-8083-28)

Weather radar observations and their resultant images are graphical displays of precipitation and non-precipitation targets detected by weather radars. Weather Surveillance Radar-1988 Doppler (WSR-88D), also known as next generation weather radar (NEXRAD), displays these targets on a variety of products, which can be found on the websites of all NWS Weather Forecast Offices (WFO), the Aviation Weather Center (AWC), Storm Prediction Center (SPC), and various flight planning and weather service providers.

7. Explain what the colors on radar images represent.
(FAA-H-8083-28)

The colors on radar images represent the reflective power of the precipitation target. In general, the amount of radar power received is proportional to the intensity of the precipitation. This reflective power, commonly referred to by meteorologists as *reflectivity*, is measured in terms of decibels (dBZ). Each reflectivity image includes a color scale that describes the relationship among reflectivity value, color on the radar image, and precipitation intensity. The color scale and decibel scale can vary depending on the service provider and website.

8. What are the different types of radar images?
(FAA-H-8083-28)

The NWS produces a variety of radar products including radar mosaics, composite reflectivity, base reflectivity, and echo tops products.

9. Briefly describe how radar mosaic images are created.
(FAA-H-8083-28)

A radar mosaic consists of multiple single-site radar images combined to produce a radar image on a regional or national scale. Regional and national mosaics can be found on the websites of the NWS, AWC, and all NWS WFOs as well as commercial aviation weather providers. Radar mosaics can be assembled from composite reflectivity, base reflectivity, and echo tops, depending on the website or data provider.

10. **Define the term *composite reflectivity*.** (FAA-H-8083-28)

    Because the highest precipitation intensity can be at any altitude, the composite reflectivity product is needed. Composite reflectivity is the maximum echo intensity (reflectivity) detected within a column of the atmosphere above a location. During its tilt sequence, the radar scans through all of the elevation slices to determine the highest decibel value in the vertical column, then displays that value on the product. When compared with base reflectivity, the composite reflectivity can reveal important storm structure features and intensity trends of storms.

11. **Define the term *base reflectivity*.** (FAA-H-8083-28)

    The base reflectivity product is a display of both the location and intensity of reflectivity data from the lowest elevation angle, or 0.5 degrees above the horizon. The base reflectivity product is one elevation scan, whereas composite reflectivity looks at all elevation scans. Base reflectivity products are available several minutes sooner than composite reflectivity products. Precipitation at any location may be heavier than depicted on the base reflectivity image because it is occurring above the lowest elevation angle.

12. **Describe the four most common types of satellite imagery available to pilots.** (FAA-H-8083-28)

    Four types of satellite imagery are commonly used: GeoColor, visible, infrared (IR), and water vapor. Visible imagery is only useful during daylight hours. IR and water vapor imagery are useful day or night.

13. **What type of information is depicted by visible satellite imagery?** (FAA-H-8083-28)

    Visible satellite images display reflected sunlight from the Earth's surface, clouds, and particulate matter in the atmosphere. Clouds usually appear white, while land and water surfaces appear in shades of gray or black.

14. Infrared (IR) images depict what types of information? (FAA-H-8083-28)

IR images (color, B&W) display temperatures of the Earth's surface, clouds, and particulate matter. Generally speaking, the warmer an object, the more IR energy it emits. When clouds are present, the temperature displayed on the IR images is that of the tops of clouds. If the temperature of the atmosphere decreases with height (which is typical), cloud-top temperature can be used to roughly determine which clouds are high-level and which are low-level. A major advantage of the IR channel is that it can sense energy at night, so this imagery is available 24 hours per day.

Analysis

1. Explain what analysis charts are and provide several examples of the charts available to pilots. (FAA-H-8083-28)

Analyses of weather information are enhanced depictions and/or interpretations of observed weather data. A weather chart is a map on which data and analyses are presented that describe the state of the atmosphere over a large area at a given moment in time. NWS analysis charts include:

a. Surface analysis chart
b. Upper-air analysis
c. Freezing level analysis
d. Icing analysis—Current Icing Product (CIP)
e. Turbulence analysis—Graphical Turbulence Guidance (GTG)
f. Real-Time Mesoscale Analysis (RTMA)

2. What is a surface analysis chart? (FAA-H-8083-28)

Surface analysis charts are analyzed charts of surface weather observations. A surface analysis chart depicts the distribution of several items, including sea-level pressure; the positions of highs, lows, ridges, and troughs; the location and type of fronts; and the various boundaries such as drylines. Pressure is given in mean sea level (MSL) on the surface analysis chart while all other elements are presented as they occur at the surface point of observation. The NWS Weather Prediction Center (WPC) issues surface analysis charts for North America eight times daily, valid at 00, 03, 06, 09, 12, 15, 18, and 21 Coordinated Universal Time (UTC).

3. What is an upper-air analysis chart (constant-pressure chart)? (FAA-H-8083-28)

Any surface of equal pressure in the atmosphere is a constant pressure surface. A constant pressure analysis chart is an upper air weather map where all information depicted is at the specified pressure of the chart. From these charts, a pilot can approximate the observed air temperature, wind, and temperature-dewpoint spread along a proposed route. These charts also depict highs, lows, troughs, and ridges aloft by the height contour patterns resembling isobars on a surface map. Five constant pressure charts are issued twice daily from observed data obtained at 00Z and 12Z.

4. Describe the information provided on a freezing level analysis chart. (FAA-H-8083-28)

The freezing level is the lowest altitude in the atmosphere over a given location at which the air temperature reaches 0°C. This altitude is also known as the height of the 0°C constant-temperature surface. A freezing level analysis graphic shows the height of the 0°C constant-temperature surface. The initial analysis is updated hourly. The colors represent the height in hundreds of feet above MSL of the lowest freezing level. Regions with white indicate the surface and the entire depth of the atmosphere are below freezing. Hatched or spotted regions (if present) represent areas where the surface temperature is below freezing with multiple freezing levels aloft.

5. What are icing analysis charts, also known as Current Icing Product (CIP) charts? (FAA-H-8083-28)

The CIP combines sensor and NWS model data to provide an hourly 3D diagnosis of the icing environment. The CIP (and its forecast counterpart, the Forecast Icing Product [FIP]), provide a broad-brush approach to describing icing intensity using estimated liquid water content, drop size, and temperature to depict ice accumulation rate. The CIP suite consists of five graphics, including icing probability, icing severity, icing severity with probability > 25 percent, icing severity with probability > 50 percent, and icing severity plus supercooled large drops (SLD). CIPs are generated for select altitudes from 1,000 feet MSL to FL300 and depict the expected conditions at the valid time shown on the chart.

6. Describe the information provided by the Graphical Turbulence Guidance (GTG) analysis chart.
(FAA-H-8083-28)

The GTG computes the results from more than 10 turbulence algorithms, then compares the results of each algorithm with turbulence observations from both PIREPs and Aircraft Meteorological Data Relay (AMDAR) data to determine how well each algorithm matches reported turbulence conditions from these sources. The GTG analysis is essentially a 0-hour GTG forecast that overlays turbulence PIREPs that correspond to the valid time of the product.

7. Describe the information provided by a Real-Time Mesoscale Analysis (RTMA) chart. (FAA-H-8083-28)

RTMA is an hourly analysis system that produces analyses of surface weather elements. RTMA temperature information is a suitable replacement for missing temperature observations for a subset of airports and is intended for use by operators, pilots, and aircraft dispatchers when an airport lacks a surface temperature report from an automated weather system (e.g., ASOS or AWOS sensor) or human observer. Airports with RTMA data available are located in Alaska, Guam, Hawaii, Puerto Rico, and the CONUS. RTMA is issued by the NWS every hour, 24 hours a day.

Forecasts

1. What is a SIGMET (WS)? (AIM 7-1-6)

A SIGMET (WS) advises of weather that is potentially hazardous to all aircraft. Significant meteorological information (SIGMET) advisories are unscheduled products that are valid for 4 hours. However, SIGMETs associated with tropical cyclones and volcanic ash clouds are valid for 6 hours. Unscheduled updates and corrections are issued as necessary. In the conterminous United States, SIGMETs are issued when the following phenomena occur or are expected to occur:

a. Severe icing not associated with thunderstorms.

b. Severe or extreme turbulence or clear air turbulence (CAT) not associated with thunderstorms.

    c. Widespread dust storms or sandstorms lowering surface visibilities to below 3 miles.

    d. Volcanic ash.

2. What is an AIRMET? (AIM 7-1-6)

Airmen's meteorological information (AIRMET) advisories report significant weather phenomena but describe conditions at intensities lower than those which require the issuance of SIGMETs. AIRMETs are intended for dissemination to all pilots in the preflight and en route phase of flight to enhance safety. AIRMET information is available in two formats: text bulletins (WA) and graphics (G-AIRMET) and are issued on a scheduled basis every 6 hours beginning at 0245 UTC. Unscheduled updates and corrections are issued as necessary. AIRMETs contain details about IFR, extensive mountain obscuration, turbulence, strong surface winds, icing, and freezing levels.

3. What is a G-AIRMET? (FAA-H-8083-28)

A graphical AIRMET (G-AIRMET) is a graphical forecast of enroute weather that may be hazardous to aircraft, but is less severe than SIGMETs. G-AIRMETs identify hazardous weather in space and time more precisely than text products, enabling pilots to maintain high safety margins while flying more efficient routes. They are issued at 03:00, 09:00, 15:00 and 21:00 UTC (with updates issued as necessary). Hazards depicted in G-AIRMETs include turbulence, low level wind shear, strong surface winds, Icing, freezing level, IFR, and mountain obscurations.

4. What are the different types of AIRMETs? (AIM 7-1-6)

There are three AIRMETs—Sierra, Tango, and Zulu:

    a. AIRMET Sierra describes IFR conditions and/or extensive mountain obscurations.

    b. AIRMET Tango describes moderate turbulence, sustained surface winds of 30 knots or greater, and/or nonconvective lowlevel wind shear.

    c. AIRMET Zulu describes moderate icing and provides freezing level heights.

5. What is a center weather advisory (CWA)?
(FAA-H-8083-28)

A center weather advisory (CWA) is an aviation warning for use by aircrews to anticipate and avoid adverse weather conditions in the en route and terminal environments. This is not a flight planning product; instead it reflects current conditions expected at the time of issuance, and/or is a short-range forecast for conditions expected to begin within 2 hours from that time. CWAs are valid for a maximum of 2 hours. If conditions are expected to continue beyond that period, a statement will be included in the CWA.

6. What is a convective outlook chart? (FAA-H-8083-28)

The NWS Storm Prediction Center (SPC) issues narrative and graphical convective outlooks to provide the CONUS NWS WFOs, the public, the media, and emergency managers with the potential for severe (tornado, wind gusts 50 knots or greater, or hail 1 inch in diameter or greater) and non-severe (general) convection, and specific severe weather threats during the following 8 days. The convective outlook defines areas of marginal risk (MRGL), slight risk (SLGT), enhanced risk (ENH), moderate risk (MDT), or high risk (HIGH) of severe weather based on a probability percentage, which varies for time periods from 1 day to 3 days, and then two probability thresholds for days 4 through 8. The day 1, day 2, and day 3 convective outlooks also depict areas of general thunderstorms (TSTMS).

7. Describe Graphical Forecasts for Aviation (GFA).
(AIM 7-1-4)

The Graphical Forecasts for Aviation (GFA) webpage is intended to provide the necessary aviation weather information to give users a complete picture of the weather that may impact flight in the CONUS, Alaska, Hawaii, Gulf of Mexico, Caribbean, and portions of the Atlantic and Pacific Oceans. The webpage contains observational data, forecasts, and warnings that can be viewed from 14 hours in the past to 18 hours in the future, including thunderstorms, clouds, flight category, precipitation, icing, turbulence, and wind. Wind, icing, and turbulence forecasts are available in 3,000-foot increments from the surface up to 30,000 feet MSL, and in 6,000-foot increments from 30,000 feet MSL to FL480 (48,000 feet MSL). Turbulence forecasts are also broken into LO (below 18,000 feet MSL) and HI (at or above 18,000 feet

MSL) graphics. A maximum icing graphic and maximum wind velocity graphic (regardless of altitude) are also available. Built with modern geospatial information tools, the GFA allows users to pan and zoom to focus on areas of greatest interest.

8. What are the different types of aviation forecasts available when selecting the "Forecast" tab of the GFA? (AIM 7-1-4)

The "Forecasts" tab will provide gridded displays of various weather parameters as well as NWS textual weather observations, forecasts, and warnings out to 15 hours. Icing, turbulence, and wind gridded products are three-dimensional. Other gridded products are two-dimensional and may represent a composite of a three-dimensional weather phenomenon or a surface weather variable, such as horizontal visibility. Forecasts are viewable out to 15 hours. Selecting the "Forecasts" tab will provide the following forecasts:

a. TAF—terminal aerodrome forecast.
b. CIG/VIS—ceiling and visibility.
c. Clouds.
d. PCPN/WX—precipitation and weather.
e. TS—thunderstorm.
f. Winds.
g. Turb—turbulence.
h. Ice.

9. Describe some of the weather products available when selecting the "Obs/Warn" tab of the GFA. (AIM 7-1-4)

Selecting the "Obs/Warn" tab provides an option to display observations and warnings for the current time and the previous 14 hours (rounded to the nearest hour). Selecting the "Obs/Warn" tab will provide the following information:

a. METAR.
b. PCPN/WX—precipitation and weather.
c. CIG/VIS—ceiling and visibility.
d. PIREP—pilot reports.
e. RAD/SAT—radar and satellite.

10. Describe the content of a terminal aerodrome forecast (TAF). (FAA-H-8083-28)

A TAF is a concise statement of the expected meteorological conditions significant to aviation for a specified time period, within a 5 SM radius from the center of an airport's runway complex (terminal). TAFs use the same weather code found in METAR weather reports, in the following format:

a. *Type of reports*—A routine forecast (TAF), an amended forecast (TAF AMD), or a corrected forecast (TAF COR).

b. *ICAO station identifier*—4-letter station identifiers.

c. *Date and time of origin*—The date/time of forecast follows the terminal's location identifier and shows the day of the month in two digits, and the time in which the forecast is completed and ready for transmission in four digits, appended with a Z to denote UTC. *Example:* 061737Z—the TAF was issued on the 6th day of the month at 1737 UTC.

d. *Valid period date and time*—The first two digits are the day of the month for the start of the TAF, followed by two digits that indicate the starting hour (UTC). The next two digits indicate the day of the month for the end of the TAF, and the last two digits are the ending hour (UTC) of the valid period. Scheduled 24- and 30-hour TAFs are issued four (4) times per day, at 0000, 0600, 1200, and 1800Z. *Example:* A 00Z TAF issued on the 9th of the month and valid for 24 hours would have a valid period of 0900/0924.

e. *Forecasts*—Winds (true north), visibility (SM), significant and vicinity weather, cloud and vertical obscuration (AGL), non-convective low-level wind shear, forecast change indicators (FM, TEMPO, and PROB).

11. What information is provided in a winds and temperatures aloft forecast (FB)? (FAA-H-8083-28)

FBs are computer prepared forecasts of wind direction, wind speed, and temperature at specified times, altitudes, and locations. They are produced four times daily for specified locations in the CONUS, Hawaii, Alaska and coastal waters, and the western Pacific Ocean. Amendments are not issued to the forecasts.

Wind forecasts are not issued for altitudes within 1,500 feet of a location's elevation.

Some of the features of FBs are:

a. Product header includes date and time observations collected, forecast valid date and time, and the time period during which the forecast is to be used.

b. Altitudes up to 15,000 feet referenced to MSL; altitudes at or above 18,000 feet are references to flight levels (FL).

c. Temperature indicated in degrees Celsius (two digits) for the levels from 6,000 through 24,000 feet. Above 24,000 feet, minus sign is omitted since temperatures are always negative at those altitudes. Temperature forecasts are not issued for altitudes within 2,500 feet of a location's elevation. Forecasts for intermediate levels are determined by interpolation.

d. Wind direction indicated in tens of degrees (two digits) with reference to true north and wind speed is given in knots (two digits). Light and variable wind or wind speeds of less than 5 knots are expressed by 9900. Forecast wind speeds of 100 through 199 knots are indicated by subtracting 100 from the speed and adding 50 to the coded direction. For example, a forecast of 250 degrees, 145 knots, is encoded as 7545. Forecast wind speeds of 200 knots or greater are indicated as a forecast speed of 199 knots. For example, 7799 is decoded as 270 degrees at 199 knots or greater.

12. What information does a freezing level graphics chart provide? (FAA-H-8083-28)

Freezing level graphics are used to assess the lowest freezing level heights and their values relative to flight paths. The chart uses colors to represent the height in hundreds of feet MSL of the lowest freezing level(s). The initial analysis and 3-hour forecast graphics are updated hourly. The 6-, 9-, and 12-hour forecast graphics are updated every three hours.

13. What are constant pressure level forecasts?
(FAA-H-8083-28)

Constant pressure level forecasts are a computer model's depiction of select weather (e.g., wind) at a specified constant pressure level (e.g., 300 millibars [mb]), along with the altitudes (in meters) of the specified constant pressure level.

They are used to provide an overview of weather patterns at specified times and pressure altitudes and are the source for wind and temperature aloft forecasts. Pressure patterns cause and characterize much of the weather. Typically, lows and troughs are associated with clouds and precipitation while highs and ridges are associated with fair weather, except in winter when valley fog may occur. The location and strength of the jet stream can be viewed at 300 mb, 250 mb, and 200 mb levels.

Constant Pressure Level	Approx. Altitude (MSL)
925 mb	2,500 ft
850 mb	5,000 ft
700 mb	10,000 ft
500 mb	18,000 ft
300 mb	30,000 ft
250 mb	34,000 ft
200 mb	39,000 ft

14. What are short-range surface prognostic charts?
(FAA-H-8083-28)

Short-range surface prognostic (prog) charts provide a forecast of surface pressure systems, fronts and precipitation for a 2½ day period. They cover a forecast area of the 48 contiguous states and coastal waters, and are prepared by the NWS Weather Prediction Center (and available on the AWC website). Predicted conditions are divided into five forecast periods: 12, 18, 24, 48 and 60 hours. Each chart depicts a snapshot of weather elements expected at the specified valid time. Charts are issued four times a day and can be used to obtain an overview of the progression of surface weather features during the included periods.

15. Describe a U.S. low-level significant weather prognostic chart. (FAA-H-8083-28)

Low-level significant weather (SIGWX) charts provide a forecast of aviation weather hazards, primarily intended as guidance products for preflight briefings. The forecast domain covers the continental U.S. and the coastal waters for altitudes FL240 and below. Each depicts a snapshot of weather expected at the specified valid time. The charts depict weather flying categories, turbulence, and freezing levels, and are issued four times per day in two types: a 12-hour and a 24-hour prog.

16. Describe a mid-level significant weather chart. (FAA-H-8083-28)

This chart provides a forecast and an overview of significant enroute weather phenomena over a range of flight levels from 10,000 feet MSL to FL450, and associated surface weather features. It is a "snapshot" of weather expected at the specified valid time and depicts numerous weather elements that can be hazardous to aviation. The AWC issues the 24-hour mid-level significant weather chart four times daily.

17. What information may be obtained from the U.S. high-level significant weather prognostic charts? (FAA-H-8083-28)

High-level significant weather (SIGWX) charts provide a forecast of significant enroute weather phenomena over a range of flight levels from FL250 to FL630, and associated surface weather features. Each chart depicts a "snap-shot" of weather expected at the specified valid time. Conditions routinely appearing on the chart are:

a. Thunderstorms and cumulonimbus clouds.
b. Moderate or severe turbulence.
c. Moderate or severe icing.
d. Jet streams.
e. Tropopause heights.
f. Tropical cyclones.
g. Severe squall lines.
h. Volcanic eruption sites.
i. Widespread sandstorms and dust storms.

18. **What information can a pilot obtain from current and forecast icing products (CIP and FIP)?** (FAA-H-8083-28)

Current icing product (CIP)—Provides an hourly three-dimensional diagnosis of the icing environment; information is displayed on a suite of twelve graphics available for the 48 contiguous United States, much of Canada and Mexico, and their respective coastal waters. CIP is a supplementary weather product for enhanced situational awareness only. The CIP product suite is issued hourly 15 minutes after the hour by the AWC.

Forecast icing potential (FIP)—Provides a three-dimensional forecast of icing potential (or likelihood) using numerical weather prediction model output. It may be used as a higher resolution supplement to AIRMETs and SIGMETs but is not a substitute for them. The forecast area covers the 48 contiguous states, much of Canada and Mexico, and their respective coastal waters. The FIP is issued every hour and generates an hourly forecast for 3 hours into the future.

19. **What are several examples of weather charts that you would use to obtain information on high-altitude weather?** (AC 61-107)

a. *Constant pressure charts*—Provide information on pressure systems, temperature, winds, and temperature/dewpoint spread at the 850 mb, 700 mb, 500 mb, 300 mb, and 200 mb levels. All five charts are issued every 12 hours.

b. *Prognostic charts*—Provide forecast winds, temperature, and expected movement of weather over the 6-hour valid time of the chart.

c. *Observed tropopause charts*—Provide jet stream, turbulence, and temperature/wind/pressure reports at the tropopause over each station.

d. *Tropopause wind prognostic charts*—Helpful in determining jet stream patterns and the presence of CAT and wind shear.

e. *Tropopause height vertical wind shear charts*—Helpful in determining jet stream patterns and the presence of CAT and wind shear. Dashed lines indicate wind shear.

Note: Pilots should consult all weather charts, including those designed for low levels. High-altitude flight allows a pilot to over-fly most adverse weather, but pilots must consider low-altitude weather for arrival, departure, and enroute emergencies that require an immediate diversion.

C. Meteorology

Atmospheric Composition and Stability

1. What gases is the atmosphere composed of? (AC 61-107)

The atmosphere is a mixture of gases in constant motion, composed of approximately 78 percent nitrogen, 21 percent oxygen, and 1 percent other gases (carbon dioxide, argon). The atmosphere also constantly absorbs and releases water vapor, which causes changes in the weather.

2. What is the troposphere? (FAA-H-8083-28)

The troposphere begins at the Earth's surface and extends up to about 11 kilometers (36,000 feet) high. As the gases in this layer decrease with height, the air becomes thinner. Therefore, the temperature in the troposphere also decreases with height. As you climb higher, the temperature drops from about 15°C (59°F) to −56.5°C (−70°F). Almost all weather occurs in this region.

3. Does the vertical depth of the troposphere change? (FAA-H-8083-28)

The vertical depth of the troposphere varies due to temperature variations which are closely associated with latitude and season. It decreases from the Equator to the poles, and is higher during summer than in winter. At the Equator, it is around 18–20 kilometers (11–12 miles) high, at 50°N and 50°S latitude, 9 kilometers (5.6 miles), and at the poles, 6 kilometers (3.7 miles) high.

4. What is the tropopause? (FAA-H-8083-28)

The transition boundary between the troposphere and the stratosphere is called the tropopause. Both the tropopause and the troposphere are known as the lower atmosphere.

5. Why is knowledge of the location of the tropopause important to flight crews? (FAA-H-8083-25)

The location of the tropopause is important because it is commonly associated with the location of the jet stream and possible clear air turbulence.

6. What is the stratosphere? (FAA-H-8083-28)

The stratosphere extends from the tropopause up to 50 kilometers (31 miles) above the Earth's surface. This layer holds 19 percent of the atmosphere's gases, but very little water vapor. Temperature increases with height as radiation is increasingly absorbed by oxygen molecules, leading to the formation of ozone. The temperature rises from an average −56.6°C (−70°F) at the tropopause to a maximum of about −3°C (27°F) at the stratopause due to this absorption of ultraviolet radiation. The increasing temperature also makes it a calm layer, with movements of the gases being slow.

7. Explain the advantages and disadvantages of commercial aircraft conducting cruise flight in the lower stratosphere. (FAA-H-8083-28)

Commercial aircraft often cruise in the lower stratosphere to avoid atmospheric turbulence and convection in the troposphere. Severe turbulence during the cruise phase of flight can be caused by the convective overshoot of thunderstorms from the troposphere below. The disadvantages of flying in the stratosphere can include increased fuel consumption due to warmer temperatures, increased levels of radiation, and increased concentration of ozone.

8. What factor primarily determines the type and vertical extent of clouds? (FAA-H-8083-28)

The stability of the atmosphere.

9. How do you determine atmospheric stability? (FAA-H-8083-28)

Changes in atmospheric stability are inversely related to temperature (density) changes with height. If temperature lapse rates increase, then stability decreases. Conversely, if temperature lapse rates decrease, then stability increases. Most of these changes occur as a result of the movement of air, but diurnal (day/night) temperature variations can play a significant role. Several stability indexes and other quantities exist that evaluate atmospheric stability and the potential for convective storms. The most common of these are lifted index (LI) and convective available potential energy (CAPE). Observed CAPE values in thunderstorm environments often exceed 1,000 joules per kilogram, and in extreme cases may exceed 5,000 joules per kilogram.

10. List the effects of stable and unstable air on clouds, turbulence, precipitation and visibility. (FAA-H-8083-28)

	Stable	Unstable
Clouds	Stratiform	Cumuliform
Turbulence	Smooth	Rough
Precipitation	Steady	Showery
Visibility	Fair to Poor	Good

11. Explain the difference between a stable atmosphere and an unstable atmosphere. (FAA-H-8083-25)

The stability of the atmosphere depends on its ability to resist vertical motion. A stable atmosphere makes vertical movement difficult, and small vertical disturbances dampen out and disappear. In an unstable atmosphere, small vertical air movements tend to become larger, resulting in turbulent airflow and convective activity. Instability can lead to significant turbulence, extensive vertical clouds, and severe weather.

12. Explain how the lifted index (LI) relates to atmospheric stability. (FAA-H-8083-28)

The LI is the temperature difference between an air parcel (usually at the surface) lifted adiabatically and the temperature of the environment at a given pressure (usually 500 millibars) in the atmosphere. A positive value indicates a stable column of air and a negative value indicates an unstable column of air. A value of zero indicates a neutrally stable column of air.

Wind

1. Describe several examples of adverse winds affecting an aircraft during a takeoff or landing. (FAA-H-8083-28)

Crosswinds—Not correctly compensating for a crosswind is a major cause of runway excursions; if a pilot does not correctly compensate for a crosswind, the aircraft may drift off side of runway.

Gusts—A fluctuation of wind speed with variations of 10 knots or more between peaks and lulls. Gusty winds at the point of touchdown provide significant challenges to a safe landing.

Tailwinds—Result in a longer takeoff roll due to higher ground speed to generate sufficient lift. A tailwind will result in a smaller initial climb gradient which may be insufficient to clear obstacles. Tailwinds during landing increase landing distance especially on a wet runway and will also result in a longer landing roll due higher ground speed at touchdown.

Variable wind/sudden wind shift—A variable wind is a wind that changes direction frequently, while a sudden wind shift is a line or narrow zone along which there is an abrupt change of wind direction. Both, even at low wind speeds, can make takeoffs and landings difficult. A headwind can quickly become a crosswind or tailwind.

Wind shear—The change in wind speed and/or direction, usually in the vertical. The characteristics of the wind shear profile are of critical importance in determining the impact for an aircraft on takeoff or landing.

2. **Define the term *wind shear* and state the areas it is likely to occur.** (FAA-H-8083-25, FAA-H-8083-28)

Wind shear is the sudden, drastic change in wind speed and/or direction over a small area, from one level or point to another, usually in the vertical. Wind shear occurs in all directions, but for convenience, it is measured along vertical and horizontal axes, thus becoming horizontal and vertical wind shear. It is important to remember that wind shear can affect any flight at any altitude (e.g., at upper levels near jet streams or near the ground due to convection). Low-level wind shear is commonly associated with passing frontal systems, thunderstorms, temperature inversions, and strong upper-level winds (greater than 25 knots).

3. **Explain the difference between an increasing headwind shear and a decreasing headwind shear.** (FAA-H-8083-28)

An increasing headwind (or decreasing tailwind) shear increases indicated airspeed and thus increases performance. The airplane will tend to pitch up to regain trim airspeed. An additional consideration is that this type of shear may reduce normal deceleration during flare which could cause overrun. An increasing tailwind (or decreasing headwind) shear will decrease indicated airspeed and performance capability. Due to airspeed loss, the airplane may tend to pitch down to regain trim speed.

4. **What is a mountain wave?** (FAA-H-8083-28)

A mountain wave is an atmospheric wave disturbance formed when stable air flow passes over a mountain or mountain ridge. Mountain waves are a form of mechanical turbulence which develop above and downwind of mountains. The waves remain nearly stationary while the wind blows rapidly through them. The waves may extend 600 miles or more downwind from the mountain range. Mountain waves frequently produce severe to extreme turbulence. Location and intensity varies with wave characteristics. Incredibly, vertically propagating mountain waves have been documented up to 200,000 feet (60,000 meters) and higher.

5. Which types of clouds are associated with a mountain wave? (FAA-H-8083-28)

When sufficient moisture is present in the upstream flow, mountain waves produce interesting cloud formations including: cap clouds, cirrocumulus standing lenticular (CCSL), altocumulus standing lenticular (ACSL), and rotor clouds. These clouds provide visual proof that mountain waves exist. However, these clouds may be absent if the air is too dry.

6. Describe the conditions that would be favorable for mountain waves to form. (FAA-H-8083-28)

a. Large-scale winds at ridge level, blowing perpendicular (or nearly so) to the ridge-line, are normally required.

b. Wind speeds at ridge level are normally 20 knots or greater.

c. The atmosphere is relatively stable; if there is a steep temperature lapse rate below 500 mb (an unstable atmosphere), with evidence of convection present, this type of atmospheric wave is unlikely to form.

Note: Vertically propagating waves are most likely and most intense during the winter and early spring months, when the winds at ridge level are strongest.

7. Clear air turbulence (CAT) caused by mountain waves is generally located where? (FAA-H-8083-28)

Turbine-powered aircraft operating at cruise altitudes above FL180 in the vicinity of mountainous terrain may encounter moderate or greater turbulence associated with orographic winds. This type of turbulence may be characterized by relatively rapid onset and can lead to structural damage or airframe failure.

Mountain waves can create CAT. Mountain wave CAT may extend from the mountain crests to as high as 5,000 feet above the tropopause and can range 100 miles or more downstream from the mountains.

8. What is a katabatic wind? (FAA-H-8083-28)

Katabatic winds are winds produced by the flow of cold, dense air down a slope in an area subject to radiational cooling. Mountain winds are the most common form of katabatic winds. An example of this phenomena would be the Santa Ana winds, which are warm winds descending from the Sierras into the Santa Ana Valley of California.

9. Describe how a sea breeze is created. (FAA-H-8083-28)

A sea breeze is a coastal local wind that blows from sea to land, and caused by temperature differences when the sea surface is colder than the adjacent land. Air above the land becomes warmer (less dense) than air above the water. This is because land heats up faster than water. Low-level pressure gradients develop with lower pressure over the warmer land and higher pressure over the cooler water. Low-level winds develop in the direction of the PGF. Thus, the wind blows from the water to the land. The air rises over land and sinks over water. Clouds (and precipitation) may develop in the rising air over land with cloud dissipation over the sinking air offshore.

Temperature

1. Describe the three most common temperature scales. (FAA-H-8083-28)

Celsius (°C) scale—The most commonly used temperature scale worldwide and in meteorology. The scale is based on the freezing point (0°C) and boiling point of water (100 °C) under a pressure of one standard atmosphere (approximately sea level). Each degree on the Celsius scale is exactly the same size as a degree on the Kelvin scale.

Fahrenheit (°F) scale—The United States uses Fahrenheit (°F) scale for everyday temperature measurements. In this scale, the freezing point of water is 32 degrees Fahrenheit (32 °F) and the boiling point is 212 degrees Fahrenheit (212 °F).

Kelvin (K) scale—A thermodynamic (absolute) temperature scale, where absolute zero, the theoretical absence of all thermal energy, is zero Kelvin (0 K). The Kelvin scale is a direct measure of the average kinetic molecular activity. Because nothing can be colder than absolute zero, the Kelvin scale contains no negative numbers.

2. What is the standard atmosphere at sea level?
(FAA-H-8083-25)

Standard atmosphere at sea level includes a surface temperature of 59°F or 15°C, and a surface pressure of 29.92 inHg or 1013.2 millibars.

3. What are standard atmosphere temperature and pressure lapse rates? (FAA-H-8083-25)

A standard temperature lapse rate is one in which the temperature decreases at the rate of approximately 3.5°F or 2°C per 1,000 feet up to 36,000 feet. Above this point, the temperature is considered constant up to 80,000 feet. A standard pressure lapse rate is one in which pressure decreases at a rate of approximately 1 inHg per 1,000 feet of altitude gain to 10,000 feet.

4. Define the term *temperature inversion*. (FAA-H-8083-28)

A temperature inversion, or simply inversion, is a layer in which the temperature increases with altitude. If the base of the inversion is at the surface, it is termed a surface-based inversion. If the base of the inversion is not at the surface, it is termed an inversion aloft.

5. What happens to air density as altitude increases?
(AC 61-107)

Atmospheric density in the troposphere decreases gradually with altitude, decreasing to 50 percent of its sea level value at 18,000 feet MSL. This means that at FL180 the same volume of air contains only one-half the oxygen molecules as at sea level.

Moisture/Precipitation

1. What is the definition of the term *relative humidity*, and why is knowledge of its value important?
(FAA-H-8083-28)

Relative humidity is the ratio, usually expressed as a percentage, of water vapor actually in the air parcel compared (relative) to the amount of water vapor the air parcel could hold at a particular temperature and pressure. If the relative humidity of the air is high, it can contribute to the formation of clouds, fog, haze, or smoke, resulting in diminished visibility and an inversion layer. The relationship between dewpoint and temperature defines the concept of relative humidity.

2. Define the term *dewpoint.* (FAA-H-8083-28)

The dewpoint, given in degrees, is the temperature at which the air can hold no more moisture. When the temperature of air is reduced to the dewpoint, the air is completely saturated and moisture begins to condense in the form of fog, dew, frost, clouds, rain, or snow.

3. The amount of moisture in the atmosphere is dependent on what value? (FAA-H-8083-28)

The temperature of the air. Every 20°F increase in temperature doubles the amount of moisture the air can hold. Conversely, a decrease of 20°F cuts the capacity in half.

4. What are the necessary ingredients for precipitation to form? (FAA-H-8083-28)

Precipitation formation requires three ingredients: water vapor, sufficient lift to condense the water vapor into clouds, and a growth process that allows cloud droplets to grow large and heavy enough to fall as precipitation. Significant precipitation usually requires clouds to be at least 4,000 feet thick. The vertical distribution of temperature will often determine the type of precipitation that occurs at the surface.

5. Describe the following types of precipitation: drizzle, rain, snow, ice pellets (sleet), freezing rain, hail. (FAA-H-8083-28)

Drizzle—Forms in stable air, falls from stratiform clouds, and is typically accompanied by fog. Visibility in drizzle can be less than 1 mile.

Rain—Occurs when there is a deep layer of above-freezing air based at the surface.

Snow—Precipitation in the form of ice crystals that falls at a steady rate or in snow showers; snow begins, changes in intensity, and ends rapidly; it occurs when temperature remains below freezing throughout the entire depth of the atmosphere.

Ice pellets (sleet)—Occur when there is a shallow layer aloft with above freezing temperatures and with a deep layer of below freezing air based at the surface. As snow falls into the shallow warm layer, the snowflakes partially melt. As the precipitation reenters air that is below freezing, it refreezes into ice pellets.

(continued)

Freezing rain—Occurs when there is a deep layer aloft with above freezing temperatures and with a shallow layer of below freezing air at the surface. It can begin as either rain and/or snow, but becomes all rain in the warm layer. The rain falls back into below freezing air, but since the depth is shallow, the rain does not have time to freeze into ice pellets. The drops freeze on contact with the ground or exposed objects.

Hail—Precipitation in the form of balls or other irregular lumps of ice produced by thunderstorms.

Weather System Formation, Including Air Masses and Fronts

1. What is the definition of an *air mass*? (FAA-H-8083-28)

An air mass is a large body of air with generally uniform temperature and humidity. The area from which an air mass originates is called a source region.

2. Describe the different types of fronts. (FAA-H-8083-28)

Cold front—Occurs when a mass of cold, dense, and stable air advances and replaces a body of warmer air.

Occluded front—A frontal occlusion occurs when a fast-moving cold front catches up with a slow-moving warm front. Two types: cold front occlusion and warm front occlusion.

Warm front—The boundary area formed when a warm air mass contacts and flows over a colder air mass.

Stationary front—When the forces of two air masses are relatively equal, the boundary or front that separates them remains stationary and influences the local weather for days. The weather is typically a mixture of both warm and cold fronts. Stationary fronts move at a speed of less than 5 knots.

3. What are the general characteristics of the weather a pilot would encounter when operating near a cold front? A warm front? (FAA-H-8083-25)

Cold Front—As the front passes, expected weather can include towering cumulus or cumulonimbus, heavy rain accompanied by lightning, thunder and/or hail; tornadoes possible; during passage, poor visibility, winds variable and gusting; temperature/dewpoint and barometric pressure drop rapidly.

Warm Front—As the front passes, expected weather can include stratiform clouds, drizzle, low ceilings and poor visibility; variable winds; rise in temperature.

Note: The weather associated with a front depends on the amount of moisture available, the degree of stability of the air that is forced upward, the slope of the front, the speed of frontal movement, and the upper wind flow.

4. What is a trough? (FAA-H-8083-28)

A trough (also called a trough line) is an elongated area of relatively low atmospheric pressure. At the surface when air converges into a low, it cannot go outward against the pressure gradient, nor can it go downward into the ground; it must go upward. Therefore, a trough is an area of rising air. Rising air is conducive to cloudiness and precipitation, hence the general association of low pressure and bad weather.

5. What is a ridge? (FAA-H-8083-28)

A ridge (also called a ridge line) is an elongated area of relatively high atmospheric pressure. Air moving out of a high or ridge depletes the quantity of air, therefore, these are areas of descending air. Descending air favors dissipation of cloudiness, hence the association of high pressure and good weather.

6. What is a dryline? Why is knowledge of its location important? (FAA-H-8083-28)

A dryline is a low-level boundary hundreds of miles long separating moist and dry air masses. In the U.S, it typically lies north-south across the southern and central High Plains during the spring and early summer, where it separates moist air from the Gulf of Mexico to the east and dry desert air from the southwestern states to the west. Severe and sometimes tornadic thunderstorms often develop along a dryline or in the moist air just to the east of it, especially when it begins moving eastward.

Clouds

1. **Why is knowledge of cloud types important in aviation?**
(FAA-H-8083-28)

A cloud is a visible aggregate of minute water droplets and/or ice particles in the atmosphere above the Earth's surface. Clouds are like signposts in the sky that provide information on air motion, stability, and moisture, which help pilots visualize weather conditions and potential weather hazards.

2. **Explain how clouds are formed.** (FAA-H-8083-28)

Clouds form in the atmosphere as a result of condensation of water vapor in rising currents of air or by the evaporation of the lowest layer of fog. Rising currents of air are necessary for the formation of vertically deep clouds capable of producing precipitation heavier than light intensity.

3. **Describe the four basic cloud forms observed in the Earth's atmosphere.** (FAA-H-8083-28)

Cirriform—High-level clouds that form above 20,000 feet and that are usually composed of ice crystals. They are typically thin and white in appearance. Cirrus generally occur in fair weather and point in the direction of air movement at their elevation.

Nimbus—Comes from the Latin word meaning "rain." These clouds typically form between 7,000 and 15,000 feet and bring steady precipitation. As the clouds thicken and precipitation begins to fall, the bases of the clouds tend to lower toward the ground.

Cumuliform—Clouds that look like white, fluffy cotton balls or heaps and show the vertical motion or thermal uplift of air taking place in the atmosphere. The level at which condensation and cloud formation begins is indicated by a flat cloud base, and its height will depend upon the humidity of the rising air. The more humid the air, the lower the cloud base. The tops of these clouds can reach over 60,000 feet.

Stratiform—"Stratus" is Latin for "layer" or "blanket." These clouds consist of a featureless low layer that can cover the entire sky like a blanket, bringing generally gray and dull weather. The cloud bases are usually only a few hundred feet above the ground.

Over hills and mountains, they can reach ground level where they may be called fog. Also, as fog lifts off the ground due to daytime heating, the fog forms a layer of low stratus clouds.

4. Describe the three main cloud levels found in temperate regions. (FAA-H-8083-28)

High clouds (16,500–40,000 feet)—Cirrus (Ci), cirrocumulus (Cc), and cirrostratus (Cs) are high-level clouds; typically thin and white in appearance, composed almost entirely of ice crystals.

Middle clouds (6,500–23,000 feet)—Altocumulus (Ac), altostratus (As), and nimbostratus (Ns) are mid-level clouds composed primarily of water droplets, and can also be composed of supercooled liquid water droplets and/or ice crystals when temperatures are below freezing.

Low clouds (surface–6,500 feet)—Cumulus (Cu), towering cumulus (TCu), stratocumulus (Sc), stratus (St), and cumulonimbus (Cb) are low clouds composed of water droplets, and can also be composed of supercooled liquid water droplets and/or ice crystals when temperatures are below freezing

5. Are there any hazards associated with operation in or through high clouds? (FAA-H-8083-28)

Cirrus (Ci)—Cirrus clouds are found in stable air above 30,000 feet MSL; appear as delicate filaments of white (or mostly white) patches or narrow bands; composed almost entirely of ice crystals; cirrus clouds have little effect on aircraft and contain no significant icing or turbulence.

Cirrocumulus (Cc)—Appear as a thin, white patch, sheet, or layer of cloud without shading, and is composed of very small elements in the form of grains, ripples, etc.; can be composed of highly super-cooled water droplets, as well as small ice crystals, or a mixture of both; usually, the droplets are rapidly replaced by ice crystals. Pilots can expect some turbulence and icing.

Cirrostratus (Cs)—Appear as a whitish veil, usually fibrous (hair-like) but sometimes smooth, that may totally cover the sky, and that often produces halo phenomena, either partial or complete. Cirrostratus clouds are composed primarily of ice crystals and contain little, if any, icing and no turbulence.

6. Explain the hazards associated with operating an aircraft near or in towering cumulus or cumulonimbus clouds. (AC 61-107)

Clouds with extensive vertical development (e.g., towering cumulus and cumulonimbus clouds) indicate a deep layer of unstable air and contain moderate to heavy turbulence with icing. The bases of these clouds are found at altitudes associated with low to middle clouds but their tops can extend up to 60,000 feet MSL or more.

Note: Cumulonimbus clouds are thunderstorm clouds that present a particularly severe hazard that pilots should circumnavigate. Hazards associated with cumulonimbus clouds include embedded thunderstorms, severe or extreme turbulence, lightning, icing, and dangerously strong winds and updrafts.

Turbulence

1. What are the three major types of turbulence? (FAA-H-8083-28)

a. *Convective*—Turbulent vertical motions that result from convective currents and the subsequent rising and sinking of air.

b. *Mechanical*—Turbulence caused by obstructions to the wind flow, such as trees, buildings, mountains, etc. Obstructions to the wind flow disrupt smooth wind flow into a complex snarl of eddies.

c. *Wind shear*—Wind shear generates turbulence between two wind currents of different directions and/or speeds. Wind shear may be associated with either a wind shift or a wind speed gradient at any level in the atmosphere.

2. Describe the visual indications a pilot would see indicating convective turbulence. (FAA-H-8083-28)

Billowy cumuliform clouds, usually seen over land during sunny afternoons, are signposts in the sky indicating convective turbulence. The cloud top usually marks the approximate upper limit of the convective current. A pilot can expect to encounter turbulence beneath or in the clouds, while air generally is smooth above the clouds. When convection extends to great heights, it develops larger towering cumulus clouds and cumulonimbus with anvil-like tops. The cumulonimbus gives visual warning of violent convective turbulence.

Jetstream

1. What is the jet stream? (AC 61-107)

The jet stream is a narrow band of high-altitude winds, near or in the tropopause, that results from large temperature contrasts over a short distance (typically along fronts), creating large pressure gradients aloft. The jet stream usually travels in an easterly direction between 50 and 200 knots. The speed of the jet stream is greater in the winter than in the summer months because of greater temperature differences. It generally drops more rapidly on the polar side than on the equatorial side.

2. What are the names of the three main jet streams? (FAA-H-8083-28)

The polar front jet stream, the subtropical jet stream, and the polar night jet stream.

3. Where are the polar front and subtropical jet streams located with respect to global circulation? (FAA-H-8083-28)

The 50°–60°N/S latitude region is where the polar jet is located, and the subtropical jet is located around 30°N latitude. The location of the polar front jet stream is a significant factor affecting daily weather patterns across the United States.

4. How does the location of the jet stream move with a change of seasons? (FAA-H-8083-28)

Jet streams follow the sun, in that as the sun's elevation increases each day in the spring, the jet streams shift north moving into Canada by summer. As autumn approaches and the sun's elevation decreases, the jet stream moves south into the United States, helping to bring cooler air to the country.

5. Where can a pilot obtain information on the location and strength of the jet stream? (FAA-H-8083-28)

SIGWX charts provide invaluable information to dispatchers and flight crews on the forecast position of jet streams as well as other information such as tropopause heights, thunderstorm and cumulonimbus clouds, moderate or severe turbulence, moderate or severe icing, turbulence, and fronts. The mid-level SIGWX chart provides a forecast of significant enroute weather from 10,000 feet MSL to FL450. The high-level SIGWX chart provides a forecast of significant enroute weather from FL250 to FL630. The location and strength of the jet stream can also be viewed on an upper air analysis chart (constant pressure) at 300 mb, 250 mb, and 200 mb levels.

6. Where is wind shear and turbulence associated with a jet stream located? (AC 61-107)

Wind shear is a sudden change of wind velocity and/or direction. Horizontal wind shear and turbulence are frequently found on the northern side of the jet stream. Horizontal wind changes of 40 knots within 150 nautical miles (NM) or vertical wind shear of 6 knots or greater per 1,000 feet usually indicate moderate to severe turbulence and should be avoided.

Clear Air Turbulence

1. What is *clear air turbulence* (CAT)? (FAA-H-8083-28)

CAT is defined as sudden severe turbulence occurring in cloudless regions that causes violent buffeting of aircraft. CAT is a higher altitude turbulence (normally above 15,000 feet) particularly between the core of a jet stream and the surrounding air. This includes turbulence in cirrus clouds, within and in the vicinity of standing lenticular clouds, and in some cases in clear air in the vicinity of thunderstorms. Generally, though, CAT definitions exclude turbulence caused by thunderstorms, low-altitude temperature inversions, thermals, strong surface winds, or local terrain features.

2. Where is CAT encountered? (FAA-H-8083-28)

Locations where clear air turbulence can be found include:

a. At the base of a deep, upper trough, especially just downwind of an area of strong temperature advection.

b. Along the centerline of a trough area, where there is a strong horizontal wind shear between the jet core and winds to the poleward side of the jet core.

c. In the west side of a trough in the vicinity of a wind maxima as the maxima passes along the trough.

d. In the region of confluence between two jet streams, where the wind shear effect between the two jet streams is highly turbulent.

e. Near the sloping tropopause above the core, in the jet stream front below the core, and on the low pressure side of jet streams stronger than 110 knots at the core.

f. Above and to the lee of mountain wave ranges.

g. In areas where the flight path traverses a strong jet stream in the vicinity of mountainous terrain.

h. In curving jet streams that curve around a deep pressure trough.

i. In wind shift areas associated with pressure troughs and ridges.

3. In flight planning, what weather information can be used in determining the location of CAT? (FAA-H-8083-28)

Use of graphical forecasts portraying pilot reports and areas of probable turbulence is essential. Look for urgent (UUA) PIREPs since they contain information about severe or extreme turbulence (including CAT). In-flight weather advisories (e.g., SIGMETs and AIRMETs) are used to disseminate important information on atmospheric turbulence, both convective and CAT.

4. **What procedure should be followed if CAT is inadvertently encountered?** (AC 61-107)

    a. *Airspeed*—Airspeed is critical for any type of turbulent air penetration. Use the AFM-recommended turbulence penetration target speed or, if unknown, fly an airspeed below maneuvering speed.

    b. *Autopilot*—If severe turbulence is penetrated with the autopilot on, the altitude hold mode should be off. If the autopilot has a pitch hold mode, it should be engaged. With the autopilot off, the yaw damper should be engaged.

    c. *Attitude and heading*—Keep wings level and maintain the desired pitch attitude and approximate heading. If large attitude changes occur, avoid abrupt or large control inputs.

5. **What is the best source of information on the location of CAT?** (AIM 7-1-23)

    The best source of information on CAT are PIREPs. Any pilot encountering CAT should report the time, location and intensity as soon as possible to that area's controlling facility (ATC, FSS, etc.).

Thunderstorms and Microbursts

1. **What are the three ingredients a thunderstorm cell requires to form?** (FAA-H-8083-28)

    a. *Sufficient water vapor*—Must be present to produce unstable air (commonly measured using dewpoint).

    b. *Unstable air mass*—Virtually all showers and thunderstorms form in an air mass that is classified as conditionally unstable. A conditionally unstable air mass requires a lifting mechanism strong enough to release the instability.

    c. *Lifting mechanism*—Include converging winds around surface lows and troughs, fronts, upslope flow, drylines, outflow boundaries generated by prior storms, and local winds, such as sea breeze, lake breeze, land breeze, and valley breeze circulations.

2. What are the three stages of thunderstorm development? (FAA-H-8083-28)

During its lifecycle, a thunderstorm cell progresses through three stages:

a. *Towering cumulus*—Characterized by a strong convective updraft.

b. *Mature*—Precipitation beginning to fall from the cloud base signals that a downdraft has developed and a cell has entered the mature stage.

c. *Dissipating*—Downdrafts characterize the dissipating stage and the storm dies rapidly.

3. What are the three principal types of thunderstorms? (FAA-H-8083-28)

Single cell—Consists of only one cell and is easily circumnavigated by pilots, except at night or when embedded in other clouds. Single cell thunderstorms are rare; almost all thunderstorms are multicell.

Multicell (cluster and line)—Consists of a cluster of cells at various stages of their life cycle. With an organized multicell cluster, as the first cell matures, it is carried downwind and a new cell forms upwind to take its place. A multicell cluster may have a lifetime of several hours (or more).

Supercell—A dangerous convective storm that consists primarily of a single, quasi-steady rotating updraft that persists for an extended period of time. It has a very organized internal structure that enables it to produce especially dangerous weather for pilots who encounter them. Updraft speeds may reach 9,000 feet per minute (100 knots). Nearly all supercells produce severe weather (e.g., large hail or damaging wind), and about 25 percent produce a tornado.

4. **Describe the factors that affect a thunderstorm's motion.** (FAA-H-8083-28)

Storm motion equals the combined effects of both advection and propagation. Advection is the component of storm motion due to individual cells moving with the average wind throughout the vertical depth of the cumulonimbus cloud. The wind at FL180 (500 mb) usually provides a good approximation. Propagation is the component of storm motion due to old cell dissipation and the new cell development. Storm motion may deviate substantially from the motion of the individual cells which comprise the storm.

5. **What are squall line thunderstorms?** (FAA-H-8083-28)

A squall line is a nonfrontal, narrow band of active multicell thunderstorms. Often it develops ahead of a cold front in moist, unstable air, but it may also develop in unstable air far removed from any front. The line may be too long to easily detour and too wide and severe to penetrate. It often contains severe steadystate thunderstorms and presents the single most intense weather hazard to aircraft. It usually forms rapidly, reaching a maximum intensity during the late afternoon and the first few hours of darkness.

6. **What are microbursts?** (AIM 7-1-24)

Microbursts are small-scale intense downdrafts that, upon reaching the surface, spread outward in all directions from the downdraft center. This causes both vertical and horizontal wind shears that can be extremely hazardous to all types and categories of aircraft, especially at low altitudes. Due to their small size, short life span, and the fact that they can occur over areas without surface precipitation, microbursts are not easily detectable using conventional weather radar or wind shear alert systems.

7. **Where are microbursts most likely to occur?** (AIM 7-1-24)

Microbursts can be found almost anywhere convective activity is present. They may be embedded in heavy rain associated with a thunderstorm, or in light rain in benign-appearing virga. When there is little or no precipitation at the surface accompanying the microburst, a ring of blowing dust may be the only visual clue of its existence.

8. What are some basic characteristics of a microburst? (AIM 7-1-24)

Size—Less than 1 mile in diameter as it descends from the cloud base; can extend 2.5 miles in diameter near ground level.

Intensity—Downdrafts as strong as 6,000 feet per minute; horizontal winds near the surface can be as strong as 45 knots resulting in a 90-knot wind shear (headwind to tailwind change for traversing aircraft).

Duration—An individual microburst will seldom last longer than 15 minutes from the time it strikes the ground until dissipation. Sometimes microbursts are concentrated into a line structure, and under these conditions activity may continue for as long as an hour.

9. After a reported microburst has occurred and passed over an airport, should a pilot consider it safe to take off or land? (FAA-H-8083-28)

More than one microburst can occur in the same weather system. Pilots are therefore cautioned to be alert for additional microbursts if one has already been encountered or observed. If several microbursts are present, a series of horizontal vortices can form near the ground due to several microbursts being embedded in one another. Conditions associated with these vortices may produce very powerful updrafts and roll forces in addition to downdrafts.

Icing and Freezing Level Information

1. Name the three types of structural ice that may occur in flight. (FAA-H-8083-28)

Rime—A rough, milky, and opaque ice formed by the instantaneous freezing of small, supercooled water droplets after they strike the aircraft. Rime icing formation favors colder temperatures, lower liquid water content, and small droplets. It grows when droplets rapidly freeze upon striking an aircraft. The rapid freezing traps air and forms a porous, brittle, opaque, and milky-colored ice.

Clear—or glaze ice, is a glossy, clear, or translucent ice formed by the relatively slow freezing of large, supercooled water droplets. Clear icing conditions exist more often in an environment with

(continued)

warmer temperatures, higher liquid water contents, and larger droplets. It forms when only a small portion of the drop freezes immediately while the remaining unfrozen portion flows or smears over the aircraft surface and gradually freezes.

Mixed—A mixture of clear ice and rime ice and forms as an airplane collects both rime and clear ice due to small-scale variations in liquid water content, temperature, and droplet sizes. Mixed ice appears as layers of relatively clear and opaque ice when examined from the side. Mixed icing poses a similar hazard to an aircraft as clear ice. It may form horns or other shapes that disrupt airflow and cause handling and performance problems.

Note: In general, rime icing tends to occur at temperatures colder than −15°C, clear when the temperature is warmer than −10°C, and mixed ice at temperatures in between. This is only general guidance. The type of icing will vary depending on the liquid water content, droplet size, and aircraft-specific variables.

2. Why is clear icing more hazardous than other forms of icing? (FAA-H-8083-28)

It tends to form horns near the top and bottom of the airfoils leading edge, which greatly affects airflow. This results in an area of disrupted and turbulent airflow that is considerably larger than that caused by rime ice. Since it is clear and difficult to see, the pilot may not be able to quickly recognize that it is occurring. It can be difficult to remove since it can spread beyond the deicing or anti-icing equipment, although in most cases it is removed nearly completely by deicing devices.

3. Explain the factors that affect the formation of structural ice. (FAA-H-8083-28)

The meteorological quantities most closely related to icing type and severity are:

a. *Supercooled liquid water content (SLWC)*—Important in determining how much water is available for icing. The highest quantities can be found in cumuliform clouds with the lowest quantities in stratiform clouds.

b. *Temperature*—For icing to occur, the outside air temperature must be below 0°C. As clouds get colder, SLWC decreases until only ice crystals remain. Almost all icing occurs in temperatures between 0°C and −20°C, with about half of all reports occurring between −8°C and −12°C.

c. *Altitude*—The peak of occurrence is near 10,000 feet, with approximately half of incidents occurring between 5,000 feet and 13,000 feet.

d. *Droplet size*—Small droplets tend to impact the airfoil near the plane's leading edge. Larger drops, including freezing rain and freezing drizzle, can cross the streamlines and impact farther back.

d. *Aircraft type/design*—Commercial jet aircraft are generally less vulnerable to structural icing than light turboprop aircraft due to their rapid airspeed, powerful deicing equipment, and tendency to cruise at higher altitudes where temperatures are typically too cold for icing. Conversely, light turboprop aircraft are more susceptible to icing because they typically fly at lower altitudes where icing is more common and at slower speeds.

e. *Airspeed*—The rate of supercooled water droplet impact increases with airspeed, which acts to increase ice accumulation, but this is counteracted by the increase of airframe skin surface heating due to friction. Typically, airframe icing is negligible at speeds above 575 knots.

4. Describe the types of icing found in stratiform and cumuliform clouds. (FAA-H-8083-28)

Stratified clouds—Both rime and mixed are found in stratiform clouds. Icing in middle and low-level stratiform clouds is confined, on the average, to a layer between 3,000 and 4,000 feet thick. A change in altitude of only a few thousand feet may take the aircraft out of icing conditions, even if it remains in clouds. The main hazard lies in the great horizontal extent of stratiform clouds layers. High-level stratiform clouds (i.e., at temperatures colder than −20°C) are composed mostly of ice crystals and produce little icing.

Cumuliform clouds—Icing is usually clear or mixed with rime in the upper levels. The icing layer is smaller horizontally, but greater vertically than in stratiform clouds. Icing is more variable in cumuliform clouds because the factors conducive to icing depend on the particular cloud's stage of development. Icing

(continued)

intensities may range from a trace in small cumulus to severe in a large towering cumulus or cumulonimbus, especially in the upper portion of the cloud where the updraft is concentrated and supercooled large drops (SLDs) are plentiful.

5. Why do most icing reports occur in the vicinity of fronts? (FAA-H-8083-28)

For significant icing to occur above the front, the warm air must be lifted and cooled to saturation at temperatures below zero, making it contain supercooled water droplets. The supercooled water droplets freeze on impact with an aircraft. If the warm air is unstable, icing may be sporadic; if it is stable, icing may be continuous over an extended area. A line of showers or thunderstorms along a cold front may produce icing, but only in a comparatively narrow band along the front.

6. Where is severe clear icing most likely to occur along a front? (FAA-H-8083-28)

Severe clear icing occurs in freezing rain and/or freezing drizzle below a front. Rain forms above the frontal surface at temperatures warmer than freezing. Subsequently, it falls through air at temperatures below freezing and becomes supercooled. The SLDs freeze on impact with an aircraft. If the below freezing layer is shallow, freezing rain will occur at the surface. If the below freezing layer is deep, the supercooled droplets may freeze into ice pellets. Ice pellets indicate icing above. The icing can be severe because of the large amount of supercooled water. Icing in freezing precipitation is especially dangerous because it often extends horizontally over a broad area and a pilot may be unable to escape it by descending to a lower altitude.

7. Why is icing more likely and more severe in mountainous regions? (FAA-H-8083-28)

Mountain ranges cause upward air motions on their windward side. These vertical currents support large supercooled water droplets above the freezing level. The movement of a front across a mountain range combines frontal lift with the mountain's upslope flow effect to create extremely hazardous icing zones. The most severe icing occurs above the crests and on the ridges' windward side. This zone usually extends to about 5,000 feet above the mountaintops, but can extend much higher if cumuliform clouds develop.

8. Is icing at high altitudes a concern for flight crews? (AC 61-107)

Icing at high altitudes is not as common or extreme as it can be at low altitudes. When it does occur, the rate of accumulation at high altitudes is generally slower than at low altitudes. Rime ice is generally more common at high altitudes than clear ice, although clear ice is possible. Despite the composition of cirrus clouds, severe icing is generally not a problem although it can occur in some detached cirrus. It is more common in tops of tall cumulus buildups, anvils, and over mountainous regions.

9. Explain why a flight conducted in an area of high ice water conditions (HIWC) can be a hazardous to safety of the flight. (FAA-H-8083-28)

HIWC is a relatively new icing hazard, at least from the standpoint of research and understanding. HIWC refers to high-altitude ice crystals, which may exist in the tops and anvils of cumulonimbus clouds and thunderstorms. Under certain HIWC, turbine engine performance can be affected, including flameouts.

10. What is freezing level and where can you find information on its location? (FAA-H-8083-28)

The freezing level is the lowest altitude in the atmosphere over a given location at which the air temperature reaches 0°C. It is possible to have multiple freezing layers when a temperature inversion occurs above the defined freezing level. Potential sources of icing information for determining its location are: GFAs, PIREPS, AIRMETs, SIGMETs, convective SIGMETs, CWAs, low-level significant weather charts, surface analysis (for frontal location and freezing precipitation), and winds and temperatures aloft (for air temperature at altitude). Pilots can use graphical data including freezing level graphics, the current icing product (CIP), and forecast icing product (FIP).

Fog and Mist

1. How does fog form? (FAA-H-8083-28)

Fog forms when the temperature and dewpoint of the air become identical (or nearly so). This may occur through cooling of the air to a little beyond its dewpoint (producing radiation fog, advection fog, or upslope fog), or by adding moisture and thereby elevating the dewpoint (producing frontal fog or steam fog).

2. Name several types of fog. (FAA-H-8083-28)

a. Radiation fog
b. Mountain/valley fog
c. Advection fog
d. Upslope fog
e. Frontal fog or precipitation-induced fog
f. Steam fog
g. Freezing fog

3. What causes radiation fog to form? (FAA-H-8083-28)

Conditions favorable for radiation fog are a clear sky, little or no wind, and small temperature-dewpoint spread (high relative humidity). The fog forms almost exclusively at night or near daybreak.

4. How does mountain/valley fog form? (FAA-H-8083-28)

During overnight hours, two factors contribute to the formation of mountain/valley fog:

a. During the day, the ground absorbs heat, which is then released at night, causing the air near the ground to cool. Cooler, denser air from mountain tops sinks into valleys and accumulates there.

b. The valley gradually fills with cold air from the bottom, a process known as cold air drainage. This colder air reduces the surrounding air temperature, bringing it closer to the dewpoint and saturation. If there is enough moisture in the air, fog develops in these valleys during the night. This fog is most commonly seen in autumn and spring, and it is thickest around sunrise when surface temperatures are typically lowest.

5. What is advection fog and where is it most likely to form? (FAA-H-8083-28)

Advection fog forms when moist air moves over colder ground or water. It is most common along coastal areas but often develops deep in continental areas. Unlike radiation fog, it may occur with winds, cloudy skies, over a wide geographic area, and at any time of the day or night. It deepens as wind speed increases up to about 15 knots; wind greater than 15 knots lifts the fog into a layer of low stratus or stratocumulus.

6. Define *upslope fog.* (FAA-H-8083-28)

Upslope fog forms as a result of moist, stable air being cooled adiabatically as it moves up sloping terrain. Once the upslope wind ceases, the fog dissipates. Unlike radiation fog, it can form under cloudy skies. It is common along the eastern slopes of the Rockies and somewhat less frequent east of the Appalachians. It can often be quite dense and extend to high altitudes.

7. Explain the process that causes steam fog to form. (FAA-H-8083-28)

When very cold air moves across relatively warm water, enough moisture may evaporate from the water surface to produce saturation. As the rising water vapor meets the cold air, it immediately re-condenses and rises with the air that is being warmed from below. Because the air is destabilized, fog appears as rising filaments or streamers that resemble steam.

8. How does freezing fog form? (FAA-H-8083-28)

Freezing fog occurs when the temperature falls to 32°F (0°C) or below. The tiny, super-cooled liquid water droplets in fog can freeze instantly on exposed surfaces when surface temperatures are at or below freezing. Some surfaces that these droplets may freeze on include tree branches, stairs and rails, sidewalks, roads, and vehicles. For those flying, or even taxiing, a layer of ice can form on the aircraft, making flight very dangerous unless the aircraft is treated or has effective deicing equipment.

9. **Explain how frontal (or precipitation-induced) fog forms.**
   (FAA-H-8083-28)

   When warm, moist air is lifted over a front, clouds and
   precipitation may form. If the cold air below is near its dewpoint,
   evaporation (or sublimation) from the precipitation may saturate
   the cold air and form fog. Frontal fog can become quite dense and
   continue for an extended period of time and may extend over large
   areas, completely suspending air operations. It is most commonly
   associated with warm fronts, but can occur with other fronts
   as well.

10. **Other than fog, what are several other examples of IFR**
    weather producers? (FAA-H-8083-28)

    Other examples of common IFR producers are low clouds (stratus),
    haze, smoke, blowing obstructions to vision, and precipitation. Fog
    and low stratus restrict navigation by visual reference more often
    than all other weather phenomena.

Frost

1. **What is frost?** (FAA-H-8083-25)

   Frost is ice crystal deposits formed by sublimation when the
   temperature and dewpoint are below freezing.

2. **Describe the conditions that would be conducive to the**
   formation of frost on a parked aircraft. (AC 91-74)

   Frost can form on an airplane sitting outside on a clear night
   when there is moisture present in the air as the airplane's skin
   temperature falls below freezing due to radiation cooling. Certain
   airplanes may be more vulnerable to ice formation from cold-
   soaked fuel than others depending on how the fuel tanks are
   arranged and how much fuel they contain. On the ground, clear ice
   can form on the upper surfaces of the wing when cold-soaked fuel
   (due to aircraft prolonged operation at high altitude) remains in
   contact with the fuel tanks' upper surfaces after landing, and during
   time on the ground when the airplane is exposed to conditions
   of atmospheric moisture (for example, fog, precipitation, and
   condensation of humid air) at ambient temperatures above
   freezing. Atmospheric moisture, when in contact with cold wing

surfaces, may freeze. This can even occur if conditions remain above freezing and are not expected to be, or recognized as, icing conditions.

3. **During the preflight walk around, a pilot notices thin deposits of frost on the upper and lower surfaces of each wing. Should the pilot be concerned about these small amounts of frost?** (drs.faa.gov)

Frost has the appearance of being a minor contaminant and does not offer the same obvious signal of danger as do other types of contamination such as snow or ice. However, frost is a serious threat to the safety of aircraft operations because it always adheres to the aircraft surface, is rough, and causes significant lift degradation and increased drag. An aircraft should be thoroughly cleaned and free of frost prior to beginning a flight.

It is imperative that takeoff not be attempted unless the PIC has ascertained, as required by regulation, that all critical surfaces of the aircraft are free of adhering ice, snow, or frost formations.

4. **Explain how frost adhering to an aircraft's wings can affect an aircraft's performance and flight characteristics.** (AC 120-58)

The reduction of lift and increase in drag significantly increase stall speed, reduce controllability, and alter aircraft flight characteristics. Thicker or rougher frozen contaminants can have increasing effects on lift, drag, stall speed, stability and control, with the primary influence being surface roughness located on critical portions of an aerodynamic surface. These adverse effects on the aerodynamic properties of the airfoil may result in sudden departure from the commanded flight path and may not be preceded by any indications or aerodynamic warning to the pilot. Test data indicates that ice, snow, or frost formations having a thickness and surface roughness similar to medium or coarse sandpaper on the leading edge and upper surface of a wing can reduce wing lift by as much as 30 percent and increase drag by 40 percent.

Note: It is imperative that takeoff not be attempted unless the PIC has ascertained, as required by regulation (14 CFR §121.629, §135.227), that all critical surfaces of the aircraft are free of adhering frost, ice, or snow formations.

Obstructions to Visibility

1. Describe several types of obstructions to visibility that may occur in the atmosphere. (AIM 7-1-29)

There are eight types of obscuration phenomena in the METAR code (obscurations are any phenomena in the atmosphere, other than precipitation, that reduce horizontal visibility):

FG	fog (visibility less than 5/8 mile)
HZ	haze
FU	smoke
PY	spray
BR	mist (visibility 5/8 – 6 miles)
SA	sand
DU	dust
VA	volcanic ash

2. When will obstructions to vision be omitted from forecasts and an ATIS broadcast? (FAA-H-8083-28, AIM 4-1-13)

Obstructions to vision are only forecast when the prevailing visibility is less than 7 SM or, in the opinion of the forecaster, is considered operationally significant. The ceiling/sky condition, visibility, and obstructions to vision may be omitted from the ATIS broadcast if the ceiling is above 5,000 feet and the visibility is more than 5 miles.

3. Why is flight through volcanic ash so dangerous? (FAA-H-8083-28)

Flying into a volcanic ash cloud can be exceedingly dangerous. Volcanic ash is composed of silica (glass). When ash is ingested into a jet engine, it melts to produce a soft sticky molten product that adheres to the compressor turbine blades and fuel injectors/igniters. With no air going into the engine, the fuel cannot ignite, the engine comes to a slow spinning stop by spooling down, and a flameout occurs. As the aircraft exits the ash cloud and into colder temperatures, the cooled, hardened silicas on the turbine blades become dislodged, allowing the fan blades to start rotating, and allow for an engine relight as the air starts moving through the engine again.

4. **What are actions pilots and dispatchers can take to mitigate the risk of an encounter with volcanic ash?** (drs.faa.gov)

   When conducting preflight planning, volcanic ash advisories (VAA) should be consulted to ensure the route is clear of any VA contaminant. Volcanic ash forecast transport and dispersion (VAFTAD) charts are also available. These charts depict volcanic ash cloud locations in the atmosphere following an eruption and also forecast dispersion of the ash concentrations over 6- and 12-hour time intervals. For operations conducted under Part 121, the route, planned cruise altitudes, and driftdown altitudes for engine failure or decompression should remain clear of VA. Operations conducted under Parts 91, 91 subpart K, 125, or 135 should consider the same route restrictions.

5. **Explain how smoke can be hazardous to aviation.** (FAA-H-8083-28)

   Smoke is a suspension in the air of small particles produced by combustion due to fires, industrial burning, or other sources. It may transition to haze when the particles travel 25–100 miles (40–160 kilometers) and become more widely scattered throughout the atmosphere after larger particles have settled. Not only can smoke reduce visibility to zero, many of its compounds are highly toxic and/or irritating. The most dangerous is carbon monoxide, which can lead to carbon monoxide poisoning, sometimes with supporting effects of hydrogen cyanide and phosgene.

6. **Define the term *haze*.** (FAA-H-8083-28)

   Haze is a suspension in the air of extremely small particles invisible to the naked eye and sufficiently numerous to give the air an opalescent appearance. It occurs in stable air and is usually only a few thousand feet thick, but may extend upwards to 15,000 feet.

7. **How does haze affect visibility?** (FAA-H-8083-28)

   A haze layer has a definite ceiling above which in-flight (air-to-air) visibility is unrestricted. At or below this level, the slant range (air-to-ground) visibility is poor. Visibility in haze varies greatly, depending on whether the pilot is facing into or away from the sun. Hazards associated with haze are obscuration of rising terrain, mountain ridges, man-made obstacles; it impairs a pilot's ability to see and avoid other air traffic;

D. Flight Deck Weather and Aeronautical Information

1. What information is provided by a Flight Information Service–Broadcast (FIS-B)? (AC 00-63)

Flight Information Service–Broadcast (FIS-B) over Universal Access Transceiver (UAT) data link service provides meteorological and aeronautical information to the flight deck for aircraft operating in the U.S. National Airspace System (NAS). These products are broadcast over the Automatic Dependent Surveillance–Broadcast (ADS-B) UAT link so pilots have timely information of regional weather and NAS status/changes that might affect flight.

FIS-B meteorological information (METI) and Aeronautical Information (AI) products provide strategic in-flight-deck information that enhances a preflight briefing; however, they may not include all the weather products or NOTAMs that a preflight briefing includes, and NOTAM information is limited to the past 30 days. Therefore, AI information obtained via FIS-B may not be relied on for a thorough preflight briefing.

2. Provide several examples of current FIS-B weather products available to pilots. (AC 00-63)

AIRMET (text/graphic), SIGMET (text/graphic), Convective SIGMET (text/graphic), METAR (text), CONUS NEXRAD (graphic), Regional NEXRAD (graphic), NOTAM (text/graphic), PIREP (text), SUA Status (text), TAF (text), Winds and Temperatures Aloft (text), and FIS-B Outage Notification (text).

3. What limitations should pilots consider when using data link products such as digital weather and aeronautical information for display in the cockpit? (AC 00-63)

a. *Product latency*—Be aware of the product time or "valid until" time on the particular data link information displayed in the flight deck. Since initial processing and transmission of NEXRAD data can take several minutes, pilots must assume that data link weather information will always be a minimum of 7 to 8 minutes older than shown on the time stamp. Pilots must only use data link weather radar images for broad strategic avoidance of adverse weather. Pilots operating Part 121 domestic or flag flights should contact their dispatcher for verification of adverse non-forecast weather information. This is particularly important when adverse weather phenomena are encountered and a change to the route or alternate may be required.

b. *Coverage areas/service volume*—Coverage limitations are associated with the type of data link network in use. For example, ground-based systems that require a line-of-sight may have relatively limited coverage below 5,000 feet AGL. Satellite-based data link weather systems can have limitations stemming from whether the network is in geosynchronous orbit or low earth orbit (LEO). Also, NWS NEXRAD coverage has gaps, especially in the western states.

c. *Content/format*—Since service providers often refine or enhance data link products for flight deck display, pilots must be familiar with the content, format, and meaning of symbols and displays (e.g., the legend) in the specific system.

4. How is airborne weather radar used by pilots when operating in the vicinity of thunderstorms? (FAA-H-8083-28)

Airborne weather radar is used for detecting and avoiding severe weather—not for penetrating it. Whether to fly into an area of radar echoes depends on echo intensity, spacing between the echoes, and the capabilities of the pilot and the aircraft.

5. Explain the limitations of airborne weather radar. (FAA-H-8083-28)

The ability of airborne weather radar to detect weather phenomena is limited in both direction and range. Weather radar detects only precipitation drops; it does not detect turbulence. Therefore, the radar display provides no assurance of avoiding turbulence. The radar display also does not provide assurance of avoiding instrument weather conditions from clouds and fog.

A phenomenon called attenuation may exist when a cell absorbs or reflects all of the radio signals sent by the radar system. Attenuation may prevent the radar from detecting additional cells that might lie behind the first cell. This is often referred to as a radar "shadow."

(continued)

Note: Recently manufactured transport category aircraft are now being equipped with forward looking wind shear detection equipment incorporating airborne doppler weather radar systems that can detect turbulence and wind shear.

6. If it becomes necessary to avoid an area of moderate radar echoes, what hazard should all pilots be aware of? (FAA-H-8083-28)

It is important to remember that while hail always gives a radar echo, it may fall several miles from the nearest visible cloud, and hazardous turbulence may extend to as much as 20 miles from the echo edge.

7. What minimum distances should be maintained from intense or extreme radar echoes? (FAA-H-8083-28)

Avoid heavy or extreme level echoes by at least 20 miles (i.e., such echoes should be separated by at least 40 miles before flying between them). Pilots may reduce the distance for avoiding weaker echoes.

8. If a pilot is unable to avoid penetrating a thunderstorm, what procedures are recommended before entering the storm? (FAA-H-8083-28)

a. If using automatic pilot, disengage altitude hold mode and speed hold mode. The automatic altitude and speed controls will increase maneuvers of the aircraft thus increasing structural stress.

b. Verify that jet engine anti-ice is on. Icing can be rapid at any altitude and cause almost instantaneous power failure and/or loss of airspeed indication.

c. To avoid the most critical icing, establish a penetration altitude below the freezing level or above the level of $-15°C$.

d. If using airborne radar, tilt the antenna up and down occasionally. This will permit the detection of other thunderstorm activity at altitudes other than the one being flown.

e. Ensure flight crew and passengers are seated and seatbelts fastened. Secure all loose objects.

E. Low-Visibility Operations

1. When are low-visibility operations in effect at an airport? (AC 120-57)

The movement of aircraft or vehicles on the airport paved surfaces when visibility conditions are reported to be less than 1,200 feet RVR.

2. What is the significance of LVO/SMGCS to a pilot? (AIM 4-3-19, AC 120-57)

A "low visibility operations surface movement guidance and control system," commonly known as LVO/SMGCS (pronounced "LVO SMIGS") describes a plan at U.S. airports where scheduled air carriers are authorized to conduct taxi operations when the visibility is less than 1,200 feet RVR. A LVO/SMGCS plan facilitates the safe movement of aircraft and vehicles on the airport by establishing more rigorous control procedures and requiring enhanced visual aids. There are currently two levels of SMGCS—operations less than 1,200 feet RVR to 500 feet RVR and operations less than 500 feet RVR.

3. Are flight crews required to comply with LVO/SMGS plans? (FAA-H-8083-16)

Both flight and ground crews, Part 121 and 135 operators, are required to comply with SMGCS plans when implemented at their specific airport. All airport tenants are responsible for disseminating information to their employees and conducting training in low visibility operating procedures. Anyone operating in conjunction with the SMGCS plan must have a copy of the low visibility taxi route chart for their given airport as these charts outline the taxi routes and other detailed information concerning low visibility operations.

4. What is Airport Surface Detection Equipment–Model X surveillance (ASDE-X)? (PC/G)

ASDE-X is equipment that enables ATC to detect aircraft, vehicular traffic, and other objects, on the surface of an airport, and present the image on a tower display. The ASDE-X system utilizes X-band surface movement radar, multilateration, and ADS-B to track movement.

5. Define the term *runway visual range* (RVR). (AC 120-129)

RVR is an instrumentally derived value measured by transmissometers or forward-scatter meters. RVR is calibrated by reference to runway lights and/or the contrast of objects.

6. What is controlling RVR? (AC 120-129)

The controlling RVR(s) are those reported values of one or more RVR reporting locations (TDZ, mid, rollout) used to determine if operating minima are met for the purpose of takeoff initiation, approach initiation, or in some cases, approach continuation. For instrument approaches, the controlling RVR(s) are as specified by the operator's authorization.

7. When is RVR controlling? (AC 120-29)

All U.S. Category I operating minimums below 1/2 SM (RVR2400) and all Category II and III operating minimums are based on RVR. Where RVR is used, the controlling RVR for Category I minima is touchdown RVR. All other readings are advisory. For Category II minima, controlling RVR is as specified by the operations specifications (ops specs).

8. How can a flight crew determine if they may conduct a particular low-visibility operation? (drs.faa.gov)

They should refer to the certificate holder's ops specs.

9. What are the lowest authorized ILS Category I, II, and III minimums with all required ground and airborne systems components operative? (AIM 1-1-9)

a. Category I: DH 200 feet and RVR 2,400 feet (with TDZ and centerline lighting, RVR 1,800 feet).

b. Category II: DH 100 feet and RVR 1,200 feet.

c. Category IIIa: No DH or DH below 100 feet and RVR not less than 700 feet.

d. Category IIIb: No DH or with a DH below 50 feet and RVR less than 700 feet, but not less than 150 feet.

e. Category IIIc: No DH and no RVR limitation.

Note: Special authorization and equipment required for Categories II and III.

F. Flight Risk Assessment Tools

1. What is a Flight Risk Assessment Tool (FRAT)? (FAA InFO 07015)

A FRAT is a preflight planning tool that uses a series of questions in each of the major risk categories (PAVE) to help a pilot identify and quantify risk for a flight. The tool enables proactive hazard identification, is easy to use, and can visually depict risk. It is an invaluable tool in helping pilots make better go/no-go decisions and should be a part of every flight.

2. Describe three established risk assessment tools that require assessment of the pilot, the aircraft, and the environment for the mission. (FAA FITS)

a. *Pilot-Aircraft-Environment-Duration-Urgency (PAEDU)* is the quickest to apply and results in a numeric result. It is the risk assessment methodology of the FAA's ADM program and enables the pilot to assess the risk of a flight by evaluating the presence of risk factors in each of these five areas and then assessing the risk for the area on a scale of 1 to 4.

b. *Pilot-Aircraft-enVironment-External (PAVE)* is more detailed (and these details also apply to the PAEDU method) and results in a more detailed but qualitative analysis. The PAVE Checklist works like any checklist that you would use in your aircraft. However, you should expand the use of the PAVE to your flight planning as well, and take special consideration to each line item before your final decision to fly. The PAVE checklist will give you a step-by-step approach to assessing your knowledge, but leaves the final go-no-go decision to the PIC.

c. *Flight Risk Assessment Tool (FRAT)* assigns a number to various risk factors regarding the pilot, aircraft, and environment. Each element is scored for the flight, and the totals and grand total determined. Then, the pilot is advised on the appropriate course of action depending on the grand total and whether the flight is VFR or IFR. These actions are: Go, for lowest grand total; Consider Alternate Actions; Consult Experienced CFI or Mentor; and Don't Go, for the highest grand total. *See* FAA InFO 07015.

High Altitude
Aerodynamics

4

A. High Altitude Operations

1. High altitude flight operations are those operations conducted above what altitude? (AC 61-107)

14 CFR §61.31(g) considers all flight operations conducted above 25,000 feet MSL to be high altitude.

2. Certain airspace and FAA regulatory requirements for the high altitude environment become effective at different altitudes below 25,000 feet MSL. What are several examples? (AC 61-107)

Pilots of high-altitude aircraft are subject to two principal types of airspace at altitudes above 10,000 feet MSL:

a. Class E airspace which extends from the surface up to FL180.

b. Class A airspace which extends from FL180 to FL600.

Pilots should be familiar with all regulatory requirements prior to operating in each of these types of airspace.

3. Define the term *energy*. (FAA-H-8083-30)

Energy is the capacity of a physical system to perform work. There are three types of energy: kinetic, potential, and chemical.

4. Define the three types of energy: *kinetic, potential*, and *chemical*. (FAA-H-8083-30, AURTA)

Kinetic energy—The energy of motion, sometimes thought of as the energy of speed; it increases with increasing airspeed.

Potential energy—The energy that is stored in an object, sometimes thought of as energy at rest; it is proportional to altitude.

Chemical energy—The energy that is released from a chemical reaction; the fuel in the aircraft fuel tanks is chemically converted to energy (thrust).

5. What does the term *energy state* refer to? (AURTA)

It describes how much of each kind of energy the airplane has available at any given time. Pilots who understand the airplane energy state will be in a position to know instantly what options they may have to maneuver their airplane.

6. The term *energy management* refers to what process? (AURTA)

Energy management is the process of consciously manipulating the energy state of the airplane.

7. What are the three main energy management objectives when maneuvering an airplane? (AURTA)

a. Kinetic energy stays between limits (stall and placards).

b. Potential energy stays within limits (terrain to buffet altitude).

c. Chemical energy stays above certain thresholds (not running out of fuel).

8. During maneuvering, how can the three types of energy be traded or exchanged? (AURTA)

Kinetic to potential energy—Airspeed (kinetic) can be traded for altitude (potential), as in a zoom-climb.

Potential to kinetic energy—Altitude (potential) can be traded for airspeed (kinetic), as in a dive.

Chemical energy to potential or kinetic—Can be traded for either altitude or airspeed by advancing the throttles to command more thrust than required for level flight.

9. Explain how external factors can change the aircraft's energy state and how a pilot can correct for them. (AURTA)

External factors, such as changing winds, increased drag in turns, turbulence, icing or internal factors, such as anti-ice use, autothrottle rollback, or engine malfunction or failure can cause airspeed decay. Heavily damped autothrottles, designed for passenger comfort, may not apply thrust aggressively enough to prevent a slowdown below L/D_{MAX}. At all times, pilots must ensure that flight slower than L/D_{MAX} is avoided in the high altitude environment. Proper flight planning and adherence to published climb profiles and cruise speeds will ensure that speeds slower than L/D_{MAX} are avoided.

10. **Explain the relationship between Mach number, indicated airspeed, true airspeed, and altitude for an aircraft in a climb.** (FAA-H-8083-25)

    Indicated airspeed—will decrease in relation to true airspeed as altitude increases. This is due to lower air density and less impact pressure sensed by the pitot tube(s) at higher altitudes.

    True airspeed—will increase with an increase in altitude; air density is decreased with altitude requiring a faster true airspeed in order to have the same pressure sensed by the pitot tube for the same KCAS/KIAS.

    Mach number—will increase with an increase in altitude. An increase in altitude results in a corresponding decrease in air temperature and a decrease in the speed of sound.

11. **Why is compressibility effect a significant factor in high altitude flight?** (FAA-H-8083-25)

    Compressibility and to a lesser extent, viscosity, is of paramount importance at speeds approaching the speed of sound. In these speed ranges, compressibility causes a change in the density of the air around an aircraft. During flight, a wing produces lift by accelerating the airflow over the upper surface. This accelerated air can, and does, reach sonic speeds even though the aircraft itself may be flying subsonic. When flow velocities reach sonic speeds at some location on an aircraft (such as the area of maximum camber on the wing), further acceleration results in the onset of compressibility effects such as shock wave formation, drag increase, buffeting, stability, and control difficulties. Subsonic flow principles are invalid at all speeds above this point.

12. **Define the term *Mach number* (M).** (AC 61-107)

    Mach number is a decimal number representing the true airspeed (TAS) relationship to the local speed of sound. A TAS of 75 percent of the speed of sound is given as 0.75 M, whereas 100 percent of the speed of sound is represented as Mach 1 (1.0 M). The local speed of sound varies with changes in temperature.

13. Define the term *critical Mach number* (M_cr). (AC 61-107)

Critical Mach number (M_{cr}) is the speed at which the flow of air over a portion of a specific airfoil design reaches Mach 1. This results in the formation of a shock wave and drag divergence. M_{cr} is the free stream Mach number (M) at which local sonic flow such as buffet, airflow separation, and shock waves become evident. These phenomena occur above M_{cr} and are as follows:

Subsonic—M below 0.75
Transonic—M from 0.75 to 1.20
Supersonic—M from 1.20 to 5.0
Hypersonic—M above 5.0

14. Define the term *drag divergence*. (AC 61-107)

A phenomenon that occurs when an airfoil's drag increases sharply and requires substantial increases in thrust to produce further increases in speed. Do not confuse drag divergence with M_{cr}. The drag increase is due to the unstable formation of shock waves that transform energy into heat and into pressure pulses that act to consume a major portion of the available propulsive energy. Turbulent air may produce an increase in the coefficient of drag.

15. Define the term *Mach speed*. (AC 61-107)

Mach speed is the ratio or percentage of the TAS to the speed of sound, represented by a Mach number. At sea level on a standard day (59°F/15°C), the speed of sound equals approximately 660 knots (kts) or 1,120 feet per second (ft/s). Mach 0.75 at sea level is equivalent to a TAS of approximately 498 knots (0.75 × 660 knots) or 840 feet per second. The temperature of the atmosphere normally decreases with an increase in altitude. The speed of sound is directly related only to temperature. The result is a decrease in the speed of sound up to about 36,000 feet MSL.

16. Define the term *maximum operating limit speed* (V_MO). (AC 61-107)

Expressed in knots calibrated airspeed (KCAS), V_{MO} is an airplane's maximum operating limit speed. Exceeding V_{MO} may cause aerodynamic flutter and G-load limitations to become critical during dive recovery. Structural design integrity is not predictable at velocities greater than V_{MO}.

17. **Define the term** *maximum operating speed limit* **(M$_{MO}$).**
    (AC 61-107)

    M$_{MO}$ is an airplane's maximum certificated Mach number. Any excursion past M$_{MO}$, whether intentional or accidental, may cause induced flow separation of boundary layer air over the ailerons and elevators of an airplane and result in a loss of control surface authority and/or control surface buzz or snatch.

18. **Define the terms** *aileron buzz* **and** *aileron snatch*.
    (AC 61-107)

    Aileron buzz is a very rapid oscillation of an aileron at high airspeeds on some aircraft that does not usually reach large magnitudes or become dangerous. It is often caused by shock-induced separation of the boundary layer. Aileron snatch is a violent back and forth movement of the aileron control as airflow changes over the surface.

19. **What is** *Mach tuck* **and why does it occur?** (AC 61-107, FAA-H-8083-3)

    Mach tuck is the result of an aft shift in the center of pressure, causing a nosedown pitching moment. Mach tuck is caused principally by two basic factors:

    a. *Flow separation*—Shock-wave-induced flow separation, which normally begins near the wing root, causes a decrease in the downwash velocity over the elevator and produces a tendency for the aircraft to nose down.

    b. *Center of pressure movement*—The center of pressure moves aft. This tends to unbalance the equilibrium of the aircraft in relation to its center of gravity (CG) in subsonic flight. The airplane's CG is now farther ahead of the aircraft's aerodynamic center than it was in slower flight. This dramatically increases the tendency of the airplane to pitch more nose-down.

    Note: Mach tuck develops gradually, and the condition should not be allowed to progress to the point where there is no longer enough elevator authority to prevent entry into a steep, sometimes unrecoverable, dive. An alert pilot should respond to excessive airspeed, buffeting, or warning devices before the onset of extreme nose-down forces.

20. Explain the purpose of a Mach compensating device. (AC 61-107)

Most turbojet airplanes capable of operating in the Mach speed ranges are designed with some form of trim and autopilot Mach compensating device (stick puller) to alert the pilot to inadvertent excursions beyond its certificated M_{MO}. If for any reason there is a malfunction that requires disabling the stick puller, the aircraft must be operated at speeds well below M_{MO}, as prescribed in the applicable airplane flight manual (AFM) procedures for the aircraft.

21. What is Mach buffet? (AC 61-107, FAA-H-8083-25)

Mach buffet is the airflow separation behind a shock wave pressure barrier caused by airflow over flight surfaces exceeding the speed of sound. It is important to understand that Mach buffet is a function of the speed of the airflow over the wing—not necessarily the airspeed of the airplane. Anytime that too great a lift demand is made on the wing, whether from too fast an airspeed or from too high an angle of attack (AOA) near the M_{MO}, the high speed buffet will occur.

22. What are the conditions that would increase AOA, the speed of airflow over the wing, and chances of Mach buffet? (FAA-H-8083-25)

a. *High altitudes*—The higher an aircraft flies, the thinner the air and the greater the AOA required to produce the lift needed to maintain level flight.

b. *Heavy weights*—The heavier the aircraft, the greater the lift required of the wing, and all other factors being equal, the greater the AOA.

c. *G-loading*—An increase in the G-loading on the aircraft has the same effect as increasing the weight of the aircraft. Whether the increase in G forces is caused by turns, rough control usage, or turbulence, the effect of increasing the wing's AOA is the same.

23. What is Q-corner or coffin corner? (AC 61-107)

An airplane's indicated airspeed (IAS) decreases in relation to TAS as altitude increases. As the IAS decreases with altitude, it approaches the airspeed for the low-speed buffet boundary where pre-stall buffet occurs for the airplane at a load factor of 1.0 G. The point where high-speed Mach, IAS, and low-speed buffet boundary IAS merge is the airplane's absolute or aerodynamic ceiling. Once an aircraft has reached its aerodynamic ceiling, which is higher than the altitude limit stipulated in the AFM, the aircraft can neither be made to go faster without activating the design stick puller at Mach limit nor can it be made to go slower without activating the stick shaker or pusher. This critical area of the aircraft's flight envelope is known as coffin corner. When this phenomenon is encountered, serious consequences may result, causing loss of control of the aircraft.

24. What are the two types of buffet that may be encountered in flight? (AURTA)

There are two kinds of buffet to consider in flight: low-speed buffet and high-speed buffet. As altitude increases, the indicated airspeed at which low-speed buffet occurs, increases. As altitude increases, high-speed buffet speed decreases. Therefore, at a given weight, as altitude increases, the margin between high speed and low speed buffet decreases. Proper use of buffet boundary charts or maneuver capability charts can allow the crew to determine the maximum altitude that can be flown while still respecting the required buffet margins.

25. What conditions would result in a change to the low-speed buffet and Mach buffet speeds? (AC 61-107)

Increasing either gross weight or load factor will increase the low-speed buffet and decrease Mach buffet speeds. A typical turbojet airplane flying at 51,000 feet MSL altitude at 1.0 G may encounter Mach buffet slightly above the airplane's M_{MO} (0.82 M) and low-speed buffet at 0.60 M. However, only 1.4 G (an increase of only 0.4 G) may bring on buffet at the optimum speed of 0.73 Mach and any change in airspeed, bank angle, or gust loading may reduce this straight and level flight 1.4 G protection to no protection.

26. Describe the flight characteristics that would be experienced in an airplane as the V_{MO} or M_{MO} is being approached. (FAA-H-8083-3)

a. Nose-down tendency and need for back pressure or trim.

b. Mild buffeting as airflow separation begins to occur after critical Mach speed.

c. Activation of an overspeed warning or high speed envelope protection.

27. How can pilots mitigate the risk of exceeding Mach buffet boundaries? (AC 61-107)

a. Pilots should select a maximum cruising flight altitude that will allow sufficient buffet margins for necessary maneuvering and for gust conditions likely to be encountered.

b. Pilots should be thoroughly familiar with the use of charts showing cruise maneuver and buffet limits.

c. Flight crews must be adequately trained and thoroughly educated in the critical aspect of aerodynamic factors pertinent to Mach flight at high altitudes.

28. What is a lift/drag ratio (L/D)? (FAA-H-8083-25)

The lift-to-drag ratio (L/D) is the amount of lift generated by a wing or airfoil compared to its drag. Aircraft with higher L/D ratios are more efficient than those with lower L/D ratios.

29. What is L/D_{MAX}? (AURTA)

The lowest point on the total drag curve is known as L/D_{MAX} (or V_{MD}, minimum drag speed). The speed range slower than L/D_{MAX} is known as slow flight, which is sometimes referred-to as the "back side of the power-drag curve" or the "region of reverse command". Speed faster than L/D_{MAX} is considered normal flight, or the "front side of the power-drag curve".

30. Why is flight slower than L/D_{MAX} to be avoided in the high altitude environment? (AURTA)

Flight slower than L/D_{MAX} is inherently unstable with respect to speed and thrust settings. When operating at a constant airspeed with constant thrust setting, any disturbance causing a decrease in airspeed will result in a further decrease in airspeed unless thrust is increased. Lower speeds will subject the airplane to increased drag. This increase in drag will cause a further decrease in airspeed, which may ultimately result in a stalled flight condition. Proper flight profiles and planning will ensure speeds slower than L/D_{MAX} are avoided.

31. Define the term *crossover altitude*. (AURTA)

Crossover altitude is the altitude at which a specified calibrated airspeed (CAS) and Mach value represent the same TAS value. Above this altitude, the Mach number is used to reference speeds.

32. Define the term *optimum altitude*. (AURTA)

Optimum altitude is the altitude at which the equivalent airspeed for a thrust setting will equal the square root of the coefficient of lift over the coefficient of drag. In less technical terms, it is the best cruise altitude for a given weight and air temperature. A dramatic increase in temperature will lower the optimum altitude. Therefore, when flying at optimum altitude, the flight crew should monitor temperature to ensure performance capability.

33. Explain how operating in the "ECON" or "LRC" modes affects an aircraft's optimum altitude. (AURTA)

Optimum altitude is the cruise altitude for minimum cost when operating in the most economical mode (ECON), and for minimum fuel burn when in the long range cruise (LRC) or pilot-selected speed modes. In ECON mode, optimum altitude increases as either airplane weight or cost index decreases. In LRC or selected speed modes, optimum altitude increases as either airplane weight or speed decreases. Each flight, optimum altitude continues to increase as weight decreases during the flight. For shorter trips, optimum altitude may not be achievable since the top of descent (T/D) point occurs prior to completing the climb to optimum altitude.

34. When ATC requests an increased rate of climb while operating at a high altitude, what hazard should the flight crew be aware of? (AURTA)

Airplane flight manuals and flight management systems produce optimum climb speed charts and speeds. When an increased rate of climb is required by ATC (a deviation from optimum climb speed), ensure that climb speed is not decreased below L/D_{MAX}. Evidence shows that inappropriate use of vertical speed modes is involved in the majority of slow speed events during high altitude climbs.

35. Why is it important that the flight crew be aware of outside air temperatures and thrust available when flying thrust limited jet aircraft? (AURTA)

Most jet transport airplanes are thrust limited, rather than low speed buffet limited at altitude, especially in a turn. It is imperative that crews be aware of outside temperature and thrust available. To avoid losing airspeed due to a thrust limit, use flight management systems/reduced bank angle as a routine for enroute flight if it incorporates real-time bank angle protection, or routinely select a bank angle limit of 10 to 15 degrees for cruise flight.

36. If a condition of airspeed decay occurs at altitude, what actions should the pilot flying (PF) take immediately? (AURTA)

a. If in a turn, reduce bank angle.

b. Increase thrust—select maximum continuous thrust if the airplane's autothrottle system is maintaining thrust at a lower limit.

c. Descend.

Note: If a high drag situation occurs where maximum available thrust will not arrest the airspeed decay, the only available option is to descend.

37. What is maximum altitude and how is it determined? (AURTA)

Maximum altitude is the highest altitude at which an airplane can be operated. It is determined by three basic characteristics which are unique to each airplane model. It is the lowest of:

a. *Maximum certified altitude (structural)*—Determined during certification and is usually set by the pressurization load limits on the fuselage.

b. *Thrust limited altitude*—The altitude at which sufficient thrust is available to provide a specific minimum rate of climb.

c. *Buffet or maneuver limited altitude*—The altitude at which a specific maneuver margin exists prior to buffet onset.

38. What danger may be experienced when maneuvering near limited or maximum altitudes? (AURTA)

The danger in operating near these ceilings is the potential for the speed and AOA to change due to turbulence or environmental factors that could lead to a slowdown or stall and subsequent high altitude upset. When maneuvering at or near maximum altitude there may be insufficient thrust to maintain altitude and airspeed. The airplane may initially be within the buffet limits but does not have sufficient thrust to maintain the necessary airspeed.

39. Why is it necessary to use smaller control inputs when operating at high altitudes? (AURTA)

For the same control surface movement at constant airspeed, an airplane at 35,000 feet experiences a higher pitch rate than an airplane at 5,000 feet because there is less aerodynamic damping. The change in angle of attack will be greater, creating more lift and a higher load factor. If the control system is designed to provide a fixed ratio of control force to elevator deflection, it will take less force to generate the same load factor as altitude increases.

40. Some airline load planning computers attempt to load airplanes as far aft as possible to achieve efficiency. Will an airplane loaded with an aft CG, operating at a high altitude, be more or less responsive to control pressures? Will it be more or less stable? (AURTA)

At high altitude, an aft loaded airplane will be more responsive to control pressures since it is less stable than a forward loading. The further aft an airplane is loaded, the less effort is required by the tail to counteract the nose-down pitching moment of the wing. The less effort required by the tail results in less induced drag on the entire airplane which results in the most efficient flight.

41. Explain the advantages of swept-wing aircraft when compared with straight-wing aircraft. (AC 61-107)

Sweep allows a faster speed before critical Mach is reached when compared to an equal straight wing, resulting in a more economical cruise. This occurs because the airflow now travels over a different cross-section of the airfoil. This new cross-section has less effective camber, which results in a reduced acceleration of airflow over the wing, thus allowing a higher speed before critical Mach is reached.

42. Explain the lift characteristics of swept-wing aircraft when compared with straight-wing aircraft. (AC 61-107)

The lift characteristics of straight-wing and swept-wing airplanes related to changes in AOA are more favorable for swept-wing airplanes. An increase in the AOA of the straight-wing airplane produces a substantial and constantly increasing lift vector up to its maximum coefficient of lift and, soon thereafter, flow separation (stall) occurs with a rapid deterioration of lift. By contrast, a swept wing produces a much more gradual buildup of lift.

43. What is a disadvantage of an aircraft with swept wings when compared with a straight-wing aircraft? (FAA-H-8083-25)

Swept wings tend to stall at the wing tips rather than at the wing roots, causing unstable stall characteristics and making recovery more difficult. This is because the boundary layer tends to flow spanwise toward the tips and to separate near the leading edges.

44. How can a stall situation be aggravated in a swept-wing aircraft with a T-tail? (FAA-H-8083-25)

The T-tail affords little or no pre-stall warning in the form of tail control surface buffet. Being above the wing wake, it remains effective even after the wing has begun to stall, allowing the pilot to inadvertently drive the wing into a deeper stall at a much greater AOA.

45. What will happen if the horizontal tail surfaces become buried in the wing's wake during the stall? (FAA-H-8083-25)

The elevator may lose all effectiveness, making it impossible to reduce pitch attitude and break the stall.

46. Explain the Dutch roll tendency that can occur when flying a swept-wing aircraft. (FAA-H-8083-25)

A Dutch roll is a coupled lateral/directional oscillation that is usually dynamically stable but is unsafe in an aircraft because of the oscillatory nature. If the aircraft has the right wing pushed down, the positive sideslip angle corrects the wing laterally before the nose is realigned with the relative wind. As the wing corrects the position, a lateral directional oscillation can occur resulting in the nose of the aircraft making a figure eight on the horizon as a result of two oscillations (roll and yaw), which are out of phase with each other. The damping of the oscillatory mode may be weak or strong depending on the properties of the particular aircraft.

47. Jet transport aircraft are equipped with what type of system to counter Dutch roll oscillations? (AC 61-107, FAA-H-8083-3)

A stability augmentation system is required to be installed on the aircraft to dampen the Dutch roll tendency when it is determined to be objectionable, or when it adversely affects the control stability requirements for certification. The yaw damper is a gyro-operated autocontrol system installed to provide rudder input and aid in canceling out yaw tendencies such as those in Dutch roll. The yaw damper also minimizes motion about the vertical axis caused by turbulence.

48. What is adverse yaw? (AC 61-107)

A phenomenon in which the airplane heading changes in a direction opposite to that commanded by a roll control input. It is the result of unequal lift and drag characteristics of the down-going and up-going wings. The phenomena are alleviated by tailoring the control design through use of spoilers, yaw dampers, and interconnected rudder and aileron systems.

B. Stall Prevention and Recovery Training

1. What are the desired training goals for stall prevention and recovery training? (AC 120-109)

a. Proper recognition of operational and environmental conditions that increase the likelihood of a stall event.

b. Knowledge of stall fundamentals, including factors that affect stall speed and any implications for the expected flight operations.

c. Understanding of the stall characteristics for the specific airplane.

d. Proper aeronautical decision-making skills to avoid stall events (e.g., effective analysis, awareness, resource management, mitigation strategies, and breaking the error chain through airmanship and sound judgment).

e. Proper recognition of an impending stall in varied conditions and configurations.

f. The effects of autoflight, flight envelope protection in normal and degraded modes, and unexpected disconnects of the autopilot or autothrottle/autothrust.

g. Proper recognition of when the flight condition has transitioned from the prevention phase and into the recovery phase.

h. Proper application of the stall recovery procedure.

2. How can high altitude weather increase the possibility of an aircraft stall and upset? (AURTA)

Thunderstorms, clear air turbulence, and icing at high altitudes are examples of significant weather that pilots should take into consideration in flight planning.

3. How can a wind shear encounter at high altitude cause a slowdown or stall? (AURTA)

At high altitudes the upper air currents such as the jet stream become significant. Velocities in the jet stream can be very high and can present a beneficial tailwind or a troublesome headwind. Wind shear at the boundaries of the jet stream can cause severe turbulence and unexpected changes in airspeed or Mach number. Wind shear, or other local disturbances, can cause substantial and immediate airspeed decreases in cruise, as well as climb situations.

If the airplane is performance-limited due to high altitude and subsequently encounters an area of decreasing velocity due to wind shear, in severe cases the back side of the power curve may be encountered. The pilot will have to either increase thrust or decrease angle of attack to allow the airspeed to build back to normal climb/cruise speeds. This may require trading altitude for airspeed to accelerate out of the backside of the power curve region if additional thrust is not available.

4. Define the terms *angle of attack* and *critical angle of attack*. (FAA-H-8083-3)

The angle of attack is the acute angle between the chord line of the airfoil and the direction of the relative wind. The critical angle of attack is the angle of attack at which a wing stalls regardless of airspeed, flight attitude, or weight.

5. Explain what must happen for a wing to stall.
(FAA-H-8083-3)

A stall is an aerodynamic condition which occurs when smooth airflow over the airplane's wings is disrupted, resulting in loss of lift. Specifically, a stall occurs when the AOA—the angle between the chord line of the wing and the relative wind—exceeds the wing's critical AOA. It is possible to exceed the critical AOA at any airspeed, at any attitude, and at any power setting.

6. How is the pitch angle (attitude) of an aircraft different from the aircraft's angle of attack? (FAA-H-8083-3, FAA-H-8083-15)

The aircraft's AOA is the angle between the chord line of the wing and the oncoming air, or relative wind. The pitch angle is the angle between the aircraft's longitudinal axis and the horizon and is displayed on the artificial horizon.

7. Describe an angle of attack indicator. (FAA-H-8083-31)

An angle of attack indicator is an instrument that measures the angle between the local airflow around the direction detector and the fuselage reference plane. A true AOA indicating system detects the local AOA of the aircraft and displays the information on a cockpit indicator. It also may be designed to furnish reference information to other systems on high-performance aircraft. The sensing mechanism and transmitter are usually located on the forward side of the fuselage. It typically contains a heating element to ensure ice-free operation. Signals are sent from the sensor to the cockpit or computer(s) as required. An AOA indicator may be calibrated in actual angle degrees, arbitrary units, percentage of lift used, symbols, or even fast/slow.

8. For a swept-wing turbojet airplane operating at high altitudes (above 25,000 feet), will the stalling AOA be the same as the stalling AOA at a lower altitude? (AURTA)

No. Although stalling AOA is normally constant for a given configuration, at high altitudes swept-wing turbojet airplanes may stall at a reduced AOA due to Mach effects. The pitch attitude will also be significantly lower than what is experienced at lower altitudes. Low-speed buffet will likely precede an impending stall. Thrust available to supplement the recovery will be dramatically reduced and the pitch control through elevator must be used. The goal of minimizing altitude loss must be secondary to recovering from the stall. Flight crews must exchange altitude for airspeed. Only after positive stall recovery has been achieved, can altitude recovery be prioritized.

9. **Explain how the bank angle in a turn affects an aircraft's G-loading (load factor).** (FAA-H-8083-15)

In level flight in undisturbed air, the wings are supporting not only the weight of the aircraft, but centrifugal force as well. As the bank steepens, the horizontal lift component increases, centrifugal force increases, and the load factor increases. If the load factor becomes so great that an increase in AOA cannot provide enough lift to support the load, the wing stalls. Since the stalling speed increases directly with the square root of the load factor, the pilot should be aware of the flight conditions during which the load factor can become critical. Steep turns at slow airspeed, structural ice accumulation, and vertical gusts in turbulent air can increase the load factor to a critical level.

10. **Explain the difference between an impending stall and a full stall.** (FAA-H-8083-3)

Impending stall—Occurs when the AOA causes a stall warning, but has not yet reached the critical AOA. Indications of an impending stall can include buffeting, stick shaker, or aural warning.

Full stall—Occurs when the critical AOA is exceeded. Indications of a full stall are typically that an uncommanded nose-down pitch cannot be readily arrested, and this may be accompanied by an uncommanded rolling motion. For airplanes equipped with stick pushers, its activation is also a full stall indication.

11. **Where does the stall begin on a swept-wing airplane?** (FAA-H-8083-25)

A disadvantage of swept wings is that they tend to stall at the wingtips rather than at the wing roots. This is because the boundary layer tends to flow span-wise toward the tips and to separate near the leading edges. Because the tips of a swept wing are on the aft part of the wing (behind the center of lift), a wingtip stall causes the center of lift to move forward on the wing, forcing the nose to rise further. The tendency for tip stall is greatest when wing sweep and taper are combined.

12. **How are the stalling characteristics in a swept-wing jet airplane different from those of a conventional straight-wing, low tailplane airplane?** (FAA-H-8083-3)

Straight wing—An increase in AOA produces a substantial and constantly increasing lift vector up to its maximum coefficient of lift, and soon thereafter flow separation (stall) occurs with a rapid deterioration of lift.

Swept wing—An increase in AOA produces a much more gradual buildup of lift with a less well-defined maximum coefficient of lift. This less-defined peak also means that a swept wing may not have as dramatic loss of lift at angles of attack beyond its maximum lift coefficient. However, these high-lift conditions are accompanied by high drag, which results in a high rate of descent.

13. **How are the stalling characteristics of swept-wing aircraft with a T-tail different when compared with a straight-wing, low tailplane aircraft?** (FAA-H-8083-25)

The stall situation can be aggravated by a T-tail configuration, which affords little or no pre-stall warning in the form of tail control surface buffet. The T-tail, being above the wing wake, remains effective even after the wing has begun to stall, allowing the pilot to inadvertently drive the wing into a deeper stall at a much greater AOA. If the horizontal tail surfaces then become buried in the wing's wake, the elevator may lose all effectiveness, making it impossible to reduce pitch attitude and break the stall.

14. **Describe the flight control characteristics of an aircraft experiencing a full stall.** (AC 120-109)

The aircraft will experience any one, or combination of, the following characteristics:

a. An uncommanded nose-down pitch that cannot be readily arrested, which may be accompanied by an uncommanded rolling motion.

b. Buffeting of a magnitude and severity that is a strong and effective deterrent to further increase in AOA.

c. No further increase in pitch occurs when the pitch control is held at the full aft stop for 2 seconds, leading to an inability to arrest descent rate.

d. Activation of a stick pusher.

15. How do transport category aircraft provide indication of an approaching aerodynamic stall? (AC 120-109)

The indication is provided by an alert furnished either through inherent aerodynamics, such as buffeting, or by synthetic means, such as a stick shaker or a persistent aural-and-visual cue, giving clear indications prior to a full stall to allow a pilot to prevent a full stall. Refer to 14 CFR §25.207.

16. Why is it important that pilots experience stick pusher activation during stall prevention and recovery training? (AC 120-109)

During training, pilots should experience the sudden forward movement of the control yoke/stick during a stick pusher activation. From observations, most instructors state that, regardless of previous academic training, pilots typically resist the stick pusher on their first encounter. Usually, they immediately pull back on the control yoke/stick rather than releasing pressure as they have been taught. Pilots should receive practical stick pusher training in a full flight simulator to develop the proper response (allowing the pusher to reduce AOA) when confronted with a stick pusher activation.

17. Explain the procedure for a stick pusher demonstration in a full flight simulator. (AC 120-109)

a. In level flight, reduce thrust to idle.

b. AOA should be increased to achieve the activation of the stick pusher.

c. Upon stick pusher activation, release backpressure and allow stick pusher to reduce the AOA.

d. Recover to the maneuvering speed appropriate for the airplane's configuration without exceeding the airplane's limitations.

e. There is no predetermined value for altitude loss, and maintaining altitude during recovery is not required.

18. **How does the use of the vertical speed mode (VS) on a flight director/autopilot increase risk of a stall or upset during a high altitude climb?** (AC 61-107)

Use of VS mode has considerable risk during high-altitude climb. When an aircraft is in VS mode, airplane speed is controlled by thrust. VS mode prioritizes the command VS rate; thus, speed can decay when thrust available is less than thrust required. Improper use of VS can result in speed loss with a potential for stall conditions.

19. **Why is it more difficult to recover from a stall at high altitudes (above 25,000 feet)?** (AC 61-107)

Thinner air at high altitudes has a significant impact on an airplane's flying characteristics because surface control effects, lift, thrust, drag, and horsepower are all functions of air density:

a. *Aircraft controls*—The reduced weight of air moving over control surfaces at high altitudes decreases their effectiveness. As the airplane approaches its absolute altitude, the controls feel sluggish, making altitude and heading difficult to maintain. Most airplanes that fly at or above 25,000 feet MSL are equipped with an autopilot.

b. *Horsepower*—The engine uses a determined weight of air to produce an identified amount of horsepower through internal combustion. For a given decrease of air density, horsepower decreases at a higher rate, which is approximately 1.3 times that of the corresponding decrease in air density.

c. *Speed and velocity*—For an airplane to maintain unaccelerated level flight, drag and thrust must be equal. Because density is always greater at sea level, the velocity at altitude given the same AOA will be greater than at sea level, although the IAS will not change. Therefore, an airplane's TAS increases with altitude while its IAS remains constant. In addition, an airplane's rate of climb will decrease with altitude.

20. **What effect does angle of attack have on low- and high-speed buffet?** (FAA-H-8083-3)

The AOA of the wing has the greatest effect on inducing the Mach buffet, or pre-stall buffet, at either the high- or low-speed boundaries for the airplane.

21. **Why is convergence of M_{MO} and stalling angle of attack hazardous?** (FAA-H-8083-3)

Any increase in airspeed will cause the aircraft to experience buffet and potentially cause Mach tuck. Any decrease in airspeed will cause the aircraft to experience buffet and potentially stall. The aircraft may experience airspeed changes due to environmental factors (turbulence, etc.) without pilot input.

22. **Explain what happens if the airflow over the wing is allowed to increase beyond M_{cr}.** (FAA-H-8083-3)

a. As the speed of the wing increases, a shock wave forms, becoming more severe as it moves aft on the wing. Eventually flow separation occurs behind the well-developed shock wave.

b. If allowed to progress well beyond the M_{MO}, the separation of air behind the shock wave can result in severe buffeting and possible loss of control or airplane upset.

c. Because of the changing center of lift of the wing resulting from the movement of the shock wave, the pilot experiences pitch change tendencies as the airplane moves through the transonic speeds up to and exceeding M_{MO}.

23. **After a pilot has recognized that the aircraft is in a full aerodynamic stall, why would the corrective actions necessary for stall recovery be delayed?** (AURTA)

Some of the reasons for a delayed reaction include:

a. Lack of situational awareness and crew confusion.

b. Anxiety associated with altitude violations and maintaining separation from other air traffic.

c. Previous training emphasizing prevention of altitude loss of only a few hundred feet even in the case of an impending high altitude stall.

d. Inadequate experience with high altitude manual flight control.

e. Concern for passenger and crew safety.

24. Explain the procedure for recovery from an impending stall near the airplane's maximum altitude. (AC 120-109)

a. *Disconnect autopilot and autothrottle/autothrust*—Ensure the pitch attitude does not increase when disconnecting the autopilot. This may be very important in out-of-trim situations. Manual control is essential to recovery in all situations. Leaving the autopilot or autothrottle/autothrust connected may result in inadvertent changes or adjustments that may not be easily recognized or appropriate, especially during high workload situations.

b. *Apply nose-down pitch control until impending stall indications are eliminated*—Reducing the angle of attack is crucial for recovery. This will also address autopilot-induced excessive nose-up trim. If the control column does not provide sufficient response, pitch trim may be necessary. However, excessive use of pitch trim may aggravate the condition, or may result in loss of control or high structural loads.

c. *Adjust bank angle to wings level*—This orients the lift vector for recovery.

d. *Add thrust as needed*—During a stall recovery, maximum thrust is not always needed. A stall can occur at high thrust or at idle thrust. Therefore, the thrust is to be adjusted accordingly during the recovery. For airplanes with engines installed below the wing, applying maximum thrust may create a strong nose-up pitching moment if airspeed is low. For airplanes with engines mounted above the wings, thrust application creates a helpful pitch-down tendency. For propeller-driven airplanes, thrust application increases the airflow around the wing, assisting in stall recovery.

e. *Retract speed brakes/spoilers*—This will improve lift and stall margin.

f. *Return to the desired flightpath*—Apply gentle action for recovery to avoid secondary stalls then return to desired flightpath.

25. Describe the common errors that a pilot can make when attempting to recognize and recover from an impending stall at a high altitude. (AC 120-109)

a. Recovery is attempted with thrust instead of reducing AOA.

b. Not maintaining a nose-down input until the impending stall cues are eliminated.

c. Insufficient pitch down to allow desired energy conversion of altitude to airspeed.

d. Pilot fails to promptly recover from a secondary stall.

e. Reluctance to sacrifice significant altitude.

f. Pilot fails to distinguish between high speed buffet and low speed stall.

g. Pilot increases the load factor too quickly and gets multiple impending stalls or a stick pusher activation.

h. Inappropriate use of rudder.

i. Pilot prioritizes roll control (attempting to level the wings) before reducing AOA.

j. Not disconnecting the autopilot and/or autothrottle/autothrust prior to reducing AOA.

C. Upset Prevention and Recovery Training

1. What is the main goal of upset prevention and recovery training (UPRT)? (AURTA)

The goal of UPRT training is to increase the ability of pilots to recognize and avoid situations that can lead to airplane upsets and to improve their ability to recover control of an airplane that has exceeded the normal flight regime. This will be accomplished by increasing awareness of potential upset situations and knowledge of aerodynamics and by application of this knowledge during simulator training scenarios.

2. Are Part 121 air carriers required to provide UPRT to pilots? (AC 120-111)

All Part 121 air carriers, including those who train under an advanced qualification program (AQP), are required to conduct UPRT beginning March 12, 2019. The requirement for Part 121 pilots to receive upset training is statutorily mandated in Public Law 111-216, Section 208 and the FAA does not have the authority to exempt any Part 121 air carrier from this requirement. Air carriers must include UPRT for pilots during:

a. Initial training.

b. Transition training.

c. Differences and related aircraft differences training (if differences exist).

d. Conversion training.

e. Upgrade training.

f. Requalification training (if applicable).

g. Recurrent training.

3. What is the definition of an *airplane upset*? (AURTA, AC 120-111)

An airplane upset is an airplane in flight unintentionally exceeding the parameters normally experienced in line operations or training:

a. Pitch attitude greater than 25 degrees nose up;

b. Pitch attitude greater than 10 degrees nose down;

c. Bank angle greater than 45 degrees; or

d. Within the above parameters, but flying at airspeeds inappropriate for the conditions.

4. What are several causes and contributing factors of airplane upsets? (AC 120-111)

a. *Environmentally induced upsets*—Caused by turbulence, mountain wave, wind shear, thunderstorms, microbursts, or airplane icing.

b. *Pilot-induced upsets*—Caused by misinterpretation or slow instrument crosscheck, improper adjustment of attitude and power, improper pilot input, inattention, distractions, spatial disorientation, pilot incapacitation, misunderstanding of autoflight modes or improper use of automated systems, transition from automated to manual modes due to system disconnect, and pilot-induced oscillations.

c. *Mechanically-induced upsets*—Caused by flight instrument anomalies/failures, autoflight anomalies/failures, flight control malfunctions/failures, or other system anomalies.

d. *Common illusions*—Associated with in-flight loss of control events (somatogravic illusion, the leans, Coriolis illusion, etc.).

e. *Lack of visual cues*—Situations resulting in an upset due to a lack of visual cues such as a sub-threshold roll (i.e., imperceptible roll rate, generally less than three degrees per second).

5. The majority of multi-engine turbojet airplane upsets are caused by what environmentally induced factor? (AURTA)

Wake turbulence is the leading cause of airplane upsets that are induced by the environment. Avoiding wake turbulence is the key to avoiding many airplane upsets. Pilot/ATC procedures and standards are designed to accomplish this goal, but as the aviation industry expands, the probability of an encounter increases.

6. Explain how operating near the jet stream can potentially result in an aircraft upset. (AURTA)

Wind shear at the boundaries of the jet stream can cause severe turbulence and unexpected changes in airspeed or Mach number. This wind shear, or other local disturbances, can cause substantial and immediate airspeed decreases in cruise and climb situations. If the airplane is performance limited due to high altitude and subsequently encounters an area of decreasing velocity due to wind shear, in severe cases the back side of the power curve may be encountered. The pilot will have to either increase thrust or decrease AOA to allow the airspeed to build back to normal climb/cruise speeds. This may require trading altitude for airspeed to accelerate out of the backside of the power curve region if additional thrust is not available.

7. **Explain several aircraft upset recognition and prevention training techniques.** (AC 61-138)

   a. *Divergence from flight path*—Pilots should understand that any time the airplane begins to diverge from the intended flightpath or speed they must identify what, if any, action must be taken.

   b. *Timely and appropriate intervention*—Recovery to a stabilized flightpath should be initiated as soon as a developing upset condition is recognized. The amount and rate of control input to counter a developing upset must be proportional to the amount and rate of pitch, roll and/or yaw experienced. This action may prevent what might become a more serious event.

   c. *Examples of instrumentation during developing and developed upset*—A key aspect to upset awareness, prevention, and recovery training is for pilots to recognize and prevent developing upsets and recover from developed upsets.

   d. *Effective scanning*—An effective scan is essential for pilots to identify the precursors and the initial development of the upset and using that recognition make timely and appropriate responses to return the aircraft back to the desired path.

   e. *Pitch/power/roll/yaw*—Pilots should understand how to recognize developing and developed upset conditions so they can make control inputs based on desired aircraft reaction. Control deflections at one point in the flight envelope might not be appropriate in another part of the flight envelope. Pilots should have a fundamental understanding of instrumentation and flight dynamics in pitch/power/roll/yaw in order to recognize the current state of the airplane and make the correct control inputs to arrest the divergence or recovery from the upset. The air data instrument (ADI) is the primary control instrument for recovery from an upset. Due to varying visibility conditions, one cannot depend on having adequate outside visual references.

   f. *Recovery*—An overview of actions to take to recover from an upset encompassing three basic activities: managing the energy, arresting the flightpath divergence, and recovering to a stabilized flightpath.

8. **What can pilots do to mitigate the risk of a weather-related high altitude upset occurring?** (AURTA)

Careful review of forecasts, significant weather charts, and turbulence plots are key elements in avoiding conditions that could lead to an upset. Once established in cruise flight, a prudent crew will update destination and enroute weather information. By comparing the updated information to the preflight briefing, the crew can more accurately determine if the forecast charts are accurate. Areas of expected turbulence should be carefully plotted and avoided if reports of severe turbulence are received. Trend monitoring of turbulence areas is also important. Trends of increasing turbulence should be noted and if possible avoided. Avoiding areas of potential turbulence will reduce the risk of an upset.

9. **During an aircraft upset, explain the first actions a flight crew should take when recognizing and confirming the situation.** (AURTA)

Recognize and confirm the situation by accomplishing the following key steps:

a. Communicate with crewmembers.
b. Locate the bank indicator.
c. Determine pitch attitude.
d. Confirm attitude by reference to other indicators.

10. **Pilots who have experienced an airplane upset have identified several issues associated with recovering from an upset. What are four common issues?** (AURTA)

a. *The startle factor*—Airplane upsets are infrequent; therefore, pilots are usually surprised or startled when an upset occurs. There is a tendency to react before analyzing what is happening or to fixate on one indication and fail to properly diagnose the situation.

b. *Negative G force*—Airline pilots are normally uncomfortable (for the sake of passenger comfort and safety) with aggressively unloading G forces on a large passenger airplane. This inhibition must be overcome when faced with the necessity to quickly and sometimes aggressively unload the airplane to less than 1 G.

(continued)

    c. *Full control inputs*—Flight control forces become less effective when the airplane is at or near its critical angle of attack or stall. Pilots tend not to use full control authority because they rarely are required to do so. This habit must be overcome when recovering from severe upsets.

    d. *Counter-intuitive factors*—It may be counter-intuitive to use greater unloading control forces or to reduce thrust when recovering from a high angle of attack, especially at low altitudes. If the airplane is stalled while already in a nose-down attitude, the pilot must still push the nose down (unload) in order to reduce the angle of attack. Altitude cannot be maintained in a stall and should be of secondary importance.

11. Your aircraft pitch attitude is more than 25 degrees high and is increasing. The airspeed is decreasing and your ability to maneuver the airplane is becoming increasingly difficult. How will you recover from this upset situation? (AC 120-111)

    a. Recognize and confirm the situation by announcing "Nose High." Recognizing and confirming the aircraft's energy state and the rate that it's changing will have an effect on how to handle the recovery.

    b. Disconnect the autopilot and set autothrottle off. Leaving the autopilot or autothrottle/autothrust connected may result in inadvertent changes or adjustments that may not be easily recognized or appropriate, especially during high workload situations. *Note:* a large out-of-trim condition could be encountered when the autopilot is disconnected.

    c. Apply as much as full nose-down control input as required to obtain a nose-down pitch rate. If nose-down inputs are not successful in achieving a nose-down pitch rate, pitch may be controlled by rolling the airplane. The rolling maneuver changes the pitch rate into a turning maneuver, allowing the pitch to decrease.

    d. Adjust thrust (if required). Combined with pitch trim, an additional method for achieving a nose-down pitch rate on airplanes with under-wing-mounted engines can be to reduce the power which reduces the upward pitch moment.

e. Recover to level flight when airspeed is sufficiently increasing. Establish a slightly nose-low attitude to reduce the potential for entering another upset. Roll to wings level, check airspeed, and adjust thrust and pitch as necessary.

f. The pilot monitoring (PM) should monitor airspeed and attitude throughout the recovery and announce any continued divergence.

Note: These techniques assume the airplane is not stalled. If the airplane is stalled, recovery from the stall must be accomplished first. As always, the manufacturer's procedures take precedence over the recommendations in the referenced AC.

12. When executing a nose-high recovery, why is it sometimes necessary to reduce power to achieve a nose-down pitch rate? (AURTA)

If altitude permits, flight tests have shown that an effective method for getting a nose-down pitch rate is to reduce the power on underwing-mounted engines. This reduces the upward pitch moment. In fact, in some situations for some airplane models, it may be necessary to reduce thrust to prevent the angle of attack from continuing to increase. This usually results in the nose lowering at higher speeds and a milder pitch-down. This makes it easier to recover to level flight.

13. The aircraft pitch attitude is more than 10 degrees nose-low and the airspeed is high. Describe the recovery procedure for this upset situation. (AC 120-111)

a. Recognize and confirm the situation by announcing "Nose low." Recognizing and confirming the aircraft's energy state and the rate it's changing will have an effect on how to handle the recovery.

b. Disconnect the autopilot and set autothrottle off. A large out-of-trim condition could be encountered when the AP is disconnected.

c. Recover from the stall if required. Even in a nose-low, low-speed situation, the airplane may be stalled at a relatively low pitch. Stall recovery must occur first and may require nose-down elevator, which may not be intuitive.

d. Roll in the shortest direction to wings level. Full aileron and spoiler input may be necessary to smoothly establish a recovery roll rate toward the nearest horizon.

e. Adjust thrust and drag (if required). If airspeed is low, apply thrust; if airspeed is high, reduce thrust and, if necessary, extend speed brakes.

f. Recover to level flight. Avoid a secondary stall because of premature recovery or excessive G loading

g. The PM should monitor airspeed and attitude throughout the recovery and announce any continued divergence.

Note: These techniques assume the airplane is not stalled. If the airplane is stalled, recovery from the stall must be accomplished first. As always, the aircraft manufacturer's procedures take precedence.

14. **Your airplane's bank angle is greater than 45 degrees and the pitch attitude is greater than 25 degrees nose high. The airspeed is decreasing. Explain how to recover from this upset situation. (AURTA)**

a. Recognize and confirm the situation.

b. Disengage the autopilot and autothrottle.

c. Recover from the stall if necessary.

d. Apply as much full nose-down elevator as required.

e. Use appropriate techniques:
   - Roll (adjust bank angle, not to exceed 60 degrees) to achieve a nose-down pitch rate.
   - Reduce thrust (on aircraft with underwing-mounted engines).

f. Complete the recovery:
   - Approaching the horizon, roll to wings level.
   - Check airspeed, adjust thrust if necessary.
   - Establish pitch attitude.

15. Explain the recovery procedure for the following situation. The aircraft's bank angle is greater than 45 degrees and the pitch attitude is lower than 10 degrees nose low. The airspeed is increasing. (AURTA)

a. Recognize and confirm the situation.

b. Disengage the autopilot and autothrottle.

c. Recover from the stall if necessary.

d. Roll in the shortest direction to wings level. If bank angle is greater than 90 degrees, first unload and then roll.

e. Thrust and drag—adjust if required. If airspeed is low, apply thrust; if airspeed is high, reduce thrust, and if necessary, extend speedbrakes.

f. Recover to level flight:
   • Apply nose-up elevator.
   • Apply stabilizer trim, if necessary.
   • Adjust thrust and drag as necessary.

16. During an aircraft upset, how should the pilot monitoring (PM) assist the pilot flying (PF) in the recovery procedure? (AC 120-111)

a. A PF will take action and a PM will call out the need for timely execution of recovery priorities:
   • Manage energy.
   • Arrest flightpath divergence.
   • Recover to stabilized flightpath.

b. The PM should monitor appropriate control actions taken by the PF to recover the aircraft without exceeding aircraft limitations.

c. The PM should monitor airspeed and attitude throughout the recovery and announce any continued divergence.

d. When an upset is precipitated by a stall, recover from the stall before initiating other recovery actions.

Air Carrier Operations

A. Turbine Engine Operations

1. What is the thrust to thrust lever relationship in a jet engine? (FAA-H-8083-3)

The thrust to thrust lever relationship refers to the relationship between the position of the thrust lever and the amount of thrust produced by a jet engine. In a jet engine, the amount of thrust output changes much more per increment of throttle movement at high engine speeds. If the power setting is already high, it normally takes a small amount of movement to change the power output.

2. Why is the thrust to thrust lever relationship significant for pilots transitioning to jet-powered airplanes? (FAA-H-8083-3)

In a jet engine, thrust output changes much more per increment of throttle movement at high engine speeds. If the power setting is already high, it normally takes a small amount of movement to change the power output. This is a significant difference for the pilot transitioning to jet-powered airplanes. In a situation where significantly more thrust is needed and the jet engine is at low RPM, inching the thrust lever forward will have little effect. It this situation, the pilot needs to make a smooth and significant thrust lever position change to increase the power.

3. What is the most efficient operating range for a jet engine, and how does thrust vary with RPM? (FAA-H-8083-3)

Jets operate most efficiently in the 85 percent to 100 percent range. At idle RPM of approximately 55 percent to 60 percent, they produce a relatively small amount of thrust. However, as RPM increases from 90 to 100 percent, thrust can increase by as much as the total available at 70 percent.

4. How much slower is the acceleration of a jet engine than that of a piston engine? (FAA-H-8083-3)

Acceleration of a piston engine from idle to full power is relatively rapid. The acceleration on different jet engines can vary considerably, but it is usually much slower. In some cases, the transition to full power could take up to 10 seconds. Pilots should anticipate the need for adding power from low power settings.

5. What are the definitions of a *hot start* and a *hung start*? (FAA-H-8083-3)

Hot start—This is when normal engine rotation occurs, but with exhaust temperature exceeding prescribed limits; usually caused by an excessively rich mixture in the combustor. Fuel to the engine must be terminated immediately to prevent engine damage.

Hung start—A condition where the engine is accelerating more slowly than normal is termed a hung start or false start. During a hung start/false start, the engine may stabilize at an engine RPM that is not high enough for the engine to continue to run without help from the starter. This is usually the result of low battery power or the starter not turning the engine fast enough for it to start properly.

6. What is a compressor stall? (FAA-H-8083-3)

In gas turbine engines, a compressor stall is a condition in an axial-flow compressor in which one or more stages of rotor blades fail to pass air smoothly to the succeeding stages. A stall condition is caused by a pressure ratio that is incompatible with the engine RPM. Compressor stall will be indicated by a rise in exhaust temperature or RPM fluctuation, and if allowed to continue, may result in flameout and physical damage to the engine.

7. What conditions can result in an engine compressor stall? (FAA-H-8083-32)

a. Aircraft operations outside design parameters established by manufacturer.

b. In-flight icing.

c. Foreign object damage (bird strike, runway foreign object debris, etc).

d. Abrupt pitch changes encountered in severe turbulence or during a stall.

e. Worn, dirty or contaminated compressor components.

f. Improper engine handling (fuel flow increased too rapidly, etc).

8. Define the term *compressor surge.* (FAA-H-8083-3)

A compressor surge is a severe compressor stall across the entire compressor that can result in severe damage if not quickly corrected. This condition occurs with a complete stoppage of airflow or a reversal of airflow.

9. Define the term *engine power rollback.* (AURTA, AC 20-147)

Turbine engine rollback is an uncommon anomaly consisting of an uncommanded loss of thrust (decrease in EPR or N_1), which is sometimes accompanied by an increase in EGT. Rollback can be caused by a combination of many events including moisture, icing, fuel control issues, high angle of attack disrupted airflow, and mechanical failure and usually results in flameout or core lock.

10. Explain how an engine flameout occurs. (FAA-H-8083-25)

A flameout is a condition in a gas turbine engine in which the fire in the engine goes out due to either too much or too little fuel sprayed into the combustors. Flameouts can occur due to low fuel pressure and low engine speeds, which typically are associated with high-altitude flight. This situation may also occur with the engine throttled back during a descent, which can set up the lean-condition flameout. Any interruption of the fuel supply due to prolonged unusual attitudes, a malfunctioning fuel control system, turbulence, icing, or running out of fuel may result in a flameout.

11. What does core lock refer to? (AURTA)

Core lock is a phenomenon that could, in theory, occur in any turbine engine after an abnormal thermal event (e.g. a sudden flameout at low airspeed) where the internal friction exceeds the external aerodynamic driving forces and the core of the engine stops. When this occurs, differential contraction of the cooler outside case clamps down on the hotter internal components (seals, blade tips etc.) preventing rotation or "locking the core." This seizure may be severe enough to exceed the driving force available by increasing airspeed or from the starter. If differential cooling locks the core, only time will allow the temperature difference to equalize, reduce the contact friction caused by differential contraction and allow free rotation.

12. **What items should pilots consider when an engine flameout occurs at a high altitude?** (AURTA)

    a. The first critical consideration is to obtain a safe descent speed.

    b. Then flight crews should determine engine status.

    c. If engine spools indicate zero, core lock may exist or mechanical engine damage could have occurred.

    d. If all engines have flamed out, the flight crew must obtain best L/D airspeed, instead of accelerating to windmill speed, to obtain an optimum glide ratio.

    e. Critical: the crew must follow the approved flight manual procedures, maintain sufficient airspeed to maintain core rotation.

    f. In the event the seized spool(s) begin to rotate, a relight will be contemplated and windmill airspeed may be necessary.

B. Automation

1. **Define the term *automation*.** (AC 120-35)

   Automation is the replacement of a human function, either manual or cognitive, with a machine function. This definition applies to all levels of automation in all aircraft. Effective use of automation means using that level most appropriate to support the priorities of safety, economy, and stated flight operations policies of the individual air carrier.

2. **What are several examples of automation on the flight deck?** (FAA-H-8083-16)

   Current flight deck automation includes autopilots, flight management systems, electronic flight instrument systems, and warning and alerting systems.

3. **What does the term *automation management* refer to?** (FAA-H-8083-9, AC 120-35)

   Automation management is the demonstrated ability to control and navigate an aircraft by means of automated systems installed in the aircraft. The pilot must know what to expect, how to monitor the system for proper operation, and promptly take appropriate action if the system does not perform as expected. It is the use of appropriate flight guidance to manage crew workloads and maintain situational awareness.

4. Explain the term *automation proficiency*. (AC 120-35)

Flight crewmembers must be proficient in operating their aircraft in all levels of automation. They must be knowledgeable in the selection of the appropriate degree of automation, and must have the skills needed to move from one level of automation to another.

5. Explain the different levels of automation a flight crew may use to control an aircraft during flight. (FAA Flight Deck Automation Final Report)

Automation off/full manual—The pilot is manually controlling the aircraft without the assistance of flight directors. This would be used to avoid collisions with other aircraft or to recover from an undesired aircraft state such as a stall.

Manual—The pilot is manually controlling the aircraft based on guidance assistance from the preprogrammed flight directors. This is primarily used for takeoff, initial departure, and landings.

Tactical autoflight—The aircraft's autopilot is engaged, but pilots can direct changes to heading, speed, and altitude using a control panel. Autopilot and autothrottle are engaged.

Full autoflight—The aircraft's control is fully automated based on information preprogrammed by the pilots. Autopilot and autothrottle engaged.

6. Explain what is meant by the term *automation bias* and discuss how it can increase risk. (drs.faa.gov, AC 61-98)

Automation bias is the relative willingness of a pilot to trust and use automated systems. By failing to monitor the systems and failing to check the results of the processes of those systems, the pilot becomes increasingly detached from aircraft operation, which significantly increases risk.

7. Define the term *automation dependency*. (SAFO 13002, AC 61-83)

Automation dependency is a pilot or flight crew's overreliance on the automated systems of an aircraft. Modern aircraft are commonly operated using autoflight systems (e.g., autopilot or autothrottle/autothrust). Unfortunately, continuous use of those systems does not reinforce a pilot's knowledge and skills in manual flight operations. Autoflight systems are useful tools for pilots and have improved safety and workload management, and thus enabled more precise operations. However, continuous use of autoflight systems can lead to degradation of the pilot's ability to quickly recover the aircraft from an undesired state.

8. **What are the most important aspects of managing an autopilot/FMS?** (FAA-H-8083-9)

   A pilot or flight crew must know at all times which modes are engaged, which modes are armed to engage, and must be capable of verifying that armed functions (e.g., navigation tracking or altitude capture) engage at the appropriate time.

9. **Pilots should be able to correctly select, interpret, and anticipate normal as well as inappropriate or unexpected autoflight modes. This should include the ability to?** (AC 120- 71)

   a. Correctly identify and interpret individual flight mode annunciations.

   b. Describe the respective mode's impact on the related systems and airplane operation.

   c. Understand pitch mode annunciations and their relationship to available thrust as well as the aircraft's energy state (e.g. the risk of using vertical speed mode to climb at high altitudes with limited available thrust).

10. **What information source on the instrument panel should a pilot use to determine which automation modes are active?** (AC 120-71)

    The flight mode annunciator (FMA).

11. **Explain the purpose and importance of the aircraft flight mode annunciator (FMA).** (AC 120-71)

    The FMA provides the flight crew with information on the status of the autoflight/automated systems, specifically with respect to the guidance and control functions being utilized. Whether manually controlling the aircraft, using automated systems to control the aircraft flightpath and energy, or various combinations of both, the FMA shows "who is doing what."

12. **Autoflight system mode awareness requires effective monitoring of autoflight modes. Describe several strategies that could improve monitoring of the autoflight modes.** (AC 120-71)

    a. Stay in the loop by mentally flying the aircraft even when the autopilot or other pilot is flying the aircraft.

    b. If you become distracted, ensure that you always check the FMA and your flight instruments to get back in the loop as soon as possible.

    c. Monitor the flight instruments just as you would when you are manually flying the aircraft.

    d. Be diligent in monitoring all flightpath changes—pilot actions, system modes, and aircraft responses.

    e. Always make monitoring of the pilot flying a priority task when flightpath changes are being made.

    f. Always check the FMA after a change has been selected on the autopilot mode control panel.

    g. Maintain an awareness of the autoflight systems and modes selected by the crew or automatically initiated by the flight management computer (mode awareness) to effectively monitor flightpath.

    h. Maintain an awareness of the capabilities available in engaged autoflight modes to avoid mode confusion.

    i. Effectively monitor systems and selected modes to determine that the aircraft is on the desired flightpath.

13. **In what three areas must a pilot be proficient when using advanced avionics or any automated system?** (FAA-H-8083-25)

    The pilot must know what to expect, how to monitor the system for proper operation, and be prepared to promptly take appropriate action if the system does not perform as expected.

C. Navigation and Flightpath Warning Systems

1. Explain the function of a flight management system (FMS). (AC 25.1329)

An FMS is an aircraft area navigation (RNAV) system and associated displays and input/output devices(s) having complex multi-waypoint lateral (LNAV) and vertical (VNAV) capability, data entry capability, database memory to store route and instrument flight procedure information, and display readout of NAV parameters. An FMS provides guidance commands to the flight guidance system (FGS) for the purpose of automatic navigation and speed control when the FGS is engaged in an appropriate mode or modes (e.g., VNAV, LNAV, RNAV).

2. Explain the purpose of a Flight Guidance System (FGS). (AC 25.1329)

The FGS is primarily intended to assist the flight crew in the basic control and tactical guidance of the airplane. The system may also provide workload relief to the pilots and provide a means to fly a flight path more accurately to support specific operational requirements, such as reduced vertical separation minimum (RVSM) or required navigation performance (RNP).

3. What are the main components of an FGS? (AC 25.1329)

An FGS is a system consisting of one or more of the following elements:

a. Autopilot.
b. Flight director.
c. Automatic thrust control.

An FGS also includes any interactions with stability augmentation and trim systems.

4. Due to traffic, ATC has instructed you to climb immediately. At the same time, your traffic collision avoidance system (TCAS) issues a resolution advisory (RA) "Descend, descend." What is your next action? (AC 120-55)

You should descend. ATC may not know when TCAS issues RAs. It is possible for ATC to unknowingly issue instructions that are contrary to the TCAS RA indications. Safe vertical separation may be lost during TCAS coordination when one aircraft maneuvers opposite the vertical direction indicated by TCAS and the other aircraft maneuvers as indicated by TCAS. As a result, both aircraft may experience excessive altitude excursions in vertical chase scenarios due to the aircraft maneuvering in the same vertical direction. Accordingly, during an RA, do not maneuver contrary to the RA based solely upon ATC instructions. ATC may not be providing separation service or be communicating with the aircraft causing the RA.

5. A TCAS RA requires you to deviate from an ATC clearance. After the traffic conflict is resolved, what will ATC expect you to do next? (AC 120-55)

In responding to a TCAS RA that directs a deviation from assigned altitude, communicate with ATC as soon as practicable after responding to the RA. When the RA is cleared, the flight crew should advise ATC that they are returning to their previously assigned clearance or should acknowledge any amended clearance issued.

6. Describe several system and operational limitations of a TCAS system. (AC 120-55)

System limitations include the inability of TCAS to detect non-transponder-equipped aircraft and not issue RAs for traffic without an altitude-reporting transponder. Operational limitations include some RAs inhibit altitudes, certain RAs being inhibited by aircraft performance constraints, the inability to comply with an RA due to aircraft performance limitations after an engine failure, and appropriate response to RAs in limiting performance conditions, such as during heavy weight takeoff or while en route at maximum altitude for a particular weight.

7. **Describe various conditions under which certain functions of TCAS are inhibited.** (AC 120-55)

   a. "INCREASE DESCENT" RAs are inhibited below 1,450 (±100) feet AGL.

   b. "DESCEND" RAs are inhibited below 1,100 (±100) feet AGL.

   c. All RAs are inhibited below 1,000 (±100) feet AGL.

   d. All TCAS aural annunciations are inhibited below 500 (±100) feet AGL. This includes the aural annunciation for traffic advisories (TAs).

   e. Altitude and configuration under which climb and increase climb RAs are inhibited. A pilot should know if their aircraft type issues climb and increase climb RAs when operating at the aircraft's certified ceiling. If your aircraft type provides RA climb and increase climb commands at certified ceiling, the commands are to be followed.

8. **Should a pilot's response to a TCAS RA have priority over other cockpit warnings such as stall warning, wind shear, or enhanced ground proximity warning system (EGPWS) or terrain awareness warning system (TAWS) alerts?** (AC 120-55)

   If a TCAS RA maneuver is contrary to other critical cockpit warnings, pilots should respect those other critical warnings as defined by TCAS certification and training. Responses to stall warning, wind shear, and EGPWS/TAWS take precedence over a TCAS RA, particularly when the aircraft is below 2,500 feet AGL.

9. **Are pilots required to make a written report of a TCAS RA?** (NTSB 830.5)

   The NTSB requires immediate notification for airborne collision and avoidance system (ACAS) resolution advisories issued when an aircraft is being operated on an IFR flight plan and compliance with the advisory is necessary to avert a substantial risk of collision between two or more aircraft or in Class A airspace.

10. **What are the three main improvements of TAWS over existing GPWS systems?** (AC 23-18)

    TAWS equipment improved on GPWS systems by providing the flight crew with:

    a. Earlier aural and visual warning of impending terrain.
    b. Forward looking capability.
    c. Continued operation in the landing configuration.

11. **Describe the forward looking terrain avoidance (FLTA) feature of TAWS equipment.** (AC 23-18)

    The FLTA function looks ahead of the airplane along and below the airplane's lateral and vertical flight path and provides suitable alerts if a potential controlled flight into terrain (CFIT) threat exists.

12. **What is a TAWS premature descent alert (PDA)?** (AC 23-18)

    A TAWS PDA uses the airplane's current position and flight path information, as determined from a suitable navigation source and airport database, to determine if the airplane is hazardously below the normal (typically 3 degree) approach path for the nearest runway as defined by the alerting algorithm.

13. **Explain why TAWS-equipped aircraft continue to experience incidents and accidents involving terrain.** (AC 23-18, FAA InFO 23003)

    TAWS sometimes gives nuisance alerts that desensitize the pilot to TAWS alerts, which can result in the pilot's decision to ignore a valid alert. Most TAWS systems offer a terrain inhibit switch that allows the pilot to silence TAWS alerts. There have been cases in which pilots have used the inhibit switch or ignored TAWS alerts, thinking they were nuisance alerts, when in fact the alerts were valid indications of a dangerous situation.

14. **What is a TAWs nuisance alert?** (AC 23-18, FAA InFO 23003)

    A nuisance alert is an inappropriate alert occurring during normal safe procedures, that occurs as a result of a design performance limitation of TAWS. Most TAWS systems contain software logic that attempts to recognize and remain silent in situations in which proximity to terrain is normal. This logic is partly based on the aircraft's distance from the runway of intended landing. For example, flying at an altitude of 200 feet AGL when 3,500 feet away from the runway is a reasonable alert, but flying at an altitude of 200 feet AGL when 5 miles from the runway is not a reasonable alert. TAWS logic attempts to silence itself in normal situations and sound in abnormal situations.

15. Explain the term *required navigational performance* (RNP). (AIM 1-2-2, FAA-H-8083-15)

While both RNAV navigation specifications (NavSpecs) and RNP NavSpecs contain specific performance requirements, RNP is RNAV with the added requirement for onboard performance monitoring and alerting (OBPMA). RNP is also a statement of navigation performance necessary for operation within a defined airspace. The United States currently supports three standard RNP levels: RNP 0.3—Approach; RNP 1.0—Departure, Terminal; RNP 2.0—En route. RNP levels are actual distances from the centerline of the flightpath, which must be maintained for aircraft and obstacle separation. A critical component of RNP is the ability of the aircraft navigation system to monitor its achieved navigation performance, and to identify for the pilot whether the operational requirement is or is not being met during an operation. The RNP capability of an aircraft will vary depending upon the aircraft equipment and the navigation infrastructure. For example, an aircraft may be eligible for RNP 1, but may not be capable of RNP 1 operations due to limited NAVAID coverage or avionics failure.

16. How is ADS-B In information used for traffic situational awareness? (AC 90-114)

Most ADS-B In systems will include a flight deck traffic display depicting the relative position and related information of ADS-B-equipped aircraft presented on a plan view. This traffic display is only one component of the input and output devices collectively known as a cockpit display of traffic information (CDTI). The traffic display may be on a dedicated display or integrated into and presented on an existing display (e.g., navigation display (ND) or multifunction display (MFD)). In many installations, a moving map depicting key surface elements of the airport may be displayed when on the ground or within a predefined altitude/distance from an airport while airborne.

17. Does use of the CDTI relieve a flight crew of their responsibility to see and avoid other air traffic? (AC 90-114, 14 CFR 91.113)

No. The traffic display information should only be used to supplement what can be seen out the window (OTW), except when authorized to conduct certain ADS-B In operations such as ADS-B In Trail or CDTI assisted visual separation (CAVS) procedures. Pilots must always conduct OTW scans to see and avoid as required under 14 CFR §91.113(b). Unless specifically certified for the function, the traffic display is not intended for collision avoidance or self-separation.

18. Explain why certain ground and airborne traffic will not appear on an ADS-B traffic display. (AC 90-114)

Not all ground and airborne traffic will appear on the traffic display. The traffic display can only display properly equipped ADS-B Out traffic broadcasting on the received frequencies, and, depending on the operating location, Automatic Dependent Surveillance–Rebroadcast (ADS-R), ADS-R Same Link Rebroadcast (ADS-R SLR), TIS-B, and/or traffic alert and collision avoidance system (TCAS) (if installed) traffic. Additionally, the completeness of the traffic situational awareness information is affected by range, signal quality, and proper installation and function of the ADS-B Out system on the traffic aircraft.

19. Why is it important for flight crews to establish crew coordination procedures on the use of the CDTI and ADS-B In information prior to flight? (AC 90-114)

In crewed aircraft, it's important to establish and utilize crew coordination procedures to minimize head-down time.

20. In TCAS-equipped aircraft, does ADS-B In traffic display information replace guidance from a traffic advisory (TA) and/or RA? (AC 90-114)

No. CDTI traffic information does not replace any TA and/or RA provided by the aircraft's TCAS. RA response must be based on the TCAS display and approved procedures.

21. **Explain the term** *CDTI-assisted visual separation* **(CAVS).** (AC 90-114)

    CAVS (CDTI-assisted visual separation) is an ADS-B In application that assists the flight crew in maintaining separation from ADS-B Out-equipped aircraft during visual separation. Currently, CAVS authorization is only for the approach phase of flight when cleared by ATC to maintain visual separation from specific traffic.

22. **Describe how a flight crew should use CAVS during a visual approach to an airport.** (AC 90-114)

    Currently, CAVS may only be used during the approach phase of flight when cleared by ATC to maintain visual separation from specific traffic. Because of the accuracy and integrity of displayed traffic on ADS-B In systems approved for CAVS, CAVS information may be used as a substitute for continuous visual observation of traffic-to-follow (TTF) under specified conditions.

    Note: CAVS does not relieve the pilot of the responsibility to see and avoid other aircraft. ATC maintains separation responsibility from all other aircraft and for the orderly flow of traffic to the runway.

23. **What are ADS-B in-trail procedures (ITP)?** (AC 90-114)

    ITP are designed primarily for use in non-radar oceanic airspace to enable appropriately equipped ADS-B In aircraft to perform flight level changes previously unavailable with procedural separation minima applied. FAA authorization is required for all U.S. aircraft operators to conduct ITP operations using ADS-B In.

D. High Altitude Emergencies

1. **Explain what happens when an aircraft cabin decompresses.** (FAA-H-8083-25)

    Decompression is the inability of the aircraft's pressurization system to maintain the designed aircraft cabin pressure. For example, an aircraft is flying at an altitude of 29,000 feet but the aircraft cabin is pressurized to an altitude equivalent to 8,000 feet. If decompression occurs, the cabin pressure may become equivalent to that of the aircraft's altitude of 29,000 feet. The rate at which this occurs determines the severity of decompression.

2. **What are the two main causes of aircraft decompression?** (AC 61-107)

Decompression can be caused by a malfunction of the pressurization system itself or structural damage to the aircraft.

3. **Describe the signs of a rapid decompression in the cockpit.** (AC 61-107)

a. A cabin fog may occur because of the rapid drop in temperature and the change in relative humidity.

b. Air will escape from the lungs through the nose and mouth because of a sudden lower pressure outside of the lungs.

c. Differential air pressure on either side of the eardrum will occur but should clear automatically.

d. Exposure to wind blast and extremely cold temperatures.

4. **Explain the three types of aircraft decompression.** (AC 61-107)

Explosive decompression—A change in cabin pressure faster than the lungs can decompress. Most authorities consider any decompression that occurs in less than 0.5 seconds as explosive and potentially dangerous. This type of decompression is more likely to occur in small volume pressurized aircraft than in large pressurized aircraft and often results in lung damage. To avoid potentially dangerous flying debris in the event of an explosive decompression, properly secure all loose items such as baggage and oxygen cylinders.

Rapid decompression—A change in cabin pressure where the lungs can decompress faster than the cabin. The risk of lung damage is significantly lower in this decompression compared to an explosive decompression.

Gradual or slow decompression—A gradual or slow decompression is dangerous because it may not be detected. Automatic visual and aural warning systems generally provide an indication of a slow decompression.

5. What are the dangers of decompression?
(FAA-H-8083-25)

a. Proper use of oxygen equipment must be accomplished quickly to avoid hypoxia. Unconsciousness may occur in a very short time. The time of useful consciousness (TUC) is considerably shortened when a person is subjected to a rapid decompression, which causes a rapid reduction of pressure on the body leading to a quick exhalation of the oxygen in the lungs.

b. At higher altitudes where the pressure differential is greater, being tossed or blown out of the airplane is a danger if one is near an opening during a decompression. Those who must be near an opening should always wear safety harnesses or seatbelts when in pressurized aircraft.

c. Evolved gas decompression sickness (the bends).

d. Exposure to windblast and extreme cold.

6. Describe the general procedures required after experiencing a decompression at a high altitude.
(AC 61-107)

Immediately don oxygen masks and breathe 100 percent oxygen slowly. Descend to a safe altitude. If supplemental oxygen is not available, initiate an emergency descent to an altitude below 10,000 feet MSL. If symptoms of hypoxia are experienced and persist, land as soon as possible.

7. Why is slow decompression as dangerous as or more dangerous than a rapid or explosive decompression?
(AC 61-107)

During a slow decompression, the typical indications of a decompression (noise, flying debris, etc.) may not be evident. Furthermore, the insidious nature of hypoxia and depression of mental function decreases the ability to recognize the emergency and undertake appropriate recovery procedures. For those reasons, a slow decompression is the most dangerous, and the aviator must always be on guard against this insidious threat.

8. **Define the term *time of useful consciousness* (TUC).** (FAA-H-8083-25)

   TUC describes the maximum time the pilot has to make rational, life-saving decisions and carry them out at a given altitude without supplemental oxygen. As altitude increases above 10,000 feet, the symptoms of hypoxia increase in severity, and the TUC rapidly decreases. The TUC varies from 1 to 2 minutes at 30,000 feet MSL to only 9 to 15 seconds at 40,000 feet MSL.

9. **Pressurized aircraft that meet the requirements of 14 CFR Part 23 or 25 have cabin altitude warning systems that activate at what altitude?** (AC 61-107)

   10,000 feet. Pressurized aircraft meeting the more stringent requirements of Part 25 have automatic passenger oxygen mask dispensing devices that activate before exceeding 15,000 foot cabin altitude.

10. **When operating above FL250, activation of a cabin altitude warning would require flight crewmembers be capable of donning O$_2$ masks in what length of time?** (14 CFR 25.1447)

    Five seconds. The mask must be immediately available to the flight crewmember when seated at his station, and installed so that it can be placed on the face from its ready position with one hand, properly secured, sealed, and supplying oxygen upon demand, within five seconds and without disturbing eyeglasses or causing delay in proceeding with emergency duties.

11. **What are the four major physiological problems the flight crew and passengers would experience if the cabin suddenly decompressed from a cabin altitude of 7,000 feet to the aircraft's cruise altitude of 35,000 feet in 30 seconds?** (AC 61-107, CAMI)

    Hypoxia, decompression sickness, hypothermia, and spatial disorientation.

12. Explain altitude decompression sickness (DCS).
(FAA-H-8083-25)

DCS describes a condition characterized by a variety of symptoms resulting from exposure to low barometric pressures that cause inert gases (mainly nitrogen), normally dissolved in body fluids and tissues, to come out of physical solution and form bubbles. Nitrogen is an inert gas normally stored throughout the human body in physical solution. If the nitrogen is forced to leave the solution too rapidly, bubbles form in different areas of the body causing a variety of signs and symptoms. The most common symptom is joint pain, which is known as "the bends."

13. What actions should be taken if a pilot or passenger experiences altitude-induced DCS? (FAA-H-8083-25)

a. Put on oxygen mask immediately and switch the regulator to 100 percent oxygen.

b. Begin an emergency descent and land as soon as possible. Even if the symptoms disappear during descent, land and seek medical evaluation while continuing to breathe oxygen.

c. If one of the symptoms is joint pain, keep the affected area still; do not try to work pain out by moving the joint around.

d. Upon landing, seek medical assistance from an FAA medical officer, AME, military flight surgeon, or a hyperbaric medicine specialist. Be aware that a physician not specialized in aviation or hypobaric medicine may not be familiar with this type of medical problem.

e. Definitive medical treatment may involve the use of a hyperbaric chamber operated by specially trained personnel.

f. Delayed signs and symptoms of altitude-induced DCS can occur after return to ground level regardless of presence during flight.

14. Briefly describe the flight crew's actions in the event of a cabin fire at altitude. (AC 61-107, AC 120-80)

Because of the highly combustible composition of oxygen, if a fire breaks out during a flight at high altitude, pilots should initiate an immediate descent to an altitude that does not require oxygen. Additional procedures would include:

a. Immediately don oxygen masks and verify that the regulator is set to 100 percent.

b. Plan for an immediate descent and landing at the nearest suitable airport.

c. Do not use smoke/fume elimination procedures to combat a fire.

d   Do use smoke/fume elimination procedures to evacuate pollutants.

e. Do not reset circuit breakers, unless required for safe flight.

Note: Studies and experience indicate that flight crewmembers should begin planning for an emergency landing as soon as possible after the first indication of fire. Delaying the aircraft's descent by only a couple of minutes might make the difference between a successful landing and evacuation, and the complete loss of an aircraft and its occupants.

15. What general procedures are recommended when inadvertently flying through thunderstorm activity or known severe turbulence? (AC 61-107)

a. *Airspeed*—Critical for any type of turbulent air penetration. Use the AFM-recommended turbulence penetration target speed or, if unknown, fly an airspeed below maneuvering speed. Use of high airspeeds can result in structural damage and injury to passengers and crewmembers. Severe gusts may cause large and rapid variations in IAS. Do not chase airspeed.

b. *Altitude*—Penetration should be at an altitude that provides adequate maneuvering margins in case severe turbulence is encountered to avoid the potential for catastrophic upset.

c. *Autopilot*—If severe turbulence is penetrated with the autopilot on, the altitude hold mode should be off. If the autopilot has a pitch hold mode, it should be engaged. The autopilot pitch hold mode can usually maintain pitch more successfully than a pilot under stress. With the autopilot off, the yaw damper should be engaged. Controllability of the aircraft in turbulence becomes more difficult with the yaw damper off. Rudder controls should be centered before engaging the yaw damper.

d. *Lightning*—When flight through a thunderstorm cannot be avoided, turn up the intensity of panel and cabin lights so lightning does not cause temporary blindness. White lighting in the cockpit is better than red lighting during thunderstorms.

e. *Attitude and heading*—Keep wings level and maintain the desired pitch attitude and approximate heading. Do not attempt to turn around and fly out of the storm because the speed associated with thunderstorms usually makes such attempts unsuccessful. Use smooth, moderate control movements to resist changes in attitude. If large attitude changes occur, avoid abrupt or large control inputs. Avoid, as much as possible, use of the stabilizer trim in controlling pitch attitudes. Do not chase altitude.

E. Crew Communications

1. Explain the importance of effective communication in crew coordination and what crewmembers can do to improve their coordination during a flight. (AC 120-48)

Effective communication is a prerequisite for crew coordination between all crewmembers. Improving coordination between crewmembers lies not only in improving communication between them, but also in increasing their knowledge and awareness of each other's duties at each stage of the flight so they can be sensitive to each other's level of workload. This knowledge helps to avoid miscommunication, unrealistic expectations, and inappropriate requests of each other. During emergencies, each crewmember should know what to expect from the other crewmembers so they can work together effectively.

2. **What are some of the factors that can influence crew interpersonal communications?** (AC 120-51)

   External factors include communication barriers such as rank, age, gender, and organizational culture, including the identification of inadequate standard operating procedures (SOPs). Internal factors include speaking skills, listening skills, decision-making skills, conflict resolution techniques, and the use of appropriate assertiveness and advocacy.

3. **Describe several crewmember behaviors that help to ensure that necessary information is provided at the appropriate time, decisions are clearly communicated and understood, and crewmembers are actively engaged in the decision-making process.** (AC 120-51)

   a. Operational decisions are clearly stated to other crewmembers.

   b. Crewmembers acknowledge their understanding of decisions.

   c. "Bottom lines" for safety are established and communicated.

   d. The big picture and the game plan are shared within the team, including flight attendants and others as appropriate.

   e. Crewmembers are encouraged to state their own ideas, opinions, and recommendations.

   f. Efforts are made to provide an atmosphere that invites open and free communications.

   g. Initial entries and changed entries to automated systems are verbalized and acknowledged.

4. **What are several behavioral markers associated with crewmembers promoting the best course of action, even when it involves conflict with others?** (AC 120-51)

   a. Crewmembers speak up and state their information with appropriate persistence until there is some clear resolution.

   b. A "challenge and response" environment is developed.

   c. Questions are encouraged and are answered openly and nondefensively.

   d. Crewmembers are encouraged to question the actions and decisions of others.

e. Crewmembers seek help from others when necessary.

f. Crewmembers question status and programming of automated systems to confirm situation awareness.

5. Why is the preflight briefing considered the most important procedure for setting the stage for good coordination between flightcrew members and flight attendants? (AC 120-48)

The preflight briefing is considered the single most important procedure for setting the stage for good coordination between flightcrew members and flight attendants because it sets the expectations and tone for the flight. Conducting relevant and timely briefings, including feedback, supports effective communication. Additionally, most airlines consider the preflight briefing to be a standard operating procedure (SOP), highlighting its importance in ensuring safe and effective operations.

6. An effective captain's briefing addresses coordination, planning, and problems. Describe some of the behavioral markers of an effective captain's briefing. (AC 120-51)

a. Establishes an environment for open communications (e.g., the captain calls for questions or comments, answers questions directly, listens with patience, etc.).

b. Is interactive and emphasizes the importance of questions, critique, and the offering of information.

c. Establishes a "team concept" (e.g., the captain uses "we" language, encourages all to participate and to help with the flight).

d. Covers pertinent safety and security issues.

e. Identifies potential problems such as weather, delays, and abnormal system operations.

f. Provides guidelines for crew actions centered on standard operating procedures (SOP). Division of labor and crew workload is addressed.

g. Includes the cabin crew as part of the team.

h. Sets expectations for handling deviations from SOPs.

(continued)

i. Establishes guidelines for the operation of automated systems (e.g., when systems will be disabled, which programming actions must be verbalized and acknowledged).

j. Specifies duties and responsibilities with regard to automated systems for the pilot flying (PF) and the pilot monitoring (PM).

7. What information should be covered in the takeoff/departure and approach/landing briefings?
(FAA-S-ACS-11)

If the operator, aircraft manufacturer, or training provider has not specified a briefing, the briefing must cover the items appropriate for the conditions, such as: departure runway, departure procedure, power settings, speeds, abnormal or emergency procedures prior to or after reaching decision speed (i.e., V_1 or V_{MC}), emergency return intentions, go-around/rejected landing procedures, initial rate of descent, and what is expected of the other crewmembers during the takeoff and landing.

8. Give several examples of the type of information a good cockpit/cabin preflight briefing should contain.
(AC 120-48)

The preflight briefing should include, but is not limited to, the following topics:

a. Crew introductions/crew complement

b. Passenger count

c. Weather conditions

d. Security information

e. Aviation safety inspector (ASI), Federal Air Marshal (FAM), Federal Flight Deck Officer (FFDO), law enforcement officer (LEO), or jump seat riders

f. Preflight inspections, write-ups, or maintenance issues

g. Flight deck entry/exit procedures and jump seat and oxygen operation

h. Issues related to taxi, takeoff, and landing (e.g., short/long taxi)

i. Chimes used for normal and emergency signals

9. **Describe the types of briefings and debriefings that occur regularly during line operations.** (AC 121-42)

   a. Preflight briefing of the crew, including flight attendants if applicable, prior to the first flight of the day.

   b. Preflight briefing of the flight crew prior to a flight for which a higher than normal workload is expected due to circumstances such as icing conditions, items deferred per the minimum equipment list (MEL), and takeoff or landing from a special airport.

   c. Briefing of the flight crew prior to the PIC taking a rest break.

   d. Debriefing of the flight crew after a flight for which a higher than normal workload was encountered.

F. Checklist Philosophy

1. **Explain how a *challenge-do-verify* checklist is performed.** (drs.faa.gov)

   The challenge-do-verify (CDV) method consists of a crewmember making a challenge before an action is initiated, taking the action, and then verifying that the action item has been accomplished. The CDV method is most effective when one crewmember issues the challenge and the second crewmember takes the action and responds to the first crewmember, verifying that the action was taken. This method requires that the checklist be accomplished methodically, one item at a time, in an unvarying sequence.

2. **What are the advantages and disadvantages of using the CDV method for checklist accomplishment?** (drs.faa.gov)

   The primary advantage of the CDV method is the deliberate and systematic manner in which each action item must be accomplished. The CDV method keeps all crewmembers involved (in the loop), provides for concurrence from a second crewmember before an action is taken, and provides positive confirmation that the action was accomplished. The disadvantages of the CDV method are that it is rigid and inflexible and that crewmembers cannot accomplish different tasks at the same time.

3. Explain how to accomplish a *do-verify* checklist. (drs.faa.gov)

The do-verify (DV) method (or clean-up method) consists of the checklist being accomplished in a variable sequence without a preliminary challenge. After all of the action items on the checklist have been completed, the checklist is then read again while each item is verified. The DV method allows the flight crew to use flow patterns from memory to accomplish a series of actions quickly and efficiently. Each individual crewmember can work independently, which helps balance the workload between crewmembers. The DV method has a higher inherent risk of an item on the checklist being missed than does the CDV method.

4. What is the significance of immediate action items found on some checklists? (drs.faa.gov)

An immediate action item (also known as a memory item) is an action that must be accomplished so expeditiously (in order to avoid or stabilize a hazardous situation) that time is not available for a crewmember to refer to a manual or checklist. Crewmembers must be so familiar with these actions that they can perform them correctly and reliably from memory. Situations that require immediate action include, but are not limited to the following:

a. Imminent threat of crewmember incapacitation.

b. Imminent threat of loss of aircraft control.

c. Imminent threat of destruction of a system or component that makes continued safety of the flight and subsequent landing improbable.

5. Why do emergency checklists require the pilots to "call for checklist" after completion of the immediate action items? (drs.faa.gov)

After completion of the immediate action items, and the emergency has been brought under control, the pilot should call for the actual checklist, so as to verify that all initial immediate action items on the emergency checklist were accomplished. Only after this is done should the remainder of the checklist be completed. This procedure ensures that the emergency is dealt with quickly and efficiently and that all immediate action items are completed first.

6. Describe some of the common errors that flight crews make when using checklists. (AC 120-71)

a. Crew overlooked item(s) on the checklist.

b. Crew failed to verify settings visually.

c. Operator or aircraft manufacturer checklist contained error(s) or was incomplete.

d. Failing to complete a step after an interruption.

e. Failing to complete a checklist.

f. Completing the wrong checklist

g. Difficulty in finding a checklist.

h. Becoming disoriented within the checklist.

i. Difficulty in confirming that the checklist action was carried out correctly.

j. Problems in understanding and interpreting the checklist.

k. Difficulty in determining who should be carrying out the checklist actions (PF vs. PM).

7. How can a flight crew prevent making errors when using checklists? (AC 120-71)

a. Remember to use the checklist.

b. Check every item, every time.

c. Slow down and confirm significant items.

d. Deliberately read the checklist.

e. If interrupted, restart from the beginning.

8. What is the function of standard callouts made by flight crews? (AC 120-71, AFM)

Standard callouts for basic operations should be established to ensure that the flight crew functions as a well-coordinated team and maintains the situational awareness necessary for safe operation of the aircraft. The PM should be assigned the responsibility for monitoring the flight progress and for providing callouts to the PF for each significant transition point, event, or failure condition.

9. What are examples of standard callouts for basic IFR operations? (AC 120-71, AFM)

a. During climb to assigned altitude, the PM should provide a callout when passing through the transition altitude (as a reminder to reset the altimeters) and when approaching 1,000 feet below assigned altitude.

b. During cruise, the PM should provide a callout when the aircraft altitude deviates by 200 feet or more from the assigned altitude.

c. During descent from enroute flight altitude to initial approach altitude, the PM should provide a callout when approaching 1,000 feet above the assigned altitude, an altitude where a speed reduction is required (e.g. 10,000 feet in the U.S.), 1,000 feet above the initial approach altitude (above field elevation for approaches in VFR conditions), and when passing the transition level.

10. What are examples of standard callouts for IFR Category I approaches? (AC 120-71, AFM)

a. *Beginning the final approach segment*—Prior to this, a callout should be provided to cross-check the altimeter settings and instrument indications and to confirm the status of warning flags for the flight and navigation instruments and other critical systems.

b. *Rate of descent callouts*—If the flight altitude is less than 2,000 feet AGL, the PM should provide a callout when the rate of descent exceeds 2,000 fpm. Additionally, a callout should be provided when the rate of descent exceeds 1,000 fpm if the flight altitude is less than 1,000 feet AGL.

c. *Altitude callouts*—The PM should provide a callout at 1,000 feet above the landing elevation to confirm aircraft configuration and to cross-check the flight and navigation instruments. For approaches conducted in IFR conditions, the PM should also provide a callout at 100 feet above the MDA or DH (as applicable) followed by a callout upon arriving at the MDA or DH.

d. *Airspeed callouts*—The PM should provide a callout at any point in the approach when the airspeed is below the planned speed for the existing aircraft configuration. If the aircraft has entered the final approach segment, a callout should also be provided when the airspeed exceeds 10 knots above the planned final approach speed.

e. *Visual cue callouts*—The PM should provide a callout when the visual cues required to continue the approach by visual reference are acquired, such as "approach lights" or "runway." This callout should not be made unless the available visual cues meet the requirements of 14 CFR §91.116 for descent below the MDA or DH.

f. *Destabilized approach callouts*—Any time approach becomes destabilized (approach criteria not met). The approach is destabilized if the criteria for a stabilized approach are not met and maintained.

g. *Approach profile callouts*—The PM should provide a callout if the aircraft deviates from the proper approach profile during any portion of an instrument approach.

11. What additional callouts should be made during the final approach segment of an instrument approach procedure? (AC 120-71, AFM)

a. The PM should provide a callout if the aircraft has entered the final approach segment of an ILS/MLS approach and the localizer (azimuth) displacement exceeds 1/3 dot and/or the glide-slope (elevation) displacement is greater than one dot.

b. For localizer (azimuth) based approaches, a callout should be made if the displacement exceeds 1/3 dot during the final approach segment.

c. For VOR based approaches, a callout should be made if the displacement exceeds 2 degrees during the final approach segment.

d. For performance-based approaches that include both lateral and vertical guidance, the PNF should provide a callout if the aircraft deviates from the proper approach profile during any portion of an instrument approach.

G. Operational Control

1. Define the term *operational control*. (14 CFR Part 1, AC 120-101)

Operational control, with respect to a flight, means the exercise of authority over initiating, conducting, or terminating a flight.

2. Who has operational control authority in a domestic or flag operation? (AC 120-101)

Each domestic or flag certificate holder is responsible for operational control. For such operations, the aircraft dispatcher and PIC exercise joint responsibility for the preflight planning, delay, and dispatch release of a flight. They are responsible for ensuring that all flight operations under their control are conducted safely in accordance with all applicable regulations and operations specifications.

3. Who has operational control authority in a supplemental operation? (AC 120-101)

Each supplemental certificate holder is responsible for operational control. For supplemental operations, the PIC and director of operations (DO) or designee (flight follower) are responsible for initiation, diversion, and termination of a flight in accordance with all applicable regulations and ops specs.

4. What is an aircraft dispatcher? (AC 120-101)

An aircraft dispatcher is an airman certificated under Part 65 who exercises joint responsibility with the PIC in the safe conduct of flight(s) in connection with any civil aircraft in air commerce. The aircraft dispatcher must be current and qualified for the operation being conducted. All domestic and flag operators must use certified aircraft dispatchers to directly control flight operations.

5. If a captain (PIC) is in disagreement with an aircraft dispatcher over whether a flight can be made safely, can the flight depart? (14 CFR 121.663)

A PIC may not initiate or continue a flight unless both the PIC and the aircraft dispatcher agree that the flight can be conducted safely as planned under the existing and forecast conditions.

6. **Describe some of the responsibilities of a domestic or flag aircraft dispatcher.** (AC 120-101)

   Dispatcher functions include, but are not limited to the following:

   a. Planning a flight.

   b. Preparing and disseminating the dispatch release.

   c. Monitoring the progress of each flight.

   d. Issuing additional information for the safety of flight to include weather, airport conditions, Notices to Air Missions (NOTAMs), status of navigation aides, etc.

   e. Delaying a flight, if in the opinion of the aircraft dispatcher and PIC the flight cannot be conducted safely.

   f. Canceling a potentially unsafe flight.

7. **What is a dispatch release?** (AC 120-101)

   A flight conducted under Part 121 domestic or flag rules may not depart from the point of origin unless a dispatch release contains specific authorization for the flight between specified points. The dispatch release may be for a single flight or for a series of flights with intermediate stops. It is a legal document signed by the PIC and aircraft dispatcher stating the agreed-upon conditions under which the flight will be operated safely. Regulations require the release to be amended if the agreed-upon conditions change.

8. **What is a flight follower?** (AC 120-101)

   The flight follower is typically a designee of the DO who is appropriately trained and who may be delegated the functions (i.e., authority) of initiating, continuing, diverting and terminating a flight with the PIC. However, the DO may not delegate the responsibility of initiating, continuing, continuing, diverting and terminating a flight.

9. **Explain the difference between a dispatch release and a flight release.** (AC 120-101)

   A dispatch release is a legal document required for domestic and flag operations flights. A flight release is the legal document required for supplemental operation flights.

H. Ground Operations

1. What is a runway incursion? (FAA-H-8083-16)

A runway incursion is any occurrence in the airport runway environment involving an aircraft, vehicle, person, or object on the ground that creates a collision hazard or results in a loss of required separation with an aircraft taking off, intending to take off, landing, or intending to land.

2. What are three major areas that contribute to runway incursions? (FAA-H-8083-3)

a. *Communications*—misunderstanding the given clearance; failure to communicate effectively.

b. *Airport knowledge*—failure to navigate the airport correctly; unable to interpret airport signage.

c. *Cockpit procedures for maintaining orientation*—failure to maintain situational awareness.

3. If ATC instructs an aircraft to "taxi to" an assigned takeoff runway, does that authorize the aircraft to cross all runways that the taxi route intersects? (AIM 4-3-18)

No, a clearance must be obtained prior to crossing any runway. ATC will issue an explicit clearance for all runway crossings. When assigned a takeoff runway, ATC will first specify the runway, issue taxi instructions, and state any hold short instructions or runway crossing clearances if the taxi route will cross a runway.

4. Thorough planning for taxi operations is essential for a safe operation. What information should a flight crew plan and brief prior to taxi operations? (AC 91-73, AC 120-74)

a. Review and understand airport signage, markings, and lighting.

b. Review the airport diagram, planned taxi route, and identify any hot spots.

c. Review the latest airfield NOTAMs and ATIS (if available) for taxiway/runway closures, construction activity, etc.

d. Conduct a pre-taxi/pre-landing briefing that includes the expected/assigned taxi route and any hold short lines and restrictions based on ATIS information or previous experience at the airport.

e. Plan for critical times and locations on the taxi route (complex intersections, crossing runways, etc.).

f. Plan to complete as many aircraft checklist items as possible at the gate prior to taxi.

5. How can a flight crew increase their situational awareness during airport surface operations? (SAFO 11004)

a. All pilots display the current airport diagram for immediate reference during taxi.

b. Cross reference the heading indicator to ensure turns are being made in the correct direction and you are following the assigned taxi route.

c. Exercise increased awareness when taxing between parallel runways.

d. Wait until you have exited the runway and you are sure of your taxi clearance prior to beginning an after-landing checklist, or non-essential communications.

6. What crew resource management (CRM) procedures can a flight crew use while taxiing to mitigate the risk of committing a runway incursion? (SAFO 11004)

a. Use CRM to control crew workload and reduce distractions.

b. Keep other crewmembers in the loop by announcing when going "heads down," and also reporting "back up, are there any changes?"

c. Approaching a clearance limit, verbalize the hold short clearance limit.

d. Prior to crossing any hold short line, visually check to ensure there is no conflicting traffic on the runway. Verbalize "clear right, clear left."

7. What is an airport surface hot spot?
(Chart Supplement U.S.)

A hot spot is a runway safety-related problem area on an airport that presents increased risk during surface operations. Typically, hot spots are complex or confusing taxiway-taxiway or taxiway-runway intersections. The area of increased risk has either a history of or potential for runway incursions or surface incidents due to a variety of causes, such as but not limited to: airport layout, traffic flow, airport marking, signage and lighting, situational awareness, and training. Hot spots are depicted on airport diagrams as circles or polygons designated as HS1, HS2, etc.

8. What are airport movement areas? (AC 150/5300-19)

Movement areas are the runways, taxiways, and other areas of an airport/heliport which are utilized for taxiing/hover taxiing, air taxiing, takeoff, and landing of aircraft, exclusive of loading ramps and parking areas. At those airports/heliports with a tower, specific approval for entry onto the movement area must be obtained from ATC.

9. What are standardized or coded taxi routes?
(FAA-H-8083-16)

Standardized taxi routes are coded taxi routes that follow typical taxiway traffic patterns to move aircraft between gates and runways. ATC issues clearances using these coded routes to reduce radio communication and eliminate taxi instruction misinterpretation.

10. Describe several potential challenges and barriers to effective pilot monitoring. (AC 120-71)

a. *Time pressure*—Can exacerbate high workload and increase errors. It can also lead to rushing and "looking without seeing."

b. *Lack of feedback to pilots when monitoring lapses occur*—Pilots are often unaware that monitoring performance has degraded.

c. *Design of SOPs*—SOPs may fail to explicitly address monitoring tasks.

d. *Pilots' inadequate mental model of autoflight system modes*—Pilots may not have a complete or accurate understanding of all functions and behaviors of the autoflight system.

e. *Training*—May overlook the importance of monitoring and how to do it effectively. Lack of emphasis on monitoring may occur in training and evaluation.

f. *Pilot performance*—High workload, distraction, and inattention can all lead to monitoring errors.

11. What phraseology will ATC use to instruct a pilot to taxi onto the runway and await takeoff clearance? (AIM 5-2-5)

Line up and wait (LUAW) is an ATC procedure designed to position an aircraft onto the runway for an imminent departure. The ATC instruction "line up and wait" is used to instruct a pilot to taxi onto the departure runway and line up and wait. If landing traffic is a factor during LUAW operations, ATC will inform the aircraft in position of the closest traffic within six flying miles requesting a full-stop, touch-and-go, stop-and-go, or an unrestricted low approach to the same runway.

I. Leadership and Professionalism

1. Define the term *leadership*. (AC 121-42)

Leadership can be defined as a relational process that emphasizes the ability to exercise skill to achieve a goal, is both proactive and reactive, and necessarily takes into account other members of the group. In flight operations, leadership is a proactive process by the PIC that considers other crewmembers (including flight attendants, as applicable) and uses all available resources to achieve a safe flight in a professional manner in accordance with SOPs.

2. Describe several characteristics of a good leader. (AC 121-42)

Characteristics that could influence the PICs ability to lead include confidence, focus, decisiveness, adaptability, accountability, honesty, professionalism, and the ability to inspire others. A PIC should understand how leadership characteristics can influence and improve situation awareness, proactive decision making, and communication with others, including receptivity to feedback and active listening.

3. **Describe how to apply leadership skills in the position of pilot-in-command.** (AC 61-138)

   a. *Authority*—The PIC is the final authority as to the operation of the airplane. Use that authority wisely and appropriately considering the situation.

   b. *Responsibility*—The PIC is responsible for the tone, pace, and the outcome of decisions made and will be held accountable for all outcomes. Decisions produce actions and actions have consequences. The captain is responsible for enforcing organizational, procedural, and FAA standards.

   c. *Sound decisions*—The PIC is not operating in a vacuum and should consider all available input, but is ultimately required and expected to make sound, safe decisions.

   d. *Awareness*—The PIC is expected to be operating the airplane with the "big picture" in mind. Situational awareness is paramount when making decisions.

   e. *Mentoring*—The PIC should always be preparing first officers for upgrade. Explaining operational considerations, decision making factors, and lessons learned is an essential function of a captain.

4. **Effective mentoring should include what skills?** (AC 121-43)

   a. Good listening and effective communication skills.
   b. Being approachable and responsive to protégés.
   c. Credibility and integrity.
   d. Technical expertise and job-related knowledge.
   e. Empathy and patience.

5. **Define the term *professionalism*.** (FAA-H-8083-30)

   Though not all inclusive, the following list provides major considerations and qualifications that should be included in the definition of professionalism:

   a. Professionalism exists only when a service is performed for someone or for the common good.

   b. Professionalism is achieved only after extended training and preparation.

c. Professionalism is performance based on study and research.

d. Professionalism is reasoning logically and accurately.

e. Professionalism is making good judgment decisions.

f. Professionalism is not limiting actions and decisions to standard patterns and practices.

g. Professionalism demands a code of ethics.

h. Professionalism is being true to one's values and ethics and to those being served. Anything less than a sincere performance is quickly detected and immediately destroys effectiveness.

6. What responsibility does a pilot have with regards to their own professional development? (AC 61-138)

Learning never stops: a responsible pilot will always seek more training, instruction, or professional development. Be honest with yourself and be ready to critique your performance. Know your strengths and weaknesses. First officers should always be preparing to upgrade.

7. Explain the professional responsibilities associated with being an airline transport pilot. (AC 61-138)

a. *Proficiency*—It's important to be technically proficient. It is critical that each pilot be thoroughly knowledgeable about his or her responsibilities and the aircraft.

b. *Welfare of crew and passengers*—The pilots must always have regard for the welfare of the crew and passengers. The passengers' lives and well-being are in the hands of the crew.

c. *Trust and professionalism*—It is critical that the crew's actions communicate trust and professionalism. Each action a crewmember takes is a reflection of yourself, your company, and the pilot profession.

8. Why should PICs consider adapting their personal leadership and supervision styles to different situations, including the experiences and attributes of other crewmembers? (AC 121-42)

Depending on the situation and other persons involved, an effective leader may perform different roles involving exercising or emphasizing specific leadership characteristics. PICs may have personality types that value different leadership characteristics differently, and should have evidence-based instruction recognizing the advantages and disadvantages to their default or preferred leadership style. PICs should consider how they can adapt their personal leadership and supervision styles to varying situations, including the experience and attributes of other crewmembers.

9. Define the term *normalization of deviance*. (AC 121-42)

The normalization of deviance can be defined as a gradual process during which nonstandard practices or actions become the norm through repetitive application with no corrective action.

10. Describe several examples of normalization of deviance. (AC 121-42)

a. Nonessential conversations between crewmembers during sterile flight deck contrary to 14 CFR §121.542(b).

b. Use of a personal laptop computer or tablet by a flight crewmember during cruise flight contrary to §121.542(d).

c. A pilot not using the oxygen mask when the other pilot has left the flight deck duty station when operating above FL410 contrary to §121.333(c)(3).

d. Not completing the cruise checklist.

e. Continuation of an un-stabilized approach contrary to the stabilized approach criteria stated in the air carrier/operator/program manager's SOPs.

11. How can a PIC contribute to the prevention of the normalization of deviance? (AC 121-42)

a. Acknowledge and reinforce that the SOPs are designed to achieve consistently safe flight operations through adherence by all crewmembers.

b. Recognize situations that increase vulnerability to non-standard procedures or actions, such as time pressure, complacency, fatigue, and boredom.

c. Don't tolerate non-standard procedures or actions by other crewmembers, even when the non-standard action appears minor.

d. Use the air carrier/operator/program manager's safety reporting system to report any SOP that is impractical or ineffective instead of "working around" the SOP.

J. Crew Resource Management

1. Explain the term *crew resource management* (CRM). (AC 120-51)

CRM refers to the effective use of all available resources: human resources, hardware, and information. Other groups routinely working with the cockpit crew, who are involved in decisions required to operate a flight safely, are also essential participants in an effective CRM process. These groups include but are not limited to aircraft dispatchers, flight attendants, maintenance personnel, and air traffic controllers.

2. Are Part 121 and 135 carriers required to provide CRM training to crewmembers? (AC 120-51, 14 CFR 121.419, 135.330)

All Part 121 operators are required by regulations to provide CRM training for pilots and flight attendants, and dispatch resource management (DRM) training for aircraft dispatchers. Certificate holders conducting operations under part 135 are also required to include CRM in their training programs for crewmembers, including pilots and flight attendants.

3. What are the five focus points of CRM training?
(AC 120-51)

CRM training focuses on situational awareness, communication skills, teamwork, task allocation, and decision making.

4. What are some of the characteristics of effective CRM?
(AC 120-51)

a. Effective CRM is a comprehensive system of applying human factors concepts to improve crew performance.

b. Embraces all operational personnel.

c. Can be blended into all forms of aircrew training.

d. Concentrates on crewmembers' attitudes and behaviors and their impact on safety.

e. Uses the crew as the unit of training.

f. Training that requires the active participation of all crewmembers. It provides an opportunity for individuals and crews to examine their own behavior, and to make decisions on how to improve cockpit teamwork.

5. Provide several examples of CRM skills a captain should use when exercising their authority and responsibility as PIC. (AC 120-54)

a. Distribute workload and prioritize between primary and distracting duties.

b. Communicate plans and decisions to the crew.

c. Enforce standardization, policies, and procedures.

d. Set expectations for maintaining vigilance and avoiding complacency.

e. Respond to any safety-related concern raised by any crewmember.

f. Develop and enhance the aviation skill and knowledge of junior crewmembers.

g. Review operational irregularities and establish bottom lines.

h. Communicate intentions, "bottom lines," and decisions to all crewmembers.

6. **Provide several examples of CRM skills a first officer should employ when exercising their responsibility as first officer.** (AC 120-54)

   a. Cross-check and back the captain up. This requires maintaining vigilance and flying proficiency. It also includes effective monitoring of the situation.

   b. Report to the captain any safety-related concern and request a plan or decision if none is articulated.

   c. Support decisions articulated by the captain within the limits of safety, legality, and procedure.

   d. Develop your proficiency and take the best from each captain you work with.

   e. Maintain situational awareness.

   f. Prepare, plan, and maintain vigilance—be prepared for what you can reasonably expect.

   g. Carry out actions or decisions based on priorities and crew workload established by the captain.

   h. Identify systemic traps.

   i. Be aware of the limits of human performance and the nature of human error.

   j. Establish effective communications.

   k. Conduct or contribute to briefings—keep your head in the game and work to get ahead of it.

   l. Maintain a communications loop—acknowledge commands, statements, and questions of crewmembers.

7. **What practical application provides a pilot with an effective method to practice single pilot resource management (SRM)?** (FAA-H-8083-2)

   The 5P checklist consists of the plan, the plane, the pilot, the passengers, and the programming. It is based on the idea that the pilots have essentially five variables that impact their environment and can cause the pilot to make a single critical decision or several less critical decisions that when added together can create a critical outcome. A pilot should adopt a scheduled review of each of these critical variables at points in the flight where decisions are most likely to be effective.

8. **An effective briefing, which is primarily a captain's responsibility, should address what points?** (AC 120-51)

   An effective briefing should address coordination, planning, and potential problems.

9. **CRM training is comprised of what three main components?** (AC 120-51)

   Initial indoctrination/awareness, recurrent practice and feedback, and continual reinforcement.

10. **Explain the responsibilities of the pilot flying and the pilot monitoring.** (AC 120-71)

    The pilot flying is the pilot who is controlling the path of the aircraft at any given time, in flight or on the ground. The pilot monitoring monitors the aircraft state and system status, calls out any perceived or potential deviations from the intended flightpath, and intervenes if necessary.

11. **Describe the duties that contribute to more effective monitoring by the PM.** (AC 120-71)

    a. Follow SOPs consistently.

    b. Clearly communicate deviations to the PF and other crewmembers.

    c. Effectively manage distractions.

    d. Remain vigilant.

    e. Advise the PF if the flight guidance modes or aircraft actions do not agree with expected or desired actions and intervene if necessary.

    f. Continuously compare known pitch/power settings to current flightpath performance.

    g. Consider that the PFD, ND, and other sources of information (electronic flight bag (EFB)), might be displaying incorrect information and always be on the lookout for other evidence that confirms or disconfirms the information the displays are providing.

12. **Explain effective CRM intervention strategies that can be used by the PM.** (AC 61-138)

    a. Establish a positive attitude toward monitoring and challenging errors made by the PF.

    b. Discuss the methods that can be used to enhance the monitoring and challenging functions of both PF and PM.

    c. Appropriate questioning among pilots is a desirable CRM behavior and part of a healthy safety culture.

13. **Sometimes the roles and associated tasks of the PF and PM are not clearly defined or can become confused during flight. How would you describe the roles and responsibilities of the PF and PM?** (AC 120-71)

    a. At any point in time during the flight, one pilot is the PF and one pilot is the PM.

    b. The PF is responsible for managing, and the PM is responsible for monitoring the current and projected flightpath and energy of the aircraft at all times.

    c. The PF is always engaged in flying the aircraft (even when the aircraft is under AP control) and avoids tasks or activities that distract from that engagement.

    d. Transfer of PF and PM roles should be done positively with verbal assignment and verbal acceptance to include a short brief of aircraft state.

    e. The PM supports the PF at all times, staying abreast of aircraft state and ATC instructions and clearances.

    f. The PM monitors the aircraft state and system status, calls out any perceived or potential deviations from the intended flightpath, and intervenes if necessary.

K. Safety Culture

1. What is threat and error management (TEM)? (AC 120-35)

TEM is a framework or strategy for employing the traditional CRM skill sets. TEM promotes safe operations through the continuous process of identifying, avoiding, mitigating, or managing threats (external errors, conditions, or situations), internal errors, or undesired aircraft states.

2. What are the three main components of the TEM model? (AC 120-90)

Threats, errors, and undesired aircraft states.

3. What is the definition of a *threat*? (AC 120-90)

A threat is defined as an event or error that occurs outside the influence of the flight crew (i.e., it was not caused by the crew), increases the operational complexity of a flight, and requires crew attention and management if safety margins are to be maintained.

4. What are the two categories of threats? (AC 120-90)

a. *External threats from the environment*—adverse weather, airport conditions, terrain, traffic, and ATC.

b. *Internal treats emanating from within the airline*—aircraft malfunctions and MEL items, problems, interruptions, or errors from dispatch, cabin, ground, maintenance, and the ramp.

5. What are several examples of environmental threats? (AC 120-90)

a. *Weather*—wind shear, cross winds, turbulence, t-storms, icing, density altitude.

b. *Airport*—construction, complex taxiways, lack of or confusing signs and markings, contaminated runways.

c. *ATC*—non-standard phraseology, frequency congestion, controller error.

d. *Terrain*—lack of visual references, high or rising terrain.

6. **Describe several examples of internal organizational threats.** (AC 120-90)

    a. *Dispatch*—release paperwork unavailable or error.

    b. *Cabin*—flight attendant errors, passenger event or disruption, cabin service error.

    c. *Operational pressures*—due to late aircraft, crew swaps, aircraft swap.

    d. *Aircraft*—unexpected maintenance, automation problem.

7. **What are examples of threats that would be considered highly time critical?** (AC 120-90)

    Smoke in the cockpit/cabin, a fire, any life-threatening condition (loss of cabin pressure, etc.).

8. **What is the definition of an *error*?** (AC 120-90)

    Crew error is defined as action or inaction that leads to a deviation from crew or organizational intentions or expectations. Errors in the operational context tend to reduce the margin of safety and increase the probability of adverse events. A mismanaged error is defined as an error that is linked to or induces additional error or an undesired aircraft state.

9. **What are the three main categories of errors?** (AC 120-90)

    a. *Handling errors*—flight controls, automation.

    b. *Procedural errors*—checklists, briefings, callouts.

    c. *Communication errors*—with ATC, ground, or pilot-to-pilot.

10. **How can flight crews reduce the likelihood and frequency of errors occurring on the flight deck?** (hf.faa.gov)

    Flight crews should always strive to adhere to basic CRM principles such as:

    a. *Briefings*—complete preflight and in-flight crew briefings.

    b. *Checklists*—proper completion of all checklists.

    c. *Callouts*—critical avionic settings and flight data callouts.

    (continued)

d. *Checking*—cross-checking with readback by another crew member.

e. *Procedures*—strict adherence to SOPs.

f. *Phraseology*—use of standard phraseology in clear, unambiguous messages.

11. What is an undesired aircraft state (UAS)? (AC 120-90)

A UAS is defined as a position, condition, or attitude of an aircraft that clearly reduces safety margins and is a result of actions by the flight crew. It is a safety-compromising state that results from ineffective error management.

12. Describe several examples of an undesired aircraft state. (AC 120-90)

Examples of UAS include unstable approaches, lateral deviations, firm landings, and proceeding towards wrong taxiway/runway. As with errors, UAS can be managed effectively, returning the aircraft to safe flight, or the crew action or inaction can induce an additional error, incident, or accident.

13. Describe examples of crew behaviors that are considered to be threat and error countermeasures. (AC 120-90)

a. *Planning countermeasures*—Planning, preparation, briefings, and contingency management are essential for managing anticipated and unexpected threats.

b. *Execution countermeasures*—Monitor/cross-check, taxiway/runway management, workload, and automation management are essential for error detection and error response.

c. *Review/modify countermeasures*—Evaluation of plans and inquiry are essential for managing the changing conditions of a flight.

14. Do TEM countermeasures include equipment and procedural countermeasures? (AC 120-90)

Warning systems such as GPWS and weather alerts can be considered threat countermeasures, just as checklists and well-written procedures provide the means for error avoidance and error detection.

15. What is a safety management system (SMS)?
(AC 120-92)

SMS is the formal, top-down, organization-wide approach to managing safety risk and assuring the effectiveness of safety risk controls. It includes systematic procedures, practices, and policies for the management of safety risk.

16. What are the four functional components of an SMS?
(AC 120-92)

a. *Safety policy*—Establishes senior management's commitment to continually improve safety; defines the methods, processes, and organizational structure needed to meet safety goals.

b. *Safety risk management*—Determines the need for, and adequacy of, new or revised risk controls based on the assessment of acceptable risk.

c. *Safety assurance*—Evaluates the continued effectiveness of implemented risk control strategies; supports the identification of new hazards.

d. *Safety promotion*—Includes training, communication, and other actions to create a positive safety culture within all levels of the workforce.

17. Briefly describe the following safety culture programs.
(AC 00-46, AC 120-82, AC 120-90, AC 120-92, AC 120-66)

Aviation Safety Reporting System (ASRS)—A voluntary, confidential, and non-punitive incident reporting system funded by the FAA and administered by NASA. It receives, processes, and analyzes reports of unsafe occurrences and hazardous situations that are voluntarily submitted by pilots, ATC, and others. The information is used to identify hazards and safety discrepancies in the National Airspace System. It is also used to formulate policy and to strengthen the foundation of aviation human factors safety research. (AC 00-46)

Flight operational quality assurance (FOQA)—A voluntary program for the routine collection and analysis of digital flight data generated during aircraft operations. It is another potential tool in an operator's SMS to monitor operational data and provides data analysis and assessment. (AC 120-82)

(continued)

Line operations safety audit (LOSA)—A formal process that requires expert and highly trained observers to ride the jumpseat during regularly scheduled flights to collect safety-related data on environmental conditions, operational complexity, and flight crew performance. Confidential data collection and non-jeopardy assurance for pilots are fundamental to the process. (AC 120-90)

Safety management system (SMS)—The formal, top-down, organization-wide approach to managing safety risk and assuring the effectiveness of safety risk controls. It includes systematic procedures, practices, and policies for the management of safety risk. (AC 120-92)

Aviation safety action program (ASAP)—An ASAP provides a vehicle whereby employees of participating air carriers and repair station certificate holders can identify and report safety issues to management and to the FAA for resolution, without fear that the FAA will use reports accepted under the program to take legal enforcement action against them, or that companies will use such information to take disciplinary action. (AC 120-66)

18. Describe an airline advanced qualification program (AQP). (AC 120-54)

An AQP is a voluntary alternative to the traditional regulatory requirements under Parts 121 and 135 for pilot training and checking. Under an AQP, the FAA is authorized to approve significant departures from traditional requirements, subject to justification of an equivalent or better level of safety. The program entails a systematic front-end analysis of training requirements from which explicit proficiency objectives for all facets of pilot training are derived. It replaces programmed hours with proficiency-based training and evaluation derived from a detailed job task analysis that includes CRM.

19. What is line oriented flight training (LOFT)? (AC 120-54, AC 120-35)

A line operational simulation (LOS) flight scenario designed for training purposes to provide practice in the integration of technical and CRM skills. LOFT is conducted using a complete cockpit flight crew to the maximum extent feasible and is accomplished in an FAA-certified simulation device. For additional information, see AC 120-35.

20. What is a line operational evaluation (LOE)? (AC 120-54)

An LOE is a primary proficiency evaluation that addresses the individual's ability to demonstrate technical and CRM skills appropriate to fulfilling job requirements in a full mission scenario environment. The intent of an LOE is to evaluate and verify that an individual's job knowledge, technical skills, and CRM skills are commensurate with AQP qualification standards. The LOE is conducted in a simulation device approved for its intended use in the AQP. Under extenuating circumstances, the AQP proficiency evaluation may be accomplished in an aircraft, subject to FAA approval.

21. What is a line operational simulation (LOS)? (AC 120-54)

A LOS is a simulator or FTD training session conducted in a line environment setting. LOS includes LOFT, LOE, and special purpose operational training (SPOT). For additional information, see AC 120-35.

L. Operations Specifications

1. What are operations specifications? (14 CFR 119.7, drs.faa.gov)

Operations specifications (ops specs) outline the specific operations that a Part 125 certificate holder is allowed to conduct and any deviations the certificate holder has been granted. They also supplement the operating rules and contain limitations not addressed in the regulations. Often the regulations require that certain authorizations and limitations be written in the ops specs. This could include additional requirements for emergency equipment or personnel required for that particular operation but not indicated in the regulations.

2. What operations are governed by Part 119?
(14 CFR 119.1, AC 120-49)

Part 119 establishes the general certification requirements for air carriers and commercial operators. Part 119 contains the following provisions:

a. Definitions appropriate to air operator certification.

b. Roadmap to determine the appropriate operating rules (Part 121, 125, or 135) for the kind of operations.

c. Common certification requirements for Parts 121 and 135 (i.e., ops specs, management personnel).

d. Miscellaneous safety provisions common to Parts 121 and 135 (i.e., wet leasing, emergency operations).

3. Are the operations specifications regulatory for an air carrier or commercial operator? (14 CFR 119.1, FAA-H-8083-16)

The operations specifications are an extension of the Code of Federal Regulations, making them a legal, binding contract between a properly certificated air transportation organization and the FAA for compliance with the CFRs applicable to their operation.

4. For a certificate holder conducting domestic, flag, or commuter operations, describe the type of information the specifications must contain. (14 CFR 119.49)

a. The specific location of the certificate holder's principal base of operations.

b. Business names under which the certificate holder may operate.

c. Type of aircraft, registration markings, and serial numbers of each aircraft authorized for use, each regular and alternate airport to be used in scheduled operations, and, except for commuter operations, each provisional and refueling airport.

d. The certificate holder may not conduct any operation using any aircraft or airport not listed.

e. Kinds of operations authorized.

f. Authorization and limitations for routes and areas of operations.

g. Airport limitations.

h. Time limitations, or standards for determining time limitations, for overhauling, inspecting, and checking airframes, engines, propellers, rotors, appliances, and emergency equipment.

5. What are the two types of operating certificates an air carrier may apply for? (AC 120-49)

Air carrier certificate—This certificate is issued to carriers who plan to conduct interstate, foreign, or overseas transportation, or to carry mail.

Operating certificate—This certificate is issued to operators who plan to conduct intrastate transportation.

6. What are the two operating rules that are appropriate for air carriers and commercial operators? (AC 120-49)

An air carrier will operate under Part 121, Part 135, or both, depending on whether the operation is scheduled and the size and type of aircraft used.

7. Explain the five kinds of air carrier operations. (AC 120-49)

a. Domestic (Part 121).

b. Flag (Part 121).

c. Supplemental (Part 121).

d. Commuter (Part 135).

e. On-demand (Part 135).

8. Briefly describe the different kinds of scheduled operations. (AC 120-49)

a. *Domestic (Part 121)*—Domestic operations are scheduled operations between any points within the 48 contiguous states of the United States, or within any state.

b. *Flag (Part 121)*—Flag operations are scheduled operations between any points outside the 48 contiguous states.

c. *Commuter (Part 135)*—Certificate holders with commuter authority have specific limitations on the size and type of aircraft that can be utilized. A certificate holder who has commuter authority may also conduct on-demand operations.

9. Briefly describe the different kinds of nonscheduled operations. (AC 120-49)

a. *Supplemental (Part 121)*—Supplemental operations are operations for which the departure time, departure location, and arrival location are specifically negotiated with the customer or the customer's representative; or all cargo operations.

b. *On-Demand (Part 135)*—Certificate holders with on-demand authority have specific limitations on the size of aircraft that can be utilized. They can also conduct limited scheduled operations.

Human Factors   **6**

A. Flight Physiology

1. What is hypoxia? (AC 61-107)

Hypoxia is a state of oxygen deficiency in the blood, tissues, and cells sufficient to cause an impairment of body functions.

2. Give a brief explanation of the four forms of hypoxia. (AC 61-107)

Hypoxic—Any condition that interrupts the flow of O_2 into the lungs. This is the type of hypoxia encountered at altitude due to the reduction of the partial pressure of O_2.

Hypemic—Any condition that interferes with the ability of the blood to carry oxygen, such as anemia, bleeding, carbon monoxide poisoning, smoking, certain prescription drugs.

Stagnant—Any situation that interferes with the normal circulation of the blood arriving to the cells. Heart failure, shock, and positive G-forces will bring about this condition.

Histotoxic—Any condition that interferes with the normal utilization of O_2 in the cell. Alcohol, narcotics, and cyanide all can interfere with the cell's ability to use the oxygen in support of metabolism.

3. Significant effects of hypoxic (altitude) hypoxia normally begin to affect a healthy pilot at what altitude? (AC 61-107)

The human body functions normally in the atmospheric area extending from sea level to 12,000 feet MSL. In this range, brain oxygen saturation is at a level that allows for normal functioning. Optimal functioning is 96 percent saturation. At 12,000 feet MSL, brain oxygen saturation is approximately 87 percent, which begins to approach a level that could affect human performance.

Note: While other significant effects of hypoxia usually do not occur in a healthy pilot in an unpressurized aircraft below 12,000 feet MSL, there is no assurance that this will always be the case. Furthermore, the altitude range of impairment due to hypoxia is best described as a continuum; there is no definitive altitude at which the effects of hypoxia begin or end.

4. **Describe some of the *signs* an individual with hypoxia may exhibit.** (AC 61-107)

Rapid breathing, cyanosis (bluing effect of the skin), poor coordination, lethargy, executing poor judgment, sweating, trembling, and myoclonic (muscle) spasms.

Note: Signs of hypoxia can be detected in an individual by an observer. Signs aren't a very effective tool for hypoxic individuals to use to recognize hypoxia in themselves. Symptoms of hypoxia are the sensations a person can detect while in a hypoxic state.

5. **Describe some of the common *symptoms* of hypoxia.** (AC 61-107)

Air hunger, fatigue, nausea, headache, dizziness, hot and cold flashes, tingling, visual impairment, and euphoria.

Note: A common misconception among pilots is that it is easy to recognize the symptoms of hypoxia and to take corrective action before becoming seriously impaired. While this concept may be appealing in theory, it is both misleading and dangerous for crewmembers.

6. **As a flight crewmember, you suspect that you might be experiencing hypoxia. What should you do?** (AC 61-107)

If hypoxia is suspected, immediately don an oxygen mask and breathe 100 percent oxygen slowly. Descend to a safe altitude. If supplemental oxygen is not available, initiate an emergency descent to an altitude below 10,000 feet MSL. If symptoms persist, land as soon as possible.

7. **What factors can make a pilot more susceptible to hypoxia?** (AIM 8-1-2)

a. Carbon monoxide inhaled in smoking or from exhaust fumes.

b. Anemia (lowered hemoglobin).

c. Certain medications.

d. Small amounts of alcohol.

e. Low doses of certain drugs (antihistamines, tranquilizers, sedatives, analgesics, etc.)

f. Extreme heat or cold, fever, and anxiety increase the body's demand for oxygen, and hence its susceptibility to hypoxia.

8. How can hypoxia be avoided? (AIM 8-1-2, FAA-H-8083-25)

Hypoxia is prevented by heeding factors that reduce tolerance to altitude, by enriching the inspired air with oxygen from an appropriate oxygen system, and by maintaining a comfortable, safe cabin pressure altitude. For optimum protection, pilots are encouraged to use supplemental oxygen above 10,000 feet during the day, and above 5,000 feet at night. If supplemental oxygen is not available, a fingertip pulse oximeter can be very useful in monitoring blood O_2 levels.

9. What is hyperventilation? (AC 61-107)

Hyperventilation is defined as an increase in the rate and depth of breathing that exchanges gas in the lung beyond the volumes necessary to maintain normal levels of oxygen and carbon dioxide. Hyperventilation will result in disturbances in the acid-base balance in the blood, and eventually the brain as the levels of carbon dioxide in the lungs fall.

10. What symptoms can a pilot expect from hyperventilation? (AIM 8-1-3)

As hyperventilation "blows off" excessive carbon dioxide from the body, a pilot can experience symptoms of lightheadedness, suffocation, drowsiness, tingling in the extremities, and coolness, and react to them with even greater hyperventilation. Incapacitation can eventually result from incoordination, disorientation, and painful muscle spasms. Finally, unconsciousness can occur.

11. How can a hyperventilating condition be reversed? (AIM 8-1-3)

The symptoms of hyperventilation subside within a few minutes after the rate and depth of breathing are consciously brought back to normal. The buildup of carbon dioxide in the body can be hastened by controlled breathing in and out of a paper bag held over the nose and mouth.

12. What is ear block? (AIM 8-1-2)

As the aircraft cabin pressure decreases during ascent, the expanding air in the middle ear pushes open the eustachian tube and escapes down to the nasal passages, thereby equalizing in pressure with the cabin pressure. But this is not automatic during descent, and the pilot must periodically open the eustachian tube to equalize pressure. An upper respiratory infection or a nasal allergic condition can produce enough congestion around the eustachian tube to make equalization difficult. Consequently, the difference in pressure between the middle ear and aircraft cabin can build to a level that holds the eustachian tube closed, making equalization difficult if not impossible. An ear block produces severe pain and loss of hearing that can last from several hours to several days.

13. How is ear block prevented from occurring? (AIM 8-1-2)

Ear block can normally be prevented by swallowing, yawning, tensing muscles in the throat or, if these do not work, by the combination of closing the mouth, pinching the nose closed and attempting to blow through the nostrils (Valsalva maneuver). It is also prevented by not flying with an upper respiratory infection or nasal allergic condition.

14. What is sinus block? (AIM 8-1-2)

During ascent and descent, air pressure in the sinuses equalizes with the aircraft cabin pressure through small openings that connect the sinuses to the nasal passages. Either an upper respiratory infection, such as a cold or sinusitis, or a nasal allergic condition can produce enough congestion around an opening to slow equalization, and as the difference in pressure between the sinus and cabin mounts, eventually plug the opening. Sinus block occurs most frequently during descent.

15. What are the symptoms of a sinus block condition? (AIM 8-1-2)

A sinus block can occur in the frontal sinuses, located above each eyebrow, or in the maxillary sinuses, located in each upper cheek. It will usually produce excruciating pain over the sinus area. A maxillary sinus block can also make the upper teeth ache. Bloody mucus may discharge from the nasal passages.

16. What is spatial disorientation? (FAA-H-8083-15)

Orientation is the awareness of the position of the aircraft and of oneself in relation to a specific reference point. Spatial disorientation specifically refers to the lack of orientation with regard to position in space and to other objects.

17. What causes spatial disorientation? (FAA-H-8083-15)

Orientation is maintained through the body's sensory organs in three areas:

a. *Visual*—The eyes maintain visual orientation.

b. *Vestibular*—The motion sensing system in the inner ear maintains vestibular orientation.

c. *Postural*—The nerves in the skin, joints, and muscles of the body maintain postural orientation.

When human beings are in their natural environment, these three systems work well. However, when the human body is subjected to the forces of flight, these senses can provide misleading information resulting in disorientation.

18. Describe several examples of illusions that can lead to spatial disorientation. (AIM 8-1-5)

The leans—An abrupt correction of a banked attitude, which has been entered too slowly to stimulate the motion sensing system in the inner ear, can create the illusion of banking in the opposite direction. The disoriented pilot will roll the aircraft back into its original dangerous attitude, or if level flight is maintained, will feel compelled to lean in the perceived vertical plane until this illusion subsides.

Coriolis illusion—An abrupt head movement in a prolonged constant-rate turn that has ceased stimulating the motion sensing system can create the illusion of rotation or movement in an entirely different axis. The disoriented pilot will maneuver the aircraft into a dangerous attitude in an attempt to stop rotation. This most overwhelming of all illusions in flight may be prevented by not making sudden, extreme head movements, particularly while making prolonged constant-rate turns under IFR conditions.

Elevator illusion—An abrupt upward vertical acceleration, usually by an updraft, can create the illusion of being in a climb. The disoriented pilot will push the aircraft into a nose low attitude. An abrupt downward vertical acceleration, usually by a downdraft, has the opposite effect, with the disoriented pilot pulling the aircraft into a nose up attitude.

19. What is the cause of motion sickness, and what are its symptoms? (FAA-H-8083-25)

Motion sickness, or airsickness, is caused by the brain receiving conflicting messages about the state of the body. Symptoms of motion sickness include general discomfort, nausea, dizziness, paleness, sweating, and vomiting.

20. What action should be taken if a pilot or passenger suffers from motion sickness? (FAA-H-8083-25)

If symptoms of motion sickness are experienced, directing ventilated air to the face, using supplemental oxygen, focusing on an object outside the airplane, and avoiding unnecessary head movements may help alleviate some of the discomfort.

21. What is carbon monoxide poisoning? (AIM 8-1-4)

Carbon monoxide is a colorless, odorless, and tasteless gas contained in exhaust fumes. When breathed, even in minute quantities over a period of time, it can significantly reduce the ability of the blood to carry oxygen. Consequently, effects of hypoxia occur.

22. How does carbon monoxide poisoning occur, and what symptoms should a pilot be alert for? (AIM 8-1-4)

Most heaters in light aircraft work by air flowing over the manifold. Use of these heaters while exhaust fumes are escaping through manifold cracks and seals is responsible for several nonfatal and fatal aircraft accidents from carbon monoxide poisoning each year. A pilot who detects the odor of exhaust or experiences symptoms of headache, drowsiness, or dizziness while using the heater should suspect carbon monoxide poisoning.

23. What action should be taken if a pilot suspects carbon monoxide poisoning? (AIM 8-1-4)

A pilot who suspects this condition exists should immediately shut off the heater and open all air vents. If symptoms are severe, or they continue after landing, the pilot should seek medical treatment.

24. In transport category aircraft, explain the procedures used when smoke and/or fumes are experienced in the cockpit or cabin area. (AC 120-80)

Smoke, fire, or fumes checklists should include, as the first step, that flight crewmembers don their oxygen masks and verify that the regulator is set to 100 percent. Flight crewmembers must don smoke goggles and oxygen masks at the first indication of smoke or fumes and before accomplishing any abnormal or emergency procedures associated with smoke or fume elimination in accordance with your company's approved procedures and/or the manufacturer's recommendations. Any delay might result in a crewmembers' inability to breathe and/or see.

25. Define the term *stress* and explain what the two main categories of stress are. (FAA-H-8083-25)

Stress is the body's response to physical and psychological demands placed upon it. The two main categories are:

Acute stress (short term)—Involves an immediate threat that is perceived as danger. This is the type of stress that triggers a "fight or flight" response in an individual, whether the threat is real or imagined.

Chronic stress (long term)—Defined as a level of stress that presents an intolerable burden, exceeds the ability of an individual to cope, and causes individual performance to fall sharply.

26. How does the human body react to stress?
(FAA-H-8083-25)

The body's reaction to stress includes releasing chemical hormones (such as adrenaline) into the blood and increasing metabolism to provide more energy to the muscles. Blood sugar, heart rate, respiration, blood pressure, and perspiration all increase.

27. **The term *stressor* is used to describe an element that causes an individual to experience stress. What are the three types of stressors?** (FAA-H-8083-25)

    Physical stressors—Include conditions associated with the environment, such as temperature and humidity extremes, noise, vibration, and lack of oxygen.

    Physiological stressors—Include fatigue, lack of physical fitness, sleep loss, missed meals (leading to low blood sugar levels), and illness.

    Psychological stressors—Related to social or emotional factors such as a death in the family, a divorce, a sick child, a demotion, etc. They may also be related to mental workload such as analyzing a problem, navigating an aircraft, or making decisions.

28. **What is the definition of *fatigue*?** (AC 117-3)

    Fatigue is a physiological state of reduced mental or physical performance capability resulting from lack of sleep or increased physical activity. It can reduce a crewmember's alertness and ability to safely operate an aircraft or perform safety-related duties.

29. **What are the two types of fatigue and when are they likely to occur?** (FAA-H-8083-25)

    Acute (short-term) fatigue—Occurs after a period of strenuous effort, excitement, or lack of sleep. Rest after exertion and eight hours of sound sleep ordinarily cures this condition. A proper diet is also helpful.

    Chronic (long-term) fatigue—Has psychological roots and occurs over an extended period of time. Continuous high stress levels as well as underlying disease can produce chronic fatigue. It is not relieved by proper diet and adequate rest and sleep, and usually requires treatment by a physician.

30. **How will a pilot's performance be affected by fatigue or prolonged stress?** (FAA-H-8083-25)

    Degradation of attention and concentration, impaired coordination, and decreased ability to communicate seriously influence the pilot's ability to make effective decisions.

31. Describe the common symptoms of fatigue. (AC 120-103)

Fatigue is a complex state characterized by a lack of alertness and reduced mental and physical performance, often accompanied by drowsiness. Fatigue is objectively observed as changes in many aspects of performance, including increased reaction time, lapses in attention (e.g., reaction times greater than 500 milliseconds), reduced speed of cognitive tasks, reduced situational awareness, and reduced motivation. A person's perceived fatigue levels are often lower than observed decrements in performance.

32. Explain the main causes of fatigue in commercial aviation. (AC 120-103)

a. Amount, timing, and quality of sleep each day (sleep/wake schedule).

b. Amount of time since last sleep period (continuous hours awake).

c. Time of day (circadian rhythm).

d. Operations through multiple time zones.

e. Workload and time on task.

33. Describe how fatigue associated with aviation operations is a risk factor for occupational safety and performance effectiveness. (AC 120-100)

The multiple flight legs, long duty hours, limited time off, early report times, less-than-optimal sleeping conditions, rotating and non-standard work shifts, and jet lag pose significant challenges for the basic biological capabilities of pilots, crewmembers and shift workers. Humans simply are not designed to operate effectively under the pressured 24/7 schedules that often define aviation operations, whether the operations are short-haul commercial flights, long-range transoceanic operations, or around-the-clock and shift work operations.

34. What are some of the common factors that certificate holders must manage to minimize fatigue risk in aviation operations? (AC 120-103)

a. Crew flight and duty periods, and rest breaks to reduce fatigue.

b. Additional duties assigned to flight crews that further reduce sleep opportunities.

c. Schedule changes that extend duties beyond the published schedule.

d. The duration and timing of layovers between successive flight segments.

e. Recovery days, following a trip, that permit sufficient sleep to eliminate any accumulated sleep debt prior to scheduling or performing additional flight duties.

f. Optimal utilization of available rest opportunities.

35. Explain the strategies the flight crewmembers may use to mitigate the effects of fatigue. (AC 120-100)

a. *Recovery Sleep*—The longer one works without adequate opportunity to sleep, the greater the need for recovery sleep to prevent an accumulation of fatigue across duty periods. To some extent, FAA regulations (Part 117) codify this principle and specify off-duty rest periods that are proportional to the prior flight time.

b. *Napping*—The FAA authorizes in-flight naps for flight crews if there is an augmented complement so that two pilots are on the flight deck while the augmented crewmembers are resting. Therefore, at times when some amount of sleep is possible but limited, napping is the most effective physiological strategy for restoring alertness levels.

c. *In-flight rostering and bunk sleep (flight-ops specific)*—Refers to the scheduling of augmented flight crew to assigned positions on the flight deck, freeing other flight crew to obtain in-flight rest or bunk sleep.

d. *Activity breaks*—Short breaks can serve to increase alertness by reducing the monotony of a highly automated cockpit environment. Anecdotal reports from pilots indicate that many take brief, out-of-the-seat breaks as a fatigue countermeasure.

(continued)

e. *Light*—The use of properly timed bright light can shift human circadian rhythms. The alerting effects of light may be a result of its suppression of melatonin, a neurotransmitter released in the mid- to late-evening. Therefore, light may be a powerful mitigator of the usual alertness and performance decline common to nighttime duty, especially during aviation operations.

f. *Caffeine*—Can be an effective countermeasure in improving alertness and performance levels. Caffeine takes 15–30 minutes to enter the bloodstream after consumption, and thus alertness effects do not occur immediately. However, its effects can persist up to 5 hours after ingestion.

36. Define the term *dehydration* and describe the effect it has on a pilot. (FAA-H-8083-25)

Dehydration is the term given to a critical loss of water from the body. The first noticeable effect of dehydration is fatigue, which in turn makes top physical and mental performance difficult, if not impossible.

37. What are several causal factors that increase a pilot's susceptibility to dehydration? (FAA-H-8083-25)

Causes of dehydration are hot flight decks and flight lines, wind, humidity, and diuretic drinks (coffee, tea, caffeinated soft drinks). Flying for long periods in hot summer temperatures or at high altitudes increases susceptibility to dehydration since dry air at high altitudes tends to increase the rate of water loss from the body.

38. Describe the other symptoms a dehydrated pilot will experience if the fluid lost is not replaced. (FAA-H-8083-25)

The fatigue a pilot is already experiencing from dehydration will progress to dizziness, weakness, nausea, tingling of hands and feet, abdominal cramps, and extreme thirst.

39. Define the term *heatstroke*. (FAA-H-8083-25)

Heatstroke is a condition caused by any inability of the body to control its temperature.

40. How is onset of a heatstroke recognized?
(FAA-H-8083-25)

Onset of a heatstroke may be recognized by the symptoms of dehydration, but a heatstroke condition has been known to be recognized only by a sudden, complete collapse.

41. What general guidelines can a pilot use to mitigate the risk of becoming dehydrated? (FAA-H-8083-25)

a. Carry an ample supply of water and use frequently on any long flight, whether thirsty or not.

b. Drink one quart per hour for severe heat stress conditions or one pint per hour for moderate heat stress conditions.

c. Stay ahead of the thirst—don't rely on thirst sensation as an alarm.

d. Keep the flight deck well ventilated to help dissipate excess heat.

e. Limit daily intake of diuretic drinks (coffee, tea, caffeinated soft drinks, etc.).

42. What regulations apply, and what common sense should prevail, concerning the use of alcohol? (AIM 8-1-1)

The regulations prohibit pilots from performing crewmember duties within 8 hours after drinking any alcoholic beverage or while under the influence of alcohol. However, due to the slow destruction of alcohol, a pilot may still be under its influence 8 hours after drinking a moderate amount of alcohol. Therefore, an excellent rule is to allow at least 12 to 24 hours from "bottle to throttle," depending on the amount of alcoholic beverage consumed.

43. **For a pilot who has been taking an over-the-counter (OTC) cold medication, how do the various environmental factors the pilot is exposed to in flight affect the drug's physiological impact on the pilot?** (FAA-H-8083-25)

Drugs that cause no apparent side effects on the ground can create serious problems at relatively low altitudes. Even at typical general aviation altitudes, the changes in concentrations of atmospheric gases in the blood can enhance the effects of seemingly innocuous drugs and result in impaired judgment, decision-making, and performance.

44. **Define the term *hypothermia*.** (CAMI OK-06-033)

Hypothermia is dangerously low body temperature, below 95°F (35°C). Hypothermia occurs when more heat is lost than the body can generate. It is usually caused by extended exposure to the cold.

45. **Describe the symptoms of hypothermia.** (CAMI OK-06-033)

Symptoms usually begin slowly and there is likely to be a gradual loss of mental acuity and physical ability. Common symptoms include numbness of fingers and toes, shivering, a decreased level of consciousness, slurred speech, and poor coordination. The person experiencing hypothermia may be unaware that he or she requires emergency medical treatment.

46. **What are several types of illusions in flight which may lead to errors in judgment on landing?** (AIM 8-1-5)

Runway width illusion—Narrower than usual runway creates illusion aircraft is higher than actual; pilot tends to fly a lower approach than normal.

Runway and terrain slope illusion—Upsloping runway/terrain creates illusion aircraft is higher than actual; pilot tends to fly a lower approach than normal. Downsloping runway/terrain has the opposite effect.

Featureless terrain illusion—An absence of ground features creates illusion that aircraft is higher than actual; pilot tends to fly a lower approach than normal.

Atmospheric illusions—Rain on windscreen creates illusion of being at a higher altitude; atmospheric haze creates illusion of greater distance and height from runway; pilot tends to fly a lower approach than normal.

47. Discuss the effects of nitrogen excesses from scuba diving upon a pilot or passenger in flight. (AIM 8-1-2)

A pilot or passenger who intends to fly after scuba diving should allow the body sufficient time to rid itself of excess nitrogen absorbed during diving. If not, decompression sickness due to evolved gas can occur during exposure to low altitude and create a serious inflight emergency. The recommended waiting times before flight are as follows:

Flight altitudes up to 8,000 feet:

a. Wait at least 12 hours after a dive that did not require a controlled ascent.

b. Wait at least 24 hours after a dive in which a controlled ascent was required.

Flight altitudes above 8,000 feet:

a. Wait at least 24 hours after any scuba dive.

Note: The recommended altitudes are actual flight altitudes above mean sea level and not pressurized cabin altitudes. This takes into consideration the risk of decompression of the aircraft during flight.

B. Fitness for Flight

1. What regulations govern rest requirements for flight crewmembers? (14 CFR Part 117)

14 CFR Part 117, "Flight and Duty Limitations and Rest Requirements: Flightcrew Members."

2. As a flight crewmember, you discover you have high blood pressure. You are in possession of a current medical certificate. Can you continue to exercise the privileges of your certificate? (AIM 8-1-1)

No; the regulations prohibit a pilot who possesses a current medical certificate from performing crewmember duties while the

(continued)

pilot has a known medical condition or an increase of a known medical condition that would make the pilot unable to meet the standards for the medical certificate.

3. Are flight crewmembers allowed the use of any medications while performing required duties? (AIM 8-1-1)

The regulations prohibit pilots from performing crewmember duties while using any medication that affects the faculties in any way contrary to safety. The safest rule is not to fly as a crewmember while taking any medication, unless approved to do so by the FAA.

4. Are there any over-the-counter (OTC) medications that could be considered safe to use while flying? (AIM 8-1-1)

Pilot performance can be seriously degraded by both prescribed and over-the-counter medications, as well as by the medical conditions for which they are taken. Many medications have primary effects that may impair judgment, memory, alertness, coordination, vision, and the ability to make calculations. Also, any medication that depresses the central nervous system can make a pilot more susceptible to hypoxia.

Note: The FAA has published "What Over-the-Counter (OTC) medications can I take and still be safe to fly?" online, which contains a comprehensive list of "go" and "no-go" medications that pilots may reference when assessing their fitness for flight: www.faa.gov/sites/faa.gov/files/licenses_certificates/medical _certification/medications/OTCMedicationsforPilots.pdf.

5. What are several factors that may contribute to impairment of a pilot's performance? (AIM 8-1-1)

Illness—do I have any symptoms?

Medication—have I been taking prescription or OTC drugs?

Stress—am I under psychological pressure from the job, financial or family matters/health problems?

Alcohol—have I been drinking within 8 hours?

Fatigue—am I tired and not adequately rested?

Emotion—am I emotionally upset?

6. Define the term *fit for duty*. (AC 117-2)

Fit for duty means being physiologically and mentally prepared and capable of performing assigned duties in-flight with the highest degree of safety. This function also assumes that the flight crewmember is properly rested.

7. Explain a pilot's responsibility for ensuring they are adequately rested and fit for duty. (AC 117-2)

a. Flight crewmember has the responsibility of actually sleeping during the rest opportunity.

b. Responsibility in accordance with 14 CFR §117.5—must report for flight duty period rested and prepared.

c. Obtaining quality rest—comfort, vibration, turbulence, and noise can fragment sleep.

d. Develop personal strategies for preventing and managing fatigue risk.

e. Responsibility to report fatigue.

f. Fatigue recognition and personal assessment of fatigue and identifying signs of fatigue in others.

8. Describe the Fatigue Education and Awareness Training Program. (AC 117-2)

The program, as prescribed in 14 CFR §117.9, is designed to increase awareness and understanding of fatigue, the effects of fatigue on pilots and fatigue countermeasures. Fatigue training requirements are critical to mitigating the risk of fatigue by ensuring that both flight crewmembers and certificate holders understand the effects of fatigue on the safety of flight.

9. Is fatigue education and awareness training a separate program or is it incorporated into the flight crewmember ground training? (AC 117-2)

Each Part 121 certificate holder conducting operations under Part 117 must have an FAA-approved fatigue education and awareness training program as prescribed in 14 CFR §117.9. The training program must be part of a certificate holder's FAA-approved ground training curriculum.

10. **Are flight crewmembers the only certificate holder employees required to have FEATP training?** (AC 117-2)

    All employees responsible for administering the provisions of Part 117, including flight crewmembers, dispatchers, individuals directly involved in the scheduling of flight crewmembers, individuals directly involved in operational control, and any employee providing direct management (an employee's immediate supervisor) oversight of these areas.

11. **How often must this training be conducted?** (AC 117-2)

    All employees of the certificate holder covered under 14 CFR §117.9 must be trained annually.

C. ADM Using CRM

1. **Define the term *aeronautical decision-making* (ADM).** (FAA-H-8083-25)

    ADM is a systematic approach to the mental process used by pilots to consistently determine the best course of action in response to a given set of circumstances. It is what a pilot intends to do based on the latest information he or she has.

2. **How does the use of crew resource management (CRM) support ADM?** (FAA-H-8083-25)

    The goal of all flight crews is good ADM and the use of CRM is one way to make good decisions. CRM training for flight crews is focused on the effective use of all available resources: human resources, hardware, and information supporting ADM to facilitate crew cooperation and improve decision making.

3. **Describe the elements involved in good decision making on the flight deck.** (FAA-H-8083-25, AC 60-22)

    The elements of good decision-making are:

    a. Identifying personal attitudes hazardous to safe flight.
    b. Learning behavior modification techniques.
    c. Learning how to recognize and cope with stress.
    d. Developing risk assessment skills.
    e. Using all resources.
    f. Evaluating the effectiveness of one's ADM skill.

4. **Free and open communication is essential to the decision-making process and good CRM. What are several behaviors that relate to free and open communication among crewmembers?** (AC 120-51)

   a. Operational decisions are clearly stated to other crewmembers.

   b. Crewmembers acknowledge their understanding of decisions.

   c. Bottom lines for safety are established and communicated.

   d. The big picture and the game plan are shared within the team, including flight attendants and others as appropriate.

   e. Crewmembers are encouraged to state their own ideas, opinions, and recommendations.

   f. Efforts are made to provide an atmosphere that invites open and free communications.

   g. Initial entries and changed entries to automated systems are verbalized and acknowledged.

5. **Effective CRM encourages crewmembers to speak up and state their concerns with appropriate persistence until there is a clear resolution. Describe other behavioral markers of effective CRM involving crewmember inquiry, advocacy, and assertion.** (AC 120-51)

   a. A "challenge and response" environment is developed.

   b. Questions are encouraged and are answered openly and nondefensively.

   c. Crewmembers are encouraged to question the actions and decisions of others.

   d. Crewmembers seek help from others when necessary.

   e. Crewmembers question the status and programming of automated systems to confirm situation awareness.

6. **Explain the five hazardous attitudes and the antidotes for each.** (FAA-H-8083-25)

   Resignation ("What's the use?")—I'm not helpless. I can make a difference.

   Anti-Authority ("Don't tell me")—Follow the rules. They are usually right.

   Impulsivity ("Do it quickly")—Not so fast. Think first.

   Invulnerability ("It won't happen to me")—It could happen to me.

   Macho ("I can do it")—Taking chances is foolish.

7. **What is the definition of *risk*?** (FAA-H-8083-2)

   Risk is the future impact of a hazard that is not controlled or eliminated.

8. **Define the term *risk management*.** (FAA-H-8083-9)

   Risk management is a decision-making process designed to systematically identify hazards (perceive), assess the degree of risk (process), and determine the best course of action (perform). It is a logical process of weighing the potential costs of risks against the possible benefits of allowing those risks to stand uncontrolled.

9. **What is the goal of risk management?** (FAA-H-8083-25)

   The goal of risk management is to proactively identify safety-related hazards and mitigate the associated risks. Risk management is an important component of ADM. When a pilot follows good decision-making practices, the inherent risk in a flight is reduced or even eliminated.

10. **What are the three steps used in the risk management process?** (FAA-H-8083-9)

    a. Identify the hazard.
    b. Assess the risk.
    c. Mitigate the risk.

11. Explain the four fundamental guiding principles of risk management? (FAA-H-8083-25)

a. *Accept no unnecessary risk*—Flying is not possible without risk, but unnecessary risk comes without a corresponding return.

b. *Make risk decisions at the appropriate level*—Risk decisions should be made by the person who can develop and implement risk controls. Never let anyone else—not ATC and not your passengers—make risk decisions for you. You are the PIC.

c. *Accept risk when benefits outweigh dangers (costs)*—All identified benefits should be compared against all identified costs. High risk endeavors may be undertaken when the sum of the benefits exceeds the sum of the costs.

d. *Integrate risk management into planning at all levels*—Because risk is an unavoidable part of every flight, safety requires the use of appropriate and effective risk management, not just in the preflight planning stage, but in all stages of the flight.

12. What is a hazard? (FAA-H-8083-2)

A hazard is a present condition, event, object, or circumstance that could lead to or contribute to an unplanned or undesired event such as an accident. It is a source of danger.

13. What are several examples of aviation hazards? (FAA-H-8083-2)

a. A nick in the propeller blade.

b. Improper refueling of an aircraft.

c. Pilot fatigue.

d. Use of unapproved hardware on aircraft.

14. The ability of a pilot to recognize a hazard is predicated upon what factors? (FAA-H-8083-2)

a. *Personality*—Personality can play a large part in the manner in which hazards are gauged. People who might be reckless in nature, may take this on board the flight deck.

b. *Education*—When airlines started to employ CRM on the flight deck, the program helped crews recognize hazards and provided tools for them to eliminate the hazard or minimize its impact.

(continued)

c. *Regulations*—Provide restrictions to actions and are written to produce outcomes that might not otherwise occur if the regulation were not written. They are written to reduce hazards by establishing a threshold for the hazard.

d. *Experience*—The knowledge acquired over time and that increases with time. Inexperience is a hazard if an activity demands experience of a high skill set and the inexperienced pilot attempts that activity. Experience can provide a false sense of security.

Note: No two pilots see hazards in exactly the same way, making prediction and standardization of hazards a challenge. Risk management is unique to each and every individual, since there are no two people exactly alike in skills, knowledge, training, and abilities. An acceptable level of risk to one pilot may not necessarily be the same to another pilot.

15. Describe the three models that provide a structured framework for problem-solving and decision-making. (FAA-H-8083-25)

The 5P, the 3P (using PAVE, CARE and TEAM), and the DECIDE models. They provide assistance in organizing the decision process. All of these models have been identified as helpful to the pilot in organizing critical decisions.

16. How does the 5P model provide a pilot with an effective method to practice ADM? (FAA-H-8083-9)

The 5P checklist consists of the plan, the plane, the pilot, the passengers, and the programming. It is based on the idea that the pilot has essentially five variables that impact their environment that can cause them to make a single critical decision, or several less critical decisions, that when added together can create a critical outcome.

17. Explain the use of the 5P model to assess risk associated with each of the five factors. (FAA-H-8083-2)

At key decision points, application of the 5P checklist should be performed by reviewing each of the critical variables:

Plan—weather, route, publications, ATC reroutes/delays, fuel onboard/remaining.

Plane—mechanical status, automation status, database currency, backup systems.

Pilot—illness, medication, stress, alcohol, fatigue, eating.

Passengers—pilots/non-pilots, nervous or quiet, experienced or new, business or pleasure.

Programming—autopilot, GPS, MFD/PFD; anticipate likely reroutes/clearances; questions to ask—What is it doing? Why is it doing it? Did I do it?

18. When is the use of the 5P decision-making model recommended? (FAA-H-8083-9)

The 5P concept relies on the pilot to adopt a scheduled review of the critical variables at points in the flight where decisions are most likely to be effective. These key decision points include preflight, pre-takeoff, hourly or at the midpoint of the flight, pre-descent, and just prior to the final approach fix (or, for VFR operations, just prior to entering the traffic pattern). They also should be used anytime an emergency situation arises.

19. How can the use of the PAVE checklist assist a pilot in identifying the hazards and their associated risk prior to a flight? (FAA-H-8083-9)

Use of the PAVE checklist provides pilots with a simple way to remember each category to examine for hazards/risks during flight planning. The pilot divides the risks of flight into four categories:

Pilot-in-command—general health, physical/mental/emotional state (IMSAFE checklist); currency, proficiency, recency.

Aircraft—airworthiness (inspections), equipment (required for mission, is it operative), performance capability.

enVironment—weather hazards, terrain, airports, airspace, day or night conditions.

External pressures—meetings, people waiting at destination, desire to impress someone, etc.

20. **Describe how the 3P model can be used for effective risk management before and during a flight.** (FAA-H-8083-2)

The perceive, process, and perform (3P) model for risk management offers a simple, practical, and systematic approach that can be used during all phases of flight. To use it, pilots will:

Perceive—Identify the hazards that might affect the flight, which are present events, objects, or circumstances that could contribute to an undesired future event, given set of circumstances for a flight; think through circumstances related to the PAVE risk categories. The fundamental question to ask is, "what could hurt me, my passengers, or my aircraft?"

Process—Assess the hazards by evaluating their probability and severity. What will be their impact on flight safety. Think through the Consequences of each hazard, Alternatives available, Reality of the situation, and External pressures (CARE) that might influence their analysis. Hazards must be assessed in terms of their likelihood and severity.

Perform—Mitigate the risk by performing actions that will reduce the probability and/or severity of the risk. Transfer (can the risk decision be transferred to someone else? can you consult someone?); Eliminate (is there a way to eliminate the hazard?); Accept (do the benefits of accepting risk outweigh the costs?); Mitigate (what can you do to reduce the risk?) (TEAM).

21. **Explain how often a pilot should use the 3P model of ADM throughout a flight.** (FAA-H-8083-9)

Once a pilot has completed the 3P decision process and selected a course of action, the process begins again because the circumstances brought about by the course of action require analysis. The decision-making process is a continuous loop of perceiving, processing, and performing.

22. The DECIDE model of decision-making involves which elements? (FAA-H-8083-2)

Detect a change needing attention.

Estimate the need to counter or react to a change.

Choose the most desirable outcome for the flight.

Identify actions to successfully control the change.

Do something to adapt to the change.

Evaluate the effect of the action countering the change.

23. How is the 3P model different from the DECIDE model of ADM? (FAA-H-8083-2)

The 3P process is a continuous loop of the pilot's handling of hazards. The DECIDE model and naturalistic decision making focus on particular problems requiring resolution. Therefore, pilots exercise the 3P process continuously, while the DECIDE model and naturalistic decision-making result from the 3P process.

24. Define the term *automatic decision making*. (FAA-H-8083-25)

Automatic decision making is a type of naturalistic decision-making. In an emergency situation, a pilot might not survive if he or she rigorously applies analytical models to every decision made, as there is not enough time to go through all the options. Under these circumstances a pilot quickly imagines how one or a few possible courses of action in such situations will play out and takes the first workable option they can find. While it may not be the best of all possible choices, it often yields good results.

25. In an emergency requiring an immediate decision, what does a pilot rely on when using the automatic decision-making model? (FAA-H-8083-25)

Training and experience. Automatic decision making is anchored in training and experience and is most often used in times of emergencies when there is no time to practice analytical decision making. Naturalistic or automatic decision making improves with training and experience, and a pilot will find himself or herself using a combination of decision-making tools that correlate with individual experience and training.

26. **After identifying all of the hazards affecting a planned flight by using the PAVE model, how can a pilot assess the likelihood and severity of each hazard?** (FAA-H-8083-2)

Once all of the hazards and attendant risk(s) affecting a flight have been identified, the probability and severity of the hazards (level of risk associated with them) must be assessed. The most basic tool for assessing hazards for risk is the risk assessment matrix. Several risk assessment models are available to assist the pilot in determining his or her risk before departing on a flight. The models, all taking slightly different approaches, seek the common goal of assessing risk in an objective manner.

27. **What is a risk assessment matrix?** (FAA-H-8083-25, FAA-H-8083-2)

A risk assessment matrix is a tool used to assess the likelihood of an event occurring and the severity or consequences of that event. The matrix assists a pilot in differentiating between low, medium, and high-risk flights. Although the risk assessment matrix provides a general viewpoint of a generic situation, a more comprehensive program can be made that is tailored to a pilot's flying. This program includes a wide array of aviation-related activities specific to the pilot and assesses health, fatigue, weather, capabilities, etc. The scores are added and the overall score falls into various ranges, with the range representative of actions that a pilot imposes upon himself or herself.

28. **How is the likelihood and severity of an event rated in the risk assessment matrix?** (FAA-H-8083-2)

The likelihood of an outcome can be described as:
- *Probable*—an event may occur several times.
- *Occasional*—an event may occur sometime.
- *Remote*—an event is unlikely to occur but is possible.
- *Improbable*—an event is highly unlikely to occur.

The severity of an outcome can be described as:
- *Catastrophic*—results in fatalities and/or total airframe loss.
- *Critical*—severe injury or major airframe or property damage.
- *Marginal*—minor injury or minor airframe or property damage.
- *Negligible*—less than minor injury or damage.

The Code
of Federal
Regulations

7

A. 14 CFR Part 1

1. What type of information can be found in Part 1?
(14 CFR Part 1)

Part 1 contains general definitions, abbreviations and symbols, and rules of construction used throughout Title 14 of the Code of Federal Regulations.

2. Define the term *air carrier*. (14 CFR Part 1)

An air carrier is a person who undertakes directly by lease, or other arrangement, to engage in air transportation.

3. Define the term *commercial operator*. (14 CFR Part 1)

A person who, for compensation or hire, engages in the carriage by aircraft in air commerce of persons or property, other than as an air carrier or foreign air carrier or under the authority of Part 375. Where it is doubtful that an operation is for "compensation or hire," the test applied is whether the carriage by air is merely incidental to the person's other business or is, in itself, a major enterprise for profit.

4. What is the definition of *crewmember*? (14 CFR Part 1)

A crewmember is a person assigned to perform duty in an aircraft during flight time.

5. When does a pilot's flight time begin and end?
(14 CFR Part 1)

A pilot's flight time commences when an aircraft moves under its own power for the purpose of flight and ends when the aircraft comes to rest after landing.

6. With respect to aircraft, define *operate*. (14 CFR Part 1)

Operate means to use, cause to use, or authorize to use an aircraft for the purpose of air navigation including the piloting of aircraft, with or without the right of legal control (as owner, lessee, or otherwise).

7. What does the term *operational control* refer to? (14 CFR Part 1)

The term operational control, with respect to a flight, means the exercise of authority over initiating, conducting, or terminating a flight.

8. What is the definition of the term *large aircraft*? (14 CFR Part 1)

A large aircraft is an aircraft of more than 12,500 pounds maximum certificated takeoff weight.

B. 14 CFR Part 61

1. To serve as a required pilot flight crewmember of a civil aircraft of the United States, what certificates are required to be in a pilot's physical possession or readily accessible in the aircraft? (14 CFR 61.3)

a. A pilot certificate, special purpose pilot authorization, or temporary certificate issued under Part 61.

b. A photo identification (driver's license, government or state ID, U.S. Armed Forces ID, official passport).

c. An appropriate medical certificate.

2. A pilot is required to present their pilot certificate, medical certificate, logbook or any other records required by regulations to which individuals? (14 CFR 61.3, 61.51)

a. The Administrator.

b. An authorized representative from the NTSB.

c. Any federal, state, or local law enforcement officer.

d. An authorized representative of the Transportation Security Administration.

3. After meeting the requirements for a Category II pilot authorization, how is the authorization issued? (14 CFR 61.13)

A Category II or Category III pilot authorization is issued by a letter of authorization as part of an applicant's Instrument Rating or Airline Transport Pilot Certificate.

4. **Upon original issuance of a Category II pilot authorization, what limitation applies until specific experience requirements are met?** (14 CFR 61.13)

   For Category II operations, the limitation is 1,600 feet RVR and a 150-foot decision height. The limitation is removed when the holder shows that, since the beginning of the sixth preceding month, the holder has made three Category II ILS approaches with a 150-foot decision height to a landing under actual or simulated instrument conditions.

5. **You have been convicted of driving while under the influence of alcohol and your driver's license has been suspended. When are you required to report this suspension to the FAA?** (14 CFR 61.15)

   Each person holding a certificate issued under this Part shall provide a written report of each motor vehicle action to the FAA, Civil Aviation Security Division, not later than 60 days after the motor vehicle action.

6. **When will a temporary pilot certificate expire?** (14 CFR 61.17)

   A temporary Pilot, Flight Instructor, or Ground Instructor certificate or rating is issued for up to 120 days and expires:

   a. On the expiration date shown on the certificate;

   b. Upon receipt of the permanent certificate; or

   c. Upon receipt of a notice that the certificate or rating sought is denied or revoked.

7. **A first officer (second-in-command) for a Part 121 air carrier is required to hold what minimum certification?** (14 CFR 61.23, 121.436)

   a. An ATP certificate with appropriate aircraft type rating or an ATP certificate with restricted privileges and an appropriate aircraft type rating.

   b. At least a second-class medical certificate. A second-in-command (SIC) in flag or supplemental operations requiring three or more pilots must hold a first-class medical certificate.

8. **Before a pilot may act as pilot-in-command (PIC) for a Part 121 carrier, what minimum certification and experience requirements must be met?** (14 CFR 61.23, 6.159, 121.436)

   a. Have at least 1,500 hours of total time as a pilot.

   b. Hold an ATP certificate with appropriate aircraft type rating.

   c. Hold a first-class medical certificate.

   d. Have a minimum of 1,000 flight hours in air carrier operations as an SIC in Part 121 operations, a PIC in operations under either §135.243(a)(1) or §91.1053(a)(2)(i), or any combination of these.

9. **You hold a first-class medical certificate, are 35 years old, and are exercising PIC privileges as captain for a Part 121 carrier. When will your medical certificate expire?** (14 CFR 61.23)

   The medical certificate expires at the end of the last day of the twelfth month after the month of the date of examination shown on the medical certificate.

10. **What medical certificate are you required to hold when exercising second-in-command privileges of an Airline Transport Pilot Certificate for a Part 121 carrier?** (14 CFR 61.23)

    You must hold at least a second-class medical certificate *unless* you are exercising SIC privileges of an ATP Certificate in a Part 121 flag or supplemental operation that requires three or more pilots in which case you must hold a first-class medical certificate.

11. **When is a pilot required to hold a type rating?** (14 CFR 61.31)

    A person who acts as a PIC of any of the following aircraft must hold a type rating for that aircraft:

    a. Large aircraft (aircraft of more than 12,500 pounds, maximum certificated takeoff weight).

    b. Turbojet-powered airplanes.

    c. Other aircraft specified by the Administrator through aircraft type certificate procedures.

12. **You are acting as second-in-command of an aircraft requiring two pilots. What instrument flight time can you log as SIC?** (14 CFR 61.51)

    As SIC you can log all of the flight time you are controlling the airplane solely by reference to flight instruments.

13. **What are the currency requirements when acting as pilot-in-command of an aircraft that requires more than one pilot flight crewmember or is turbojet-powered?** (14 CFR 61.58)

    To serve as PIC of an aircraft that is type certificated for more than one required pilot flight crewmember or is turbojet-powered, a person must:

    a. Within the preceding 12 calendar months, complete a PIC proficiency check in an aircraft that is type certificated for more than one required pilot flight crewmember or is turbojet-powered; and

    b. Within the preceding 24 calendar months, complete a PIC proficiency check in the particular type of aircraft in which that person will serve as PIC, that is type certificated for more than one required pilot flight crewmember or is turbojet-powered.

    Note: Does not apply to Part 91(K), 121(Y), 121, 125, 133, 135, or 137 operations.

14. **What are the requirements for a pilot to serve as SIC of an aircraft type certificated for more than one required pilot flight crewmember?** (14 CFR 61.55)

    The pilot must hold:

    a. At least a Private Pilot Certificate with the appropriate category and class rating; and

    b. An Instrument Rating or privilege that applies to the aircraft being flown if the flight is under IFR; and

    c. At least a pilot type rating for the aircraft being flown unless the flight will be conducted as domestic flight operations within United States airspace.

15. Are pilots employed by a Part 121, Part 125, or Part 135 carrier required to pass a flight review every 24 months? (14 CFR 61.56)

No. A person who has passed (within the preceding 24 months) any of the following need not accomplish the flight review: a pilot proficiency check or practical test conducted by an examiner, an approved pilot check airman, or a U.S. Armed Force, for a pilot certificate, rating, or operating privilege.

16. What proficiency checks are required before a pilot may act as PIC of an aircraft that is type certificated for more than one required pilot flight crewmember or is turbojet-powered? (14 CFR 61.58)

a. Within the preceding 12 calendar months, complete a PIC proficiency check in an aircraft that is type certificated for more than one required pilot flight crewmember or is turbojet-powered; and

b. Within the preceding 24 calendar months, complete a PIC proficiency check in the particular type of aircraft in which that person will serve as PIC, that is type certificated for more than one required pilot flight crewmember or is turbojet-powered.

17. A pilot who applies for a Category II pilot authorization must hold what certificates and ratings? (14 CFR 61.67)

a. At least a Private or Commercial Pilot Certificate with an Instrument Rating or an Airline Transport Pilot Certificate;

b. A type rating for the aircraft for which the authorization is sought if that aircraft requires a type rating; and

c. A category and class rating for the aircraft for which the authorization is sought.

18. **A pilot applying for a Category II pilot authorization must meet what experience requirements?** (14 CFR 61.67)

    An applicant for a Category II pilot authorization must have at least:

    a. 50 hours of night flight time as PIC.

    b. 75 hours of instrument time under actual or simulated instrument conditions that may include not more than—

       i. A combination of 25 hours of simulated instrument flight time in a flight simulator or flight training device; or

       ii. 40 hours of simulated instrument flight time if accomplished in an approved course conducted by an appropriately rated training center certificated under Part 142.

    c. 250 hours of cross-country flight time as PIC.

19. **By regulation, who is required to hold an ATP Certificate?** (AC 61-138)

    a. *Part 121*—Each PIC and each SIC are required to have an ATP Certificate.

    b. *Part 135*—Operations requiring the PIC to hold an ATP Certificate with an Airplane category Multi-Engine class rating are:

       • Commuter operations using multi-engine airplanes with nine or fewer passenger seats (scheduled 135).

       • On-demand operations using multi-engine airplanes with 10 or more passenger seats.

       • Turbojets.

    c. Part 91K operations require all PICs of multi-engine turbine-powered fixed-wing airplanes to hold an ATP Certificate.

20. **What are the requirements to receive an ATP Certificate with an Airplane category Multi-Engine class rating?** (14 CFR 61.153, 61.156, 61.159, 61.160)

    a. Be at least 23 years of age or, for a restricted ATP Certificate (§61.160), be at least 21 years of age.

    b. Be able to read, speak, write, and understand the English language.

    c. Be of good moral character.

d. Hold a Commercial Pilot Certificate with an Instrument Rating, a foreign ATP with instrument privileges, or a foreign commercial pilot license with instrument rating.

e. Completion of an ATP certification training program before applying for the knowledge test.

f. Pass the ATP knowledge test and practical test.

g. Have the required aeronautical experience per 14 CFR §61.159.

21. What is the purpose of an ATP Certificate with restricted privileges? (14 CFR 61.160, AC 61-139)

It makes it possible for a pilot, with reduced total time or who has not reached the minimum age (23), to obtain a restricted ATP Certificate based on academic experience. This will enable the pilot to serve as an SIC in Part 121 operations until they obtain the necessary experience. To be eligible, a pilot must meet the requirements in 14 CFR §61.153 and §61.160. The restricted privilege ATP Certificate is subject to the limitations set forth in §61.167(b).

22. A pilot who holds an ATP Certificate with restricted privileges is subject to what limitations? (14 CFR 61.167)

The pilot may not act as pilot-in-command in operations:

a. Conducted under Part 121;

b. Conducted under §91.1053(a)(2)(i);

c. Conducted under §135.243(a)(1); or,

d. Serving as SIC in flag or supplemental operations conducted under Part 121 requiring three or more pilots.

23. What are the requirements to receive an ATP Certificate with restricted privileges (restricted to serving as SIC in Part 121 Operations—multi-engine class rating only)? (14 CFR 61.153, 61.160)

a. Be at least 21 years old.

b. Hold a Commercial Pilot Certificate with Instrument Rating.

c. Successfully complete an ATP certification training program prior to taking the ATP knowledge test (this requirement takes effect after July 31, 2014).

(continued)

    d. Pass the ATP knowledge and practical tests.

    e. Meet the aeronautical experience requirements of §61.160. A pilot may be eligible if he or she was a military-trained pilot; a graduate of a four-year bachelor degree program with aviation major; a graduate of a two-year associate degree program with an aviation major; or has 1,500 hours total time as a pilot.

24. What are the total flight time requirements for an ATP Certificate with restricted privileges based on a degree with an aviation major or based on military flight time? (AC 61-139, 14 CFR 61.160)

You must have a minimum total flight time of:

    a. 750 hours as a U.S. military pilot or former U.S. military pilot.

    b. 1,000 hours for a graduate who holds a bachelor's degree with an aviation major and meets the remaining requirements of §61.160(b).

    c. 1,250 hours for a graduate who holds an associate's degree with an aviation major and meets the remaining requirements of §61.160(c).

    d. 1,250 hours for a graduate who holds a bachelor's degree with an aviation major and meets the remaining requirements of §61.160(d).

25. What is the purpose of the ATP certification training program (CTP)? (AC 61-138, 14 CFR 61.160)

The CTP will provide an applicant for an ATP certificate with an airplane category multi-engine class rating, or an ATP certificate issued concurrently with an airplane type rating, with the knowledge and competencies required to function effectively as a professional flight crewmember in an air carrier environment. Successful completion of the ATP CTP will ensure ATP applicants receive the baseline knowledge and experience to prepare them for the duties, responsibilities, and challenges of an air carrier environment.

26. What does the ATP certification training program consist of? (14 CFR 61.156)

The training consists of at least 30 hours of classroom instruction and at least 10 hours of training in a flight simulation training device (FSTD). The 30 hours of classroom instruction includes training in areas such as aerodynamics, automation, adverse weather conditions, air carrier operations, transport airplane performance, professionalism, leadership, and development. The FSTD training consists of the following: low-energy states/stalls; upset recovery techniques; adverse weather conditions including icing, thunderstorms, and crosswinds with gusts; navigation including flight management systems; and automation including autoflight.

27. When is an applicant for an ATP Certificate required to complete the ATP CTP? (14 CFR 61.156)

A person who applies for the knowledge test for an Airline Transport Pilot Certificate with an Airplane Category Multiengine Class Rating must present a graduation certificate from an authorized training provider under Parts 121, 135, 141, or 142 of this chapter certifying the applicant has completed the ATP CTP.

28. Who is authorized to conduct an ATP certification training program? (14 CFR 61.156)

The course can only be provided by Part 121, 135, 141, and 142 certificate holders.

29. What type of simulator is required for the 10 hours of ATP CTP simulator training? (14 CFR 61.156)

At least 6 hours of training in a Level C or higher full flight simulator qualified under Part 60 that represents a multi-engine turbine airplane with a maximum takeoff weight of 40,000 pounds or greater. The remaining FSTD training may be completed in a Level 4 or higher flight simulation training device.

30. Excluding briefings and debriefings, the flight instruction of other pilots in air transportation service is restricted to how many hours? (14 CFR 61.167)

More than 8 hours in any 24-consecutive-hour period or more than 36 hours in any 7-consecutive-day period.

31. **An ATP certification training program instructor must meet what certification and experience requirements?** (AC 61-138)

Specific instructor requirements for the ATP CTP can be found in 14 CFR §§121.410, 135.336, 141.33, and 142.54. All instructors of the ATP CTP must:

a. Hold an ATP Certificate with an Airplane category Multi-Engine class rating; and

b. Have at least two years of air carrier experience. Air carrier experience for the purpose of establishing eligibility to instruct the ATP CTP is defined as experience as a PIC in operations under §91.1053(a)(2)(i) or §135.243(a)(1), or as a PIC or SIC under Part 121.

C. 14 CFR Part 91

1. **Discuss 14 CFR §91.3, "Responsibility and authority of the pilot in command."** (14 CFR 91.3, 121.533)

The PIC of an aircraft is directly responsible for, and is the final authority as to, the operation of that aircraft. Under 14 CFR §121.533, the PIC of an aircraft is, during flight time, in command of the aircraft and crew and is responsible for the safety of the passengers, crewmembers, cargo, and airplane. The PIC has full control and authority in the operation of the aircraft, without limitation, over other crewmembers and their duties during flight time, whether or not he or she holds valid certificates authorizing him or her to perform the duties of those crewmembers.

2. **14 CFR §91.9 requires that a current, approved AFM be available onboard the aircraft for guidance to the flight crew during flight operations. Is there an approved substitute for the AFM in a Part 121 or 135 operation?** (14 CFR 91.9, 121.41, 135.81, drs.faa.gov)

Yes. Operators may use either the approved AFM or they may develop, obtain approval for, and use a company flight manual (CFM). A CFM is an approved aircraft flight manual that is developed by, or for, a specific operator for a specific aircraft type and that is approved by the principle operations inspector (POI), in accordance with the provisions of §121.141(b) or §135.81(c).

3. **A pilot may not act or attempt to act as a crewmember of a civil aircraft if they have consumed alcohol within 8 hours or have a blood alcohol concentration of 0.04 or greater. If you meet these requirements, are you safe to fly?** (14 CFR 91.17, AIM 8-1-1)

The regulations prohibit pilots from performing crewmember duties within 8 hours after drinking any alcoholic beverage or while under the influence of alcohol. However, due to the slow destruction of alcohol, a pilot may still be under its influence 8 hours after drinking a moderate amount of alcohol.

An excellent rule to follow is to always allow at least 12 to 24 hours from "bottle to throttle," depending on the amount of alcoholic beverage consumed.

Note: As a flight crewmember, your employer may have established more restrictive requirements concerning fitness for duty. Some airlines now require their flight crewmembers to refrain from drinking alcohol at least 12 hours before they report for work.

4. **May portable electronic devices be operated onboard an aircraft?** (14 CFR 91.21, 121.306)

Aircraft operated by a holder of an air carrier operating certificate or an aircraft operating under IFR may not allow operation of electronic devices onboard their aircraft. Exceptions are: portable voice recorders, hearing aids, heart pacemakers, electric shavers, or any other device that the operator of the aircraft has determined will not cause interference with the navigation or communication system of the aircraft on which it is to be used.

5. **What information must a pilot-in-command be familiar with before a flight?** (14 CFR 91.103)

For a flight under IFR or a flight not in the vicinity of an airport, all available information including:

NOTAMs

Weather reports and forecasts

Known ATC traffic delays

Runway lengths at airports of intended use

Alternatives available if the planned flight cannot be completed

Fuel requirements

Takeoff and landing performance data

6. What are the right-of-way rules pertaining to IFR flights? (14 CFR 91.113)

When weather conditions permit, regardless of whether an operation is under IFR or VFR, vigilance shall be maintained by each person operating an aircraft so as to see and avoid other aircraft.

7. What is the maximum speed allowed when operating inside Class B airspace, under 10,000 feet and within a Class D surface area? (14 CFR 91.117)

Unless otherwise authorized or required by ATC, no person may operate an aircraft at or below 2,500 feet above the surface within 4 NM of the primary airport of a Class C or Class D airspace area at an indicated airspeed of more than 200 knots. This restriction does not apply to operations conducted within a Class B airspace area. Such operations shall comply with the "below 10,000 feet MSL" restriction: "No person shall operate an aircraft below 10,000 feet MSL, at an indicated airspeed of more than 250 knots."

8. When operating beneath the lateral limits of Class B airspace, or in a VFR corridor designated through Class B airspace, what maximum speed is authorized? (14 CFR 91.117)

No person may operate an aircraft in the airspace underlying a Class B airspace area designated for an airport or in a VFR corridor designated through such a Class B airspace area, at an indicated airspeed of more than 200 knots (230 MPH).

9. What aircraft speed limits are permitted in the following areas? (14 CFR 91.117)

a. Turbine-powered, below 10,000 feet MSL—250 knots IAS.

b. Within Class B airspace—250 knots IAS.

c. Beneath Class B airspace—200 knots IAS.

d. Within Class C and D airspace (below 2,500 feet AGL and within 4 NM)—200 knots IAS.

10. Define the term *minimum safe altitude*. (14 CFR 91.119)

An altitude allowing, if a power unit fails, an emergency landing without undue hazard to persons or property on the surface.

11. What are the minimum safe altitudes an aircraft may be operated at in the following areas? (14 CFR 91.119)

Congested area—No lower than 1,000 feet above the highest obstacle within a horizontal radius of 2,000 feet of the aircraft.

Other than a congested area—No lower than 500 feet above the surface, except over open water or sparsely populated areas. In those cases, the aircraft may not be operated closer than 500 feet to any person, vessel, vehicle, or structure.

Open water or sparsely populated area—Not closer than 500 feet to any person, vessel, vehicle, or structure.

12. What regulations pertain to altimeter setting procedures? (14 CFR 91.121)

Below 18,000 feet MSL:

a. The current reported altimeter setting of a station along the route and within 100 NM of the aircraft.

b. If there is no station within the area described above, the current reported altimeter of an appropriate available station.

c. In the case of an aircraft not equipped with a radio, the elevation of the departure airport or an appropriate altimeter setting available before departure.

Note: If barometric pressure exceeds 31.00 inHg, set 31.00 inHg; at or above 18,000 feet MSL, set to 29.92 inHg. (*See* AIM 7-2-2.)

13. When may the pilot-in-command of an aircraft deviate from an ATC clearance? (14 CFR 91.123)

Except in an emergency, no person may, in an area in which air traffic control is exercised, operate an aircraft contrary to an ATC instruction.

14. When may ATC request a detailed report on an emergency even though a rule has not been violated? (14 CFR 91.123)

Each PIC who (though not deviating from a rule) is given priority by ATC in an emergency, shall submit a detailed report of that emergency within 48 hours to the manager of that ATC facility, if requested by ATC.

15. **At what minimum altitude is a turbine-engine powered or large airplane required to enter the traffic pattern for an airport in Class D airspace?** (14 CFR 91.129)

    A large or turbine-powered airplane shall, unless otherwise required by the applicable distance-from-cloud criteria, enter the traffic pattern at an altitude of at least 1,500 feet above the elevation of the airport and maintain at least 1,500 feet until further descent is required for a safe landing.

16. **At what minimum altitude is a turbine engine powered airplane approaching to land on a runway served by an instrument approach procedure with vertical guidance, required to operate at if the airplane is so equipped?** (14 CFR 91.129)

    Operate that airplane at an altitude at or above the glide path between the published final approach fix and the decision altitude (DA), or decision height (DH), as applicable; or if compliance with the applicable distance-from-cloud criteria requires glide path interception closer in, operate that airplane at or above the glide path, between the point of interception of glide path and the DA or the DH.

17. **You're in a CRJ-900, performing a visual approach into the primary airport within Class B airspace and have inadvertently exited Class B airspace by descending too early or at a rate steeper than the published instrument glide path. You've been cleared for the visual. Have you violated any regulations?** (SAFO 17001, 14 CFR 91.131)

    Yes, you're in violation of 14 CFR §91.131. Class B airspace is the controlled airspace surrounding the nation's busiest airports and §91.131 states: "Unless otherwise authorized by ATC, each person operating a large turbine engine-powered airplane to or from a primary airport for which a Class B airspace area is designated must operate at or above the designated floors of the Class B airspace area while within the lateral limits of that area."

18. **What are the requirements to operate within Class A airspace?** (14 CFR 91.135)

    a. Operated under IFR and in compliance with an ATC clearance received prior to entering the airspace.

    b. Equipped with instruments and equipment required for IFR operations.

    c. Flown by a pilot rated for instrument flight.

    d. Equipped with:
       - A radio providing direct pilot/controller communication on the frequency specified by ATC in the area concerned.
       - The applicable equipment specified in 14 CFR §91.215 and §91.225 (transponder regulations and ADS-B Out).

19. **What additional equipment is required when operating above Flight Level 240?** (14 CFR 91.205)

    If VOR navigational equipment is required (appropriate to the ground facilities to be used), no person may operate a U.S.-registered civil aircraft within the 50 States and the District of Columbia at or above FL240 unless that aircraft is equipped with approved distance measuring equipment (DME) or a suitable RNAV system.

20. **What minimum flight visibility and clearance from clouds are required for VFR flight in the following situations?** (14 CFR 91.155)

    Class C, D, or E Airspace

    Less than 10,000 feet MSL:
    Visibility—3 SM.
    Cloud clearance—500 feet below, 1,000 feet above, 2,000 feet horizontal.

    At or above 10,000 feet MSL:
    Visibility—5 SM.
    Cloud clearance—1,000 feet below, 1,000 feet above, 1 SM horizontal.

    (continued)

Class G Airspace

1,200 feet or less above the surface (regardless of MSL altitude):

> *Day:*
> Visibility—1 SM.
> Cloud clearance—clear of clouds.
> *Night:*
> Visibility—3 SM.
> Cloud clearance—500 feet below, 1,000 feet above,
>   2,000 feet horizontal.

More than 1,200 feet above the surface but less than 10,000 feet MSL:

> *Day:*
> Visibility—1 statute mile
> Cloud clearance—500 feet below, 1,000 feet above,
>   2,000 feet horizontal.
> *Night:*
> Visibility—3 statute miles
> Cloud clearance—500 feet below, 1,000 feet above,
>   2,000 feet horizontal.

More than 1,200 feet above the surface and at or above 10,000 feet MSL:

> Visibility—5 statute miles
> Cloud clearance—1,000 feet below, 1,000 feet above,
>   1 SM horizontal.

21. When operating an aircraft under VFR in level cruising flight at an altitude of more than 3,000 feet above the surface, what rules apply concerning specific altitudes flown? (14 CFR 91.159)

When operating above 3,000 feet AGL but less than 18,000 feet MSL on a magnetic course of 0° to 179°, fly at an odd-thousand-foot MSL altitude plus 500 feet. When on a magnetic course of 180° to 359°, fly at an even-thousand-foot MSL altitude plus 500 feet. When operating above 18,000 feet MSL, maintain the altitude or flight level assigned by ATC.

22. What are the fuel requirements for flight in IFR conditions? (14 CFR 91.167)

The aircraft must carry enough fuel (considering weather reports, forecasts and weather conditions) to complete the flight to the first airport of intended landing, fly from that airport to the alternate airport, and fly after that for 45 minutes at normal cruising speed.

23. What are the different methods for checking the accuracy of VOR equipment? (14 CFR 91.171)

a. VOT check: ±4°

b. Ground checkpoint: ±4°

c. Airborne checkpoint: ±6°

d. Dual VOR check: 4° between each other

e. Select a radial over a known ground point: ±6°

A repair station can use a radiated test signal, but only the technician performing the test can make an entry in the logbook.

24. Before a pilot can operate an aircraft in controlled airspace under IFR, what two conditions must be met? (14 CFR 91.173)

No person may operate an aircraft in controlled airspace under IFR unless that person has filed an IFR flight plan and received an appropriate ATC clearance.

25. What minimums are necessary for IFR takeoff under 14 CFR Parts 121, 125, 129, and 135? (14 CFR 91.175)

For aircraft operated under Parts 121, 125, 129 or 135, if takeoff minimums are not prescribed under Part 97 for a particular airport, the following minimums apply to takeoffs under IFR for aircraft operating under those parts:

a. For two engines or less—1 SM visibility.

b. For more than two engines—½ SM visibility.

26. When is a procedure turn not required? (AIM 5-4-9, 14 CFR 91.175)

A procedure turn is not required when:

a. ATC specifies in approach clearance "Cleared straight-in (type) approach."

b. Holding pattern replaces the procedure turn, the holding pattern must be followed.

c. Flying a DME arc.

d. Radar vectored to final approach course.

e. Procedure turn barb is absent in the plan view or the "NoPT" symbol is depicted on the initial segment being used.

f. When conducting a timed approach from a holding fix.

g. Teardrop procedure turn is depicted and a course reversal is required.

Note: If a pilot is uncertain whether the ATC clearance intends for a procedure turn to be conducted or to allow for a straight-in approach, the pilot must immediately request clarification from ATC (14 CFR §91.123).

27. When flying an instrument approach procedure, when can the pilot descend below minimum descent altitude (MDA) or DA/DH? (14 CFR 91.175)

No pilot may operate an aircraft below the authorized MDA or continue an approach below the authorized DA/DH unless:

a. The aircraft is continuously in a position from which a descent to a landing on the intended runway can be made at a normal rate of descent using normal maneuvers.

b. The flight visibility is not less than the visibility prescribed in the standard instrument approach procedure being used.

c. When at least one of the following visual references for the intended runway is distinctly visible and identifiable to the pilot:
   • The approach light system (except that the pilot may not descend below 100 feet above the touchdown zone elevation using the ALS as a reference unless the red terminating bars or the red side row bars are also distinctly visible and identifiable).
   • The threshold.

- The threshold markings.
- The threshold lights.
- Runway end identifier lights (REIL).
- Visual glideslope indicator.
- The touchdown zone or touchdown zone markings.
- The touchdown zone lights.
- The runway or runway markings.
- The runway lights.

28. Convert the following RVR values to meteorological visibility. (14 CFR 91.175)

RVR (feet)	Visibility (SM)
1,600	1/4
2,400	1/2
3,200	5/8
4,000	3/4
4,500	7/8
5,000	1
6,000	1-1/4

29. If no applicable minimum altitude is prescribed (no MEA or MOCA), what minimum altitudes apply for IFR operations? (14 CFR 91.177, Part 95)

Minimum altitudes are:

a. Mountainous terrain (designated in Part 95)—at least an altitude of 2,000 feet above the highest obstacle within a horizontal distance of 4 NM from the course to be flown.

b. Other than mountainous terrain—at least 1,000 feet above the highest obstacle within a horizontal distance of 4 NM from the course to be flown.

30. Describe the climb procedure when approaching a fix beyond which a higher minimum enroute IFR altitude (MEA) exists. (14 CFR 91.177)

A pilot may climb to a higher minimum IFR altitude immediately after passing the point beyond which that minimum altitude applies.

31. When may a pilot operate an aircraft below the published MEA? (14 CFR 91.177)

If both a MEA and a minimum obstruction clearance altitude (MOCA) are prescribed for a particular route or route segment, a person may operate an aircraft below the MEA down to, but not below, the MOCA, provided the applicable navigation signals are available. For aircraft using VOR for navigation, this applies only when the aircraft is within 22 NM of that VOR.

32. What cruising altitudes should be maintained while operating under IFR in controlled airspace (Class A, B, C, D, or E)? In uncontrolled airspace (Class G)? (14 CFR 91.179)

IFR flights within controlled airspace (Class A, B, C, D, or E) shall maintain the altitude or flight level assigned by ATC. In uncontrolled airspace (Class G), altitude is selected based on the magnetic course flown:

Below 18,000 feet MSL:

- 0° to 179° odd thousand MSL.
- 180° to 359° even thousand MSL.

18,000 feet up to but not including 29,000 feet MSL:

- 0° to 179° odd flight levels.
- 180° to 359° even flight levels.

33. The full reduced vertical separation minimum (RVSM) flight envelope extends from FL290 upward to what altitude? (14 CFR Part 91 Appendix G)

RVSM airspace extends upward to the lowest altitude of the following:

a. FL410 (the RVSM altitude limit);

b. The maximum certificated altitude for the aircraft; or

c. The altitude limited by cruise thrust, buffet, or other flight limitations.

34. How much vertical separation is provided by ATC in RVSM airspace? (14 CFR 91.180)

Within RVSM airspace, ATC separates aircraft by a minimum of 1,000 feet vertically between FL290 and FL410 inclusive.

35. Where can a pilot find information on operations in the North Atlantic (NAT) Minimum Navigation Performance Specifications Airspace?

14 CFR Part 91 and AC 91-85B, "Authorization of Aircraft and Operators for Flight in RVSM Airspace."

36. Concerning two-way radio communications failure in VFR and IFR conditions, what is the procedure for altitude, route, leaving holding fix, descent for approach, and approach selection? (14 CFR 91.185)

In VFR conditions: If the failure occurs in VFR, or if VFR is encountered after the failure, each pilot shall continue the flight under VFR and land as soon as practicable.

In IFR conditions: If the failure occurs in IFR conditions, or if VFR conditions are not within range, each pilot shall continue the flight according to the following:

a. Route:

Assigned by route assigned in last ATC clearance

Vectored go direct from point of radio failure to fix, route, airway in vector clearance

Expected by route that ATC has advised may be expected

Filed by the route filed in flight

b. Altitude (highest of following altitudes for the route segment being flown):

Minimum minimum altitude for IFR operations

Expected altitude/flight level ATC has advised to expect in a further clearance

Assigned altitude/flight level assigned in the last ATC clearance

c. Leave clearance limit:

- When the clearance limit is a fix from which the approach begins, commence descent or descent and approach as close as possible to the expect-further-clearance time if one has been received; or if one has not been received, as close as possible to the estimated time of arrival as calculated from the filed or amended (with ATC) estimated time en route.

(continued)

- If the clearance limit is not a fix from which the approach begins, leave the clearance limit at the expect-further-clearance time if one has been received; or if none has been received, upon arrival over the clearance limit, and proceed to a fix from which an approach begins and commence descent or decent and approach as close as possible to the estimated time of arrival as calculated from the filed or amended (with ATC) estimated time en route.

37. **What reports should be made to ATC without a specific request (radar and non-radar)?** (14 CFR 91.183, 91.187, AIM 5-3-3)

The pilot must report:

Missed approach; request clearance for specific action, such as another approach, alternate airport, etc.

Airspeed change; change in average KTAS at cruising altitude of 5% or 10 knots, whichever is greater.

Reaching a holding fix or point to which cleared; report time and altitude or flight level.

Vacating any previously assigned altitude or flight level.

ETA change when previous estimate in excess of 2 minutes (non-radar).

Leaving assigned holding fix or point.

Outer marker (OM) inbound or fix used in lieu of the OM (non-radar).

Unforecast weather.

Safety of flight compromised.

VFR on top, when any altitude change is made.

Final approach fix inbound (non-radar).

Radio malfunction—any loss or impairment of navigation/communication receiver capability.

Compulsory reporting points (non-radar).

500 fpm—unable to climb/descend 500 fpm.

Remember: MARVELOUS VFR C500

38. What are the flight crew and aircraft requirements to operate an aircraft in a Category II or III operation? (14 CFR 91.189)

No person may operate a civil aircraft in a Category II or III operation unless:

a. The flight crew of the aircraft consists of a PIC and a SIC who hold the appropriate authorizations and ratings prescribed in §61.3;

b. Each flight crewmember has adequate knowledge of, and familiarity with, the aircraft and the procedures to be used; and

c. The instrument panel in front of the pilot who is controlling the aircraft has appropriate instrumentation for the type of flight control guidance system that is being used.

39. What additional equipment is required when operating above Flight Level 240? (14 CFR 91.205)

If VOR navigational equipment is required (appropriate to the ground facilities to be used), no person may operate a U.S.-registered civil aircraft within the 50 States and the District of Columbia at or above FL240 unless that aircraft is equipped with approved DME or a suitable RNAV system.

40. What are the regulations concerning use of supplemental oxygen on board an aircraft? (14 CFR 91.211)

No person may operate a civil aircraft of U.S. registry:

a. At cabin pressure altitudes above 12,500 feet MSL up to and including 14,000 feet MSL, unless, for that part of the flight at those altitudes that is more than 30 minutes, the required minimum flight crew is provided with and uses supplemental oxygen.

b. At cabin pressure altitudes above 14,000 feet MSL, unless the required flight crew is provided with and uses supplemental oxygen for the entire flight time at those altitudes.

c. At cabin pressure altitudes above 15,000 feet MSL, unless each occupant is provided with supplemental oxygen.

Note: For Part 121 and 135 oxygen requirements reference Part 121 and 135 regulations.

41. What are the regulations pertaining to the use of supplemental oxygen on board a pressurized aircraft? (14 CFR 91.211)

Above FL250—at least a ten-minute supply of supplemental oxygen, in addition to any oxygen required to satisfy §91.211, is available for each occupant of the aircraft for use in the event that a descent is necessitated by loss of cabin pressurization.

Above FL350—at least one pilot at the controls of the airplane is wearing and using an oxygen mask that is secured and sealed that either supplies oxygen at all times or automatically supplies oxygen whenever the cabin pressure altitude of the airplane exceeds 14,000 feet MSL.

Note: One pilot need not wear and use an oxygen mask while at or below FL410 if two pilots are at the controls and each pilot has a quick donning type of oxygen mask that can be placed on the face within 5 seconds. Also, if for any reason at any time it is necessary for one pilot to leave the controls of the aircraft when operating at altitudes above FL350, the remaining pilot at the controls shall put on and use an oxygen mask until the other pilot has returned to that crewmember's station.

42. What instruments and equipment may not be included in a minimum equipment list? (14 CFR 91.213)

a. Instruments and equipment that are either specifically or otherwise required by the airworthiness requirements under which the aircraft is type certificated and which are essential for safe operations under all operating conditions.

b. Instruments and equipment required by an airworthiness directive to be in operable condition unless the airworthiness directive provides otherwise.

c. Instruments and equipment required for specific operations by Part 91.

43. Where is Mode C transponder and ADS-B Out equipment required? (AIM 4-1-20, 14 CFR 91.215, 91.225, 99.13)

In general, the regulations require aircraft to be equipped with an operable Mode C transponder and ADS-B Out equipment when operating:

a. In Class A, Class B, or Class C airspace areas;

b. Above the ceiling and within the lateral boundaries of Class B or Class C airspace up to 10,000 feet MSL;

c. Class E airspace at and above 10,000 feet MSL within the 48 contiguous States and the District of Columbia, excluding the airspace at and below 2,500 feet AGL;

d. Within 30 miles of a Class B airspace primary airport, below 10,000 feet MSL (Mode C Veil); and

e. For ADS-B Out: Class E airspace at and above 3,000 feet MSL over the Gulf of Mexico from the coastline of the United States out to 12 nautical miles.

f. All aircraft flying into, within, or across the contiguous United States ADIZ.

Note: Civil and military aircraft should operate with the transponder in the altitude reporting mode and ADS-B Out transmissions enabled (if equipped) at all airports, any time the aircraft is positioned on any portion of an airport movement area. This includes all defined taxiways and runways.

44. For operations conducted in Class A airspace the aircraft must be equipped with what type of ADS-B Out equipment? (14 CFR 91.225)

Extended squitter ADS-B and Traffic Information Service–Broadcast (TIS-B), operating on the radio frequency of 1090 MHz. This type of ADS-B Out equipment is commonly abbreviated as 1090ES.

45. Describe several examples of non-common carriage operations that involve the transportation of persons or property and may involve compensation, but are conducted under Part 91. (14 CFR 91.501)

Part 91 Subpart F applies to large and turbine-powered multi-engine airplanes and fractional ownership program aircraft. 14 CFR §91.501 sets conditions on the amount and types of compensation for these operations. Examples include:

a. Flights conducted by the operator of an airplane for the operator's own personal transportation, or the transportation of guests, when no charge, assessment, or fee is made for the transportation.

b. Carriage of company officials, employees, and guests of the company on an airplane operated under a time sharing, interchange, or joint ownership agreement.

c. Carriage of property (except mail) incidental to business (limited compensation for expenses).

d. Carriage of a group (with common purpose) when there is no charge, assessment or fee.

e. Fractional ownership.

46. How many fire extinguishers must be provided for use in crew, passenger, and cargo compartments for a transport category aircraft with a 70 passenger seating capacity? (14 CFR 91.513)

At least one hand fire extinguisher must be provided and located on or near the flight deck in a place that is readily accessible to the flight crew and at least two hand fire extinguishers must be conveniently located in the passenger compartment of each airplane accommodating more than 30 passengers.

47. When must the "No Smoking" and "Fasten Seatbelts" signs be turned on? (14 CFR 91.517)

They must be turned on during airplane movement on the surface, for each takeoff, for each landing, and when otherwise considered to be necessary by the PIC.

48. Before each takeoff the pilot-in-command of an airplane carrying passengers shall ensure that all passengers have been orally briefed on what information? (14 CFR 91.519)

a. Smoking.

b. Use of safety belts and shoulder harnesses.

c. Location and means for opening the passenger entry door and emergency exits.

d. Location of survival equipment.

e. Ditching procedures and the use of flotation equipment required under §91.509 for a flight over water.

f. The normal and emergency use of oxygen equipment installed on the airplane.

49. Explain how an inaccurate passenger count prior to departure could result in violation of multiple Part 91 and 121 regulations. (14 CFR 91.605, 121,189, 121.191, 121.195)

a. If the additional passengers resulted in the takeoff weight exceeding the takeoff weight specified in the AFM, then a pilot could be found in violation of §91.605 (Transport category civil airplane weight limitations) and §121.189 (Turbine engine powered takeoff limitations).

b. Weight calculations based on inaccurate data could affect engine performance calculations, including engine-out performance, weight and balance and fuel requirements. A pilot could face violations of:

- §121.189—Turbine engine powered; takeoff limitations
- §121.191—Turbine engine powered: Enroute limitations: One engine inoperative
- §121.195—Turbine engine powered: Landing limitations: Destination airports

An inaccurate passenger count could result in a pilot (and operator) facing numerous violations.

50. How is the information obtained from cockpit voice recorders (CVR) and flight data recorders used after an accident? (14 CFR 91.609)

Information obtained from the CVR is used to assist in determining the cause of accidents or occurrences in connection with the investigation under Part 830. The Administrator does not use the CVR in any civil penalty or certificate action. An operator shall keep the recorded information for at least 60 days or, if requested by the Administrator or the Board, for a longer period.

51. When conducting a flight operation of a U.S. registered civil aircraft outside the United States, what general rules apply? (14 CFR 91.703)

Each person operating a civil aircraft of U.S. registry outside of the United States shall:

a. When over the high seas, comply with ICAO Annex 2 rules and with §91.117 (aircraft speed), §91.127 (Class E airspace), §91.129 (Class D airspace), and §91.131 (Class B airspace) rules;

b. When within a foreign country, comply with the regulations relating to the flight and maneuver of aircraft there in force;

c. Except for §91.117 (aircraft speed), §91.307 (parachute operations), §91.309 (glider towing), §91.323 (increased maximum weights in Alaska), and §91.711 (special rules foreign aircraft), comply with this Part so far as it is not inconsistent with applicable regulations of the foreign country where the aircraft is operated or ICAO Annex 2; and

d. When operating within airspace designated as RVSM airspace, comply with §91.706 (RVSM airspace operations).

e. For aircraft subject to ICAO Annex 16, carry on board the aircraft documents that summarize the noise operating characteristics and certifications of the aircraft that demonstrate compliance with this Part and Part 36 (Noise Standards).

52. What requirements must be met before conducting operations within RVSM airspace? (AC 91-85, 14 CFR 91.706)

a. Aircraft is RVSM compliant (equipment requirements, maintenance requirements).

b. Pilots are trained and knowledgeable in RVSM procedures and operations.

c. Aircraft meets RVSM altitude-keeping performance.

d. Flight planning meets RVSM requirements.

D. 14 CFR Part 111

General

1. Explain the purpose of 14 CFR Part 111.

Part 111 prescribes rules governing the use of the Pilot Records Database (PRD) and implements statutory requirements to facilitate the sharing of pilot records among air carriers and other operators in a database managed by the FAA.

2. Which operators do the 14 CFR Part 111 regulations apply to? (AC 120-68, 14 CFR 111.1)

a. Part 119 certificate holders (Part 121, 125, or 135).

b. Fractional ownerships (Part 91 Subpart K operators).

c. Air tour operators who have been issued an LOA in accordance with 14 CFR §91.147.

d. Corporate flight departments operating two or more standard airworthiness airplanes that require a type rating and/or operating a turbine-powered rotorcraft, in furtherance of or incidental to a business.

e. Public aircraft operators (PAO).

f. Trustee in bankruptcy of any operator or entity described in §111.1.

3. **What is the purpose of the Pilot Records Database (PRD)?** (AC 120-68)

   The PRD is an FAA database used to facilitate the sharing of pilot records among air carriers in a clearinghouse managed by the FAA. All Part 119 certificate holders, fractional ownerships, and air tour operators holding a letter of authorization (LOA) are required to access the PRD and evaluate the available data for each individual pilot candidate prior to making a hiring decision.

4. **Which individuals are eligible to access the PRD?** (AC 120-68, 14 CFR 111.10)

   a. *Responsible person*—An individual at the air carrier serving in a required management position, which may include director of safety, director of operations, chief pilot, director of maintenance, chief inspector, or other responsible management position, who will provide supervisory control concerning the PRD process.

   b. *Authorized users*—An individual(s) who is employed by the air carrier or operator and who has been assigned access rights to the PRD on behalf of the employer by the responsible person to perform specific functions within the PRD. These access rights are conferred by various user roles.

   c. *The pilot*—An individual certificated by the FAA at the Commercial, ATP, or Remote Pilot level with an FAA medical certificate that is the subject of a record request in the PRD.

5. **Are operators allowed to collect PRD data about a pilot for a purpose other than to provide information for a hiring decision?** (14 CFR 111.20, 111.30)

   No person may use the PRD for any purpose other than to inform a hiring decision concerning a pilot or to report information on behalf of the operator, entity, or trustee. Skimming or otherwise aggregating pilot data outside of the PRD for resale or to provide a list of pre-screened pilots is strictly prohibited by both 14 CFR §111.20 and 49 U.S.C. §44703(i).

6. **What pilot certification is necessary to register for access to the PRD?** (PRD Pilot User Guide, AC 120-68)

   Only pilots holding an FAA Commercial, ATP, or Remote Pilot Certificate with a current medical certificate can register in the PRD. Because the PRD is intended to be used in the hiring process for certain operators, pilots who do not meet basic eligibility requirements for those positions are not included in the database.

7. **What is a PAR?** (PRD Pilot User Guide)

   A PRD Airman Record (PAR) is the pilot report issued by the Pilot Records Database to the requestor that includes the FAA records. The PAR is a static file; the data is frozen at the moment of consent and will not include any additional data after the consent has been granted. The same static file is viewed by the pilot and the air carrier or proxy "consumer" role.

8. **For what period of time are a pilot's records maintained in the PRD?** (14 CFR 111.40)

   Pilot records are maintained in the PRD for the life of the pilot, until the FAA receives a certified copy of the pilot's death certificate.

Access to and Evaluation of Records

1. **Which operators are required to evaluate a pilot's records in the PRD prior to making a hiring decision?** (AC 120-68, 14 CFR 111.100)

   a. Part 119 certificate holders (Part 121, 125, or 135).

   b. Fractional ownerships (Part 91 Subpart K).

   c. Air tour operators who have been issued an LOA in accordance with 14 CFR §91.147.

   d. Optional record review—corporate flight departments and public aircraft operations (PAO) may also elect to review records in accordance with 14 CFR Part 111 Subpart B, as set forth in §111.100.

2. **Before an operator may permit an individual to begin service as a pilot, what information in the PRD must be evaluated?** (14 CFR 111.105)

   a. All FAA records in the PRD as described in §111.135.

   b. All records in the PRD submitted by a reporting entity.

   c. All motor vehicle driving records obtained in accordance with §111.110.

   d. The employment history the pilot provides to the PRD.

3. **Does an operator automatically have access to a pilot's motor vehicle driving records?** (14 CFR 111.110)

   No, the reviewing entity must first obtain the written consent from the pilot, in accordance with §111.310, before requesting a National Driver Register (NDR) search for the individual's state motor vehicle driving records. After obtaining the written consent, the reviewing entity must submit a request to the NDR to determine whether any state maintains relevant records pertaining to that pilot.

4. **Are operators allowed to access the PRD without consent from the pilot?** (14 CFR 111.120)

   No reviewing entity may retrieve records in the PRD pertaining to any pilot prior to receiving that pilot's written consent authorizing the release of that pilot's information maintained in the PRD.

5. **What type of FAA pilot records are provided in the PRD?** (14 CFR 111.135)

   FAA records include:

   a. Current pilot and medical certificate information, including associated type ratings and information on any limitations to those certificates and ratings.

   b. Any failed attempt of an individual to pass a practical test required to obtain a certificate or type rating under 14 CFR Part 61.

   c. Records related to enforcement actions resulting in a violation of Title 49 of the United States Code or a regulation prescribed or order issued under that title.

d. Records related to an individual acting as PIC or SIC during an aviation accident or incident.

e. Records related to an individual's pre-employment drug and alcohol testing history and other U.S. DOT drug and alcohol testing, including:

- Verified positive drug test results.
- Alcohol misuse violations including confirmed alcohol results of 0.04 or greater.
- Refusals to submit to drug or alcohol testing.

Note: Effective December 7, 2021, all air carriers and operators required to review records in accordance with PRIA and/or Part 111, must use the PRD to obtain the related FAA records.

6. Will the PRD be the only information source an operator considers when evaluating a pilot as a new hire employee? (AC 120-68)

No. The PRD is a starting point from which additional investigation may be warranted. The records available in the PRD are intended to assist reviewing entities in making informed hiring decisions and may indicate areas of concern where additional review may be appropriate.

Reporting of Records

1. Which operators are required to report records to the PRD about individuals employed as pilots? (AC 120-68, 14 CFR 111.200)

a. Part 119 certificate holders (Part 121, 125, and 135).

b. Fractional ownerships (Part 91 Subpart K).

c. Air tour operators conducting operations in accordance with §91.147.

d. Corporate flight departments as described in §111.1.

e. Entities conducting public aircraft operations (PAO) as defined in 49 U.S.C. 40102(a)(41).

f. The trustee in bankruptcy of any operator or entity described in §111.1.

2. In addition to FAA-reported records, what additional records are operators required to report into the PRD?
(AC 120-68, 14 CFR 111.220–111.240)

Operators, entities, and trustees are required to report certain records to the PRD in accordance with Part 111 Subpart C. These records include:

a. Training, qualification, and proficiency records (§111.225).

b. Final disciplinary action records (§111.230).

c. Drug and alcohol records (§111.220).

d. Final separation from employment records (§111.235).

e. Verification of motor vehicle driving record (§111.240).

Note: Not all record types are required to be reported by all types of reporting entities. The appendices in AC 120-68 provide an explanation of the types of records to be entered into the PRD by each reporting entity in order to meet the requirements of Part 111 Subpart C.

3. After an operator has discovered or is informed of an error in a pilot's record, how long does that operator have to correct that error or inaccuracy?
(14 CFR 111.250)

The operator must correct the record in the PRD within 10 days of identification, or initiate dispute resolution in accordance with §111.250(b).

4. What actions are required of an operator who disagrees with a pilot's request for correction of a record?
(14 CFR 111.250)

The operator must:

a. Initiate an investigation of any dispute within 30 days of determining that it does not agree that the record identified is inaccurate.

b. Provide a final disposition within a reasonable amount of time to any request for dispute resolution made by an individual about PRD records.

c. Document in the PRD the final disposition of any dispute made by the pilot.

5. How will a record that has been disputed be displayed in the PRD? (AC 120-68)

When a record is marked in dispute in the PRD, it will still be displayed to reviewing entities as any other record would. However, it will be flagged as "disputed" in the PRD Airman Record (PAR). This is intended to indicate to the reviewing entity that the pilot has indicated the record is inaccurate. This will provide an opportunity for the reviewing entity and pilot to discuss the matter.

Pilot Access and Responsibilities

1. Why is it necessary for a pilot to have access to the PRD? (14 CFR 111.305)

Electronic access by the pilot to the PRD is required when:

a. The pilot seeks to review and obtain a copy of that pilot's own comprehensive PRD record.

b. The pilot gives consent to a particular operator to access that pilot's comprehensive PRD record.

c. The pilot exercises any other privileges provided by 14 CFR Part 111.

2. Once a pilot has received electronic access to the PRD, what activities can the pilot accomplish within the database? (AC 120-68, PRD Pilot User Guide)

a. Retrieve and display the pilot's current PAR assembled from various sources with a date and time stamp.

b. Grant or revoke consent for one or more air carriers to view the PAR for the purposes of employment.

c. Enter current and/or former employers for which the airman was employed as a pilot within the previous five years, at a minimum.

d. Enter the National Driver Register (NDR) request date, if available. If the airman does not request the NDR data, the air carrier must do so.

3. **Who is responsible for the accuracy of the pilot's employment history in the PRD?** (AC 120-68, 14 CFR 111.310)

   The pilot is responsible for ensuring his or her employment history is accurate when granting consent to reviewing entities. Provision of consent must include an affirmation that the employment history of the pilot for five years preceding the date of consent is accurate and complete.

4. **Is a pilot required to report all previous employers where they were employed as a professional pilot?** (PRD Pilot User Guide, 14 CFR 61.59)

   Yes. It is considered a falsification and subject to enforcement action if current and/or former employers are omitted. You are encouraged to enter as many employers for which you were employed with as a pilot if your experience extends beyond five years.

5. **After a pilot has granted the necessary consent, what period of time does an operator have to access and view that pilot's PAR?** (PRD Pilot User Guide)

   Consent is valid for a specific period of time the pilot selects (i.e., 30, 45, or 60 days) during which time the air carrier who has received access may view or download the pilot's PRD Airman Record (PAR) as often as necessary. Consent is revoked by either the expiration of the consent period which the pilot selected or by the pilot selecting to revoke the consent for a specific air carrier.

6. **What action should pilots take if they discover inaccurate or incorrect information within the PRD?** (14 CFR 111.320, AC 120-68)

   A pilot who identifies an error or inaccuracy in that pilot's PRD records must report the error or inaccuracy to the PRD in a form and manner acceptable to the FAA Administrator. The PRD includes an inaccuracy and dispute function that can be used by a pilot who discovers an employer-generated record is inaccurate.

PRD Web Resources

The following are online sources of information on the Pilot Records Database for further study.

Electronic Code of Federal Regulations: 14 CFR Part 111
www.ecfr.gov/current/title-14/chapter-I/subchapter-G/part-111

FAA Advisory Circular (AC) 120-68J: Pilot Records Database and Pilot Records Improvement Act
www.faa.gov/documentLibrary/media/Advisory_Circular/
AC_120-68J.pdf

PRD Pilot User Guides
www.faa.gov/regulations_policies/pilot_records_database/
resources/

Pilot Records Database
www.faa.gov/regulations_policies/pilot_records_database/

E. 14 CFR Part 117

1. What is 14 CFR Part 117? (14 CFR 117.1)

Part 117 prescribes flight and duty limitations and rest requirements for all flight crewmembers and certificate holders conducting passenger operations under Part 121. This regulation also applies to all flight crewmembers and Part 121 certificate holders conducting flights under Part 91 (other than subpart K) as a domestic passenger, flag passenger, or supplemental passenger operation.

2. What is the definition of *fatigue*? (14 CFR 117.3, AC 117-3)

Fatigue means a physiological state of reduced mental or physical performance capability resulting from lack of sleep or increased physical activity that can reduce a flight crewmember's alertness and ability to safely operate an aircraft or perform safety-related duties. Advisory Circular 117-3, *Fitness for Duty*, provides valuable information pertaining to awareness and understanding of fatigue, the effects of fatigue on pilots, and fatigue countermeasures.

3. Define the term *flight duty period* (FDP). (14 CFR 117.3)

An FDP is a period that begins when a flight crewmember is required to report for duty with the intention of conducting a flight, a series of flights, or positioning or ferrying flights, and ends when the aircraft is parked after the last flight and there is no intention for further aircraft movement by the same flight crewmember. An FDP includes the duties performed by the flight crewmember on behalf of the certificate holder that occur before a flight segment or between flight segments without a required intervening rest period.

4. What are several examples of tasks that would be considered part of the FDP? (14 CFR 117.3)

Examples of tasks that are part of the FDP include deadhead transportation, training conducted in an aircraft or flight simulator, and airport/standby reserve, if the above tasks occur before a flight segment or between flight segments without an intervening required rest period.

5. Define the term *rest period*. (14 CFR 117.3)

Rest period means a continuous period determined prospectively during which the flight crewmember is free from all restraint by the certificate holder, including freedom from present responsibility for work should the occasion arise.

6. Define the term *physiological night's rest*. (14 CFR 117.3)

Physiological night's rest means 10 hours of rest that encompasses the hours of 0100 and 0700 at the flight crewmember's home base, unless the individual has acclimated to a different theater. If the flight crewmember has acclimated to a different theater, the rest must encompass the hours of 0100 and 0700 at the acclimated location.

7. Is time spent deadheading considered rest time? (14 CFR 117.3)

No. All time spent in deadhead transportation is duty and is not rest.

8. **What is the definition of an *augmented flight crew*?** (14 CFR 117.3)

   An augmented flight crew is one that has more than the minimum number of flight crewmembers required by the airplane type certificate to operate the aircraft to allow a flight crewmember to be replaced by another qualified flight crewmember for in-flight rest.

9. **Who has the responsibility for ensuring that each flight crewmember is rested and working the correct number of hours?** (14 CFR 117.5)

   It is the joint responsibility of the certificate holder and the flight crewmember.

10. **What are the maximum flight time limits for crewmembers of un-augmented operations?** (14 CFR 117.11)

    Maximum flight time for the minimum required flight crew of two is limited to 8 or 9 hours depending on the start time (acclimated time of report) of the flight crewmember. Total flight time for a three-pilot flight crew cannot exceed 13 hours and total flight time for a four-pilot flight crew cannot exceed 17 hours.

11. **How many maximum flight duty period hours are allowed for un-augmented operations? Augmented operations?** (14 CFR 117.13, 117.17)

    Un-augmented—9 to 14 FDP hours based on time of start (acclimated time) and the number of flight segments.

    Augmented—13 to 19 FDP hours based on scheduled time of start (acclimated), class of rest facility, and number of pilots.

12. **Do the regulations allow the scheduled flight duty time limitations of a flight crewmember to be extended?** (14 CFR 117.19)

    Yes. With certain limitations, the PIC and the certificate holder may extend the maximum flight duty period specified by this Part up to 2 hours. The PIC and the certificate holder may also extend the maximum combined flight duty period and reserve availability period limits specified in §117.21(c)(3) and (4) for up to 2 hours.

13. How much of the time that a flight crewmember spends in airport/standby reserve is considered as part of the flight crewmember's flight duty period? (14 CFR 117.21)

For airport/standby reserve, all time spent in a reserve status is part of the flight crewmember's flight duty period.

14. What are the cumulative duty limitations on the amount of total flight time a pilot may be assigned? (14 CFR 117.23)

100 hours in any 672 consecutive hours or 1,000 hours in any 365 consecutive calendar-day period.

15. What are the cumulative duty limitations on the amount of flight duty period hours a pilot may be assigned in any 168 or 672 consecutive hours? (14 CFR 117.23)

60 flight duty period hours in any 168 consecutive hours or 190 flight duty period hours in any 672 consecutive hours.

16. What minimum number of rest period hours must be given to a pilot prior to assignment of a flight duty period? (14 CFR 117.25)

No certificate holder may schedule and no flight crewmember may accept an assignment for any reserve or flight duty period unless the flight crewmember is given a rest period of at least 10 consecutive hours immediately before beginning the reserve or flight duty period measured from the time the flight crewmember is released from duty. The 10 hour rest period must provide the flight crewmember with a minimum of 8 uninterrupted hours of sleep opportunity.

17. How is a pilot's rest period measured? (14 CFR 117.25)

It's measured from the time the flight crewmember is released from duty to the start time of the duty period following the rest period.

18. What is the minimum number of consecutive hours a pilot must be free from all duty in any 168 consecutive-hour period? (14 CFR 117.25)

Before beginning any reserve or flight duty period, a flight crewmember must be given at least 30 consecutive hours free from all duty within the past 168 consecutive-hour period.

19. What are the crew rest requirements for a flight crewmember who has been away from home base for an extended amount of time? (14 CFR 117.25)

A flight crewmember must be given a minimum of 56 consecutive hours rest upon return to home base if the flight crewmember travels more than 60° longitude during a flight duty period or a series of flight duty periods and is away from home base for more than 168 consecutive hours during this travel. The 56 hours of rest must encompass three physiological nights' rest based on local time.

20. Are there any crew rest requirements for a flight crewmember who has exceeded the applicable flight duty period while engaged in deadhead transportation? (14 CFR 117.25)

Yes, the flight crewmember must be given a rest period equal to the length of the deadhead transportation but not less than the rest required by 14 CFR §117.25 (10 consecutive hours) before beginning a FDP.

F. 14 CFR Part 121

1. What type of operations are governed by Part 121? (14 CFR 121.1)

Part 121 prescribes rules governing domestic, flag, and supplemental operations of each person who holds or is required to hold an air carrier certificate or operating certificate under 14 CFR Part 119.

2. Which manuals are required to be carried onboard a Part 121 air carrier aircraft? (14 CFR 121.133, 121.137, 121.141)

a. An airplane flight manual (AFM) or company flight manual (CFM). (14 CFR §121.141)

b. A flight operations manual (FOM). (14 CFR §121.133)

Note: 14 CFR §121.137 requires that the FOM or appropriate parts of it are readily accessible to the flight crew when performing their assigned duties.

3. **Where would a Part 121 pilot locate instructions and information on the procedures for operating a flight in periods of ice, hail, thunderstorms, turbulence, or any potentially hazardous meteorological condition?** (14 CFR Part 121.133)

The flight operations manual required by 14 CFR 121.133.

4. **Which manual would a Part 121 pilot or dispatcher reference to find instructions and information concerning continuance of flight after equipment required for the particular type of operation becomes inoperative or unserviceable en route?** (14 CFR 121.133, 121.135)

The FOM.

5. **What is the name of the manual that provides direction and guidance to ground crews for the safe and efficient performance of their duties?** (drs.faa.gov, 14 CFR 121.135, 135.23)

The general operations manual (GOM). The Part 121 and 135 regulations specify topics that an operator's GOM must address. The operator's GOM must contain the duties and responsibilities for each category of employee including sufficient policy, direction, and guidance to each employee for the safe and efficient performance of their duties. In addition, an operator's GOM must address the policies, systems, and procedures necessary to comply with ops specs provisions and safe operating practices.

6. **Who must the crew of a domestic or flag air carrier airplane be able to communicate with, under normal conditions, along the entire route of flight?** (14 CFR 121.99)

A two-way radio communication system or other approved means of communication is available over the entire route between each airplane and the appropriate dispatch office, and between each airplane and the appropriate air traffic control unit.

7. **What effective runway length is required for a turbojet powered airplane at the destination airport if the runways are forecast to be wet or slippery at the ETA?** (14 CFR 121.195)

   115 percent of the runway length required for a dry runway.

8. **What portable electronic devices may be operated during flight?** (14 CFR 121.306)

   a. Portable voice recorders.

   b. Hearing aids.

   c. Heart pacemakers.

   d. Electric shavers.

   e. Portable oxygen concentrators that comply with the requirements in §121.574.

   f. Any other portable electronic device that the Part 119 certificate holder has determined will not cause interference with the navigation or communication.

9. **When must the emergency lights on a passenger-carrying airplane be armed or turned on?** (14 CFR 121.310)

   The emergency lights must be armed or turned on during taxiing, takeoff, and landing.

10. **A crewmember interphone system is required on which airplane?** (14 CFR 121.319)

    No person may operate an airplane with a seating capacity of more than 19 passengers unless the airplane is equipped with a crewmember interphone system.

11. **What are the passenger oxygen supply requirements for a flight, in a turbine-powered aircraft, when operating above cabin pressure altitudes of 10,000 feet?** (14 CFR 121.329)

    Each certificate holder shall provide a supply of oxygen for passengers in accordance with the following:

    a. At cabin pressure altitudes above 10,000 feet, up to and including 14,000 feet—enough oxygen for that part of the flight at those altitudes that is of more than 30 minutes duration, for 10 percent of the passengers.

    b. At cabin pressure altitudes above 14,000 feet, up to and including 15,000 feet—enough oxygen for that part of the flight at those altitudes for 30 percent of the passengers.

    c. At cabin pressure altitudes above 15,000 feet—enough oxygen for each passenger carried during the entire flight at those altitudes.

12. **What are the pilot supplemental oxygen requirements for emergency descent of turbine-engine-powered airplanes with pressurized cabins?** (14 CFR 121.333)

    At flight altitudes above 10,000 feet—a minimum of a 2-hour supply of supplemental oxygen must be provided for each flight crewmember on flight deck duty.

    At flight altitudes above FL250—if it becomes necessary for one pilot to leave his/her duty station, the remaining pilot shall put on and use an oxygen mask until the other pilot has returned to the duty station. *Exception:* one pilot need not wear and use an oxygen mask if each flight crewmember on flight deck duty has a quick-donning type of oxygen mask. A flight crewmember must be able to put on and start using a quick-donning oxygen mask within 5 seconds.

13. **For the purposes of testing a flight recorder system, how much data may be erased?** (14 CFR 121.343)

    A total of 1 hour of the oldest recorded data may be erased for the purpose of testing the flight recorder or the flight recorder system.

14. In which airplanes are Class A terrain awareness and warning systems (TAWS) required? (14 CFR 121.354)

No person may operate a turbine-powered airplane unless that airplane is equipped with an approved terrain awareness and warning system that meets the requirements for Class A equipment in TSO-C151. The airplane must also include an approved terrain situational awareness display.

15. What are the airborne weather radar equipment requirements for air carriers? (14 CFR 121.357)

No person may dispatch an airplane (or begin the flight of an airplane in the case of a certificate holder that does not use a dispatch system) under IFR or night VFR conditions when current weather reports indicate that thunderstorms, or other potentially hazardous weather conditions that can be detected with airborne weather radar, may reasonably be expected along the route to be flown, unless the airborne weather radar equipment is in satisfactory operating condition.

If the airborne weather radar becomes inoperative en route, the airplane must be operated in accordance with the approved instructions and procedures specified in the operations manual for such an event.

16. When must the cockpit voice recorder be on and operative? (14 CFR 121.359)

The CVR must be operated continuously from the start of the "before starting engine" checklist to completion of final checklist upon flight termination.

17. What is the mandatory retirement age for a Part 121 airline pilot? (14 CFR 121.383)

No certificate holder may use the services of any person as a pilot on an airplane engaged in operations under this part if that person has reached his or her 65th birthday.

18. What is the minimum pilot crew required when operating under Part 121? (14 CFR 121.385)

The minimum pilot crew is two pilots, and the certificate holder shall designate one pilot as PIC and the other SIC.

19. **What is the minimum number of flight attendants required on an airplane having the following seating capacities: 30, 70, 120?** (14 CFR 121.391)

    a. For airplanes having a maximum payload capacity of more than 7,500 pounds and having a seating capacity of more than 9 but less than 51 passengers—one flight attendant.

    b. For airplanes having a maximum payload capacity of 7,500 pounds or less and having a seating capacity of more than 19 but less than 51 passengers—one flight attendant.

    c. For airplanes having a seating capacity of more than 50 but less than 101 passengers—two flight attendants.

    d. For airplanes having a seating capacity of more than 100 passengers—two flight attendants plus one additional flight attendant for each unit (or part of a unit) of 50 passenger seats above a seating capacity of 100 passengers.

20. **For the purposes of air carrier training programs, airplanes are grouped into what two categories?** (14 CFR 121.400)

    Group I—Propeller driven, including reciprocating powered, and turboprop powered.

    Group II—Turbojet powered.

21. **Define the following types of training: *initial, transition, upgrade, differences.*** (14 CFR 121.400)

    Initial training—Required for crewmembers and dispatchers who have not qualified and served in the same capacity on another airplane of the same group.

    Transition training—Required for crewmembers and dispatchers who have qualified and served in the same capacity on another airplane of the same group.

    Upgrade training—Required for flight crewmembers who have qualified and served as SIC on a particular airplane type, before they serve as PIC on that airplane.

    Conversion training—Required for flight crewmembers who have qualified and served as flight engineer on a particular airplane type, before they serve as SIC on that airplane.

Differences training—Required for crewmembers and dispatchers who have qualified and served on a particular type airplane, when the Administrator finds differences training is necessary before a crewmember serves in the same capacity on a particular variation of that airplane.

22. **How often must a crewmember actually operate the airplane emergency equipment after initial training?** (14 CFR 121.417)

Every 24 calendar months.

23. **What type of emergency training must a certificate holder provide to flight crews operating above FL250?** (14 CFR 121.417)

Emergency training in the following subjects:

a. Respiration.

b. Hypoxia.

c. Duration of consciousness without supplemental oxygen at altitudes.

d. Gas expansion.

e. Gas bubble formation.

f. Physical phenomena and incidents of decompression.

24. **Who is responsible for mentoring a new first officer in the practical and technical details of becoming a well-rounded professional airline pilot?** (14 CFR 121.419)

Air carriers conducting domestic, flag, and supplemental operations are now required to provide new-hire pilots with an opportunity to observe flight operations and become familiar with procedures before serving as a flight crewmember in operations. Additionally, air carriers are required to provide leadership and command and mentoring training for all pilots in command. The rule will mitigate incidents of unprofessional pilot behavior and reduce pilot errors that can lead to a catastrophic event.

25. Briefly describe the revised SIC to PIC upgrade curriculum requirements. (14 CFR 121.420, 121.426)

The upgrade curriculum requirements are revised to account for the evolution in Part 121 SIC qualification and experience requirements as a result of the Pilot Certification and Qualification Requirements for Air Carrier Operations Final Rule requirements.

a. *Upgrade ground training*—Must include instruction on seat dependent procedures, duty position procedures, and CRM. Upgrade ground training must also include instruction and facilitated discussion on leadership and command and mentoring.

b. *Upgrade flight training*—Must include seat dependent maneuvers and procedures, duty position maneuvers and procedures, extended envelope training, wind-shear training, and scenario-based training (SBT) incorporating CRM and leadership and command skills.

26. What requirements must be met by an airline pilot to re-establish recency of experience? (14 CFR 121.439)

A required pilot flight crewmember must have made:

a. Three takeoffs and landings within the preceding 90 days in type.

b. One takeoff with a simulated failure of the most critical powerplant.

c. One landing from an ILS approach to the lowest ILS minimums authorized for the certificate holder.

d. One landing to a full stop.

Note: Under the supervision of a check airman, the three takeoffs and landings required, may be performed in a Level B or higher FFS approved under §121.407.

27. What are the line check requirements for the pilot-in-command of a domestic air carrier? (14 CFR 121.440)

Within the preceding 12 calendar months, the PIC must have passed a line check in which they satisfactorily perform the duties and responsibilities of a PIC in one of the types of airplanes they are to fly.

28. How often must a pilot-in-command complete a proficiency check? (14 CFR 121.409, 121.441)

A PIC must complete a proficiency check within the preceding 12 calendar months in the aircraft type in which the person is to serve and, in addition, within the preceding 6 calendar months, either a proficiency check or the approved full flight simulator (FFS) course of training.

29. How often must a pilot flight crewmember other than a pilot-in-command complete a proficiency check or line-oriented training? (14 CFR 121.409, 121.441)

The pilot must have received within the preceding 24 calendar months either a proficiency check or the line oriented simulator training course under §121.409; and within the preceding 12 calendar months, either a proficiency check or any simulator training course under §121.409.

30. Describe the responsibilities shared by the aircraft dispatcher and the pilot-in-command. (14 CFR 121.533)

Joint responsibility:

- The PIC and the aircraft dispatcher are jointly responsible for the preflight planning, delay, and dispatch release of a flight.

Aircraft dispatcher responsibility:

- Monitoring the progress of each flight.
- Issuing necessary information for the safety of the flight.
- Cancelling or re-dispatching a flight if, in his or her opinion or the opinion of the PIC, the flight cannot operate or continue to operate safely as planned or released.

PIC responsibility during flight time:

- In command of the aircraft and crew and is responsible for the safety of the passengers, crewmembers, cargo, and airplane.
- Has full control and authority in the operation of the aircraft, without limitation, over other crewmembers and their duties during flight time, whether or not he or she holds valid certificates authorizing him or her to perform the duties of those crewmembers.

31. **With regard to flight crewmember duties, what operations are considered to be in the critical phase of flight?** (14 CFR 121.542)

Critical phases of flight include all ground operations involving taxi, takeoff and landing, and all other flight operations conducted below 10,000 feet, except cruise flight. No flight crewmember may engage in, nor may any PIC permit, any activity during a critical phase that could distract any flight crewmember from the performance of his or her duties or interfere in any way with the proper conduct of those duties.

32. **Do the regulations allow flight crewmembers to use a laptop or wireless communications device for personal use while at their duty station on the flight deck during flight time?** (14 CFR 121.542)

During all flight time, no flight crewmember may use, nor may any PIC permit the use of, a personal wireless communications device or laptop computer while at a flight crewmember duty station unless the purpose is directly related to operation of the aircraft, or for emergency, safety-related, or employment-related communications, in accordance with air carrier procedures approved by the Administrator.

33. **Describe situations that would be a violation of the sterile cockpit rule.** (14 CFR 121.542, FAA InFO 14006)

Duties such as company required calls made for such non-safety related purposes as ordering galley supplies and confirming passenger connections, announcements made to passengers promoting the air carrier or pointing out sights of interest, and filling out company payroll and related records are not required for the safe operation of the aircraft.

34. **Which individuals may be admitted to the flight deck?** (14 CFR 121.547)

No person may admit any person to the flight deck of an aircraft unless the person being admitted is:

a. A crewmember.

b. A FAA air carrier inspector, Department of Defense (DOD) commercial air carrier evaluator, or NTSB representative who is performing official duties.

   c. Any person who has permission of the PIC, an appropriate management official of the Part 119 certificate holder, and the FAA; and is an employee of

- the United States;
- a Part 119 certificate holder whose duties are necessary or advantageous for safe operation; or
- a FAA certificated aeronautical enterprise whose duties are necessary or advantageous for safe operation.

   d. Any person who has the permission of the PIC, an appropriate management official of the Part 119 certificate holder and the FAA.

35. Who has the responsibility of ensuring that appropriate aeronautical charts are aboard an aircraft? (14 CFR 121.549)

The PIC shall ensure that appropriate aeronautical charts containing adequate information concerning navigation aids and instrument approach procedures are aboard the aircraft for each flight.

36. What action shall the pilot-in-command take if it becomes necessary to shut down one of the two engines on an air carrier airplane? (14 CFR 121.565)

The PIC must land at the nearest suitable airport (in reference to time, not distance) at which a safe landing can be made.

37. When is the door to the flight crew compartment required to be closed and locked? (14 CFR 121.587)

The PIC of an airplane that has a lockable flight crew compartment door in accordance with §121.313 and that is carrying passengers shall ensure that the door separating the flight crew compartment from the passenger compartment is closed and locked at all times when the aircraft is being operated.

38. A domestic air carrier flight has a delay while on the ground at an intermediate airport. What period of time is allowed before a re-dispatch release is required? (14 CFR 121.593)

Except when an airplane lands at an intermediate airport specified in the original dispatch release and remains there for not more than one hour, no person may start a flight unless an aircraft dispatcher specifically authorizes that flight.

39. Prior to flight, who is responsible for briefing a domestic or flag air carrier PIC with all available weather information? (14 CFR 121.601)

Before beginning a flight, the aircraft dispatcher shall provide the PIC with all available weather reports and forecasts of weather phenomena that may affect the safety of flight, including adverse weather phenomena, such as clear air turbulence, thunderstorms, and low altitude wind shear, for each route to be flown and each airport to be used.

40. What information is an aircraft dispatcher responsible for providing to the pilot-in-command of a domestic or flag carrier during a flight? (14 CFR 121.601)

During a flight, the aircraft dispatcher shall provide the PIC any additional available information of meteorological conditions (including adverse weather phenomena, such as clear air turbulence, thunderstorms, and low altitude wind shear), and irregularities of facilities and services that may affect the safety of the flight.

41. When is a takeoff alternate airport required for departure? (14 CFR 121.617)

If the weather conditions at the airport of takeoff are below the landing minimums in the certificate holder's operations specifications for that airport, no person may dispatch or release an aircraft from that airport unless the dispatch or flight release specifies an alternate airport located within the following distances from the airport of takeoff:

a. *Aircraft having two engines*—not more than one hour from the departure airport at normal cruising speed in still air with one engine inoperative.

b. *Aircraft having three or more engines*—not more than two hours from the departure airport at normal cruising speed in still air with one engine inoperative.

42. **When is an alternate airport required for the destination airport?** (14 CFR 121.619)

No person may dispatch an airplane under IFR or over the top unless there is at least one alternate airport for each destination airport in the dispatch release. When the weather conditions forecast for the destination and first alternate airport are marginal, at least one additional alternate must be designated. However, no alternate airport is required if, for at least one hour before and one hour after the estimated time of arrival at the destination airport, the appropriate weather reports or forecasts, or any combination of them, indicate:

a. The ceiling will be at least 2,000 feet above the airport elevation; and

b. Visibility will be at least 3 miles.

43. **What are the minimum weather conditions that must exist for an airport to be listed as an alternate airport in the dispatch release for a domestic air carrier?** (14 CFR 121.625)

Except as provided in §121.624 for ETOPS alternate airports, no person may list an airport as an alternate airport in the dispatch or flight release unless the appropriate weather reports or forecasts, or any combination thereof, indicate that the weather conditions will be at or above the alternate weather minimums specified in the certificate holder's operations specifications for that airport when the flight arrives.

44. **What is Exemption 17347?** (AC 120-118, aes.faa.gov)

Exemption 17347 (was Exemption 3585) allows for a Part 121 operator to dispatch airplanes under IFR when conditional language (TEMPO, PROB, BCMG) in a one-time increment of the weather forecast states that the weather at the destination, alternate airport, or both airports could be below the authorized weather minimums at the ETA when other time increments of the weather forecast state the weather conditions will be at or above the authorized weather minimums. The exemption provides relief from

14 CFR §121.613, §121.619, and §121.625. The flight may depart provided a second alternate that is above the required minimums is filed, and enough fuel is carried to reach the most distant alternate and thereafter fly for an additional 45 minutes at normal cruise.

Note: In an effort to manage exemptions and to facilitate operator compliance with the conditions and limitations of a grant of exemption, the FAA is no longer including similarly situated certificate holders in grants of exemption. Before commencing operations in accordance with Exemption 17347, each certificate holder must obtain an approval from the appropriate FAA certificate-holding district office.

45. If an airport is not listed in a domestic air carrier's operations specifications and does not have the prescribed takeoff minimums, what will the minimum weather conditions be for takeoff? (14 CFR 121.637)

No pilot may takeoff an airplane from an airport that is not listed in the operations specifications unless the weather conditions at that airport are equal to or better than the weather minimums for takeoff prescribed in Part 97. Where minimums are not prescribed for the airport, the weather minimums of 800–2, 900–1½, or 1,000–1 are required.

46. What is the reserve fuel requirement for a domestic air carrier airplane? (14 CFR 121.639)

No person may dispatch or takeoff an airplane unless it has enough fuel to fly to the airport to which it is dispatched, and to fly to and land at the most distant alternate airport (where required) for the airport to which dispatched and thereafter, to fly for 45 minutes at normal cruising fuel consumption.

47. Under what conditions may an air carrier pilot continue an instrument approach to DA/DH or MDA, after receiving a weather report indicating that less than minimum published landing conditions exist at the airport? (14 CFR 121.651)

If a pilot has begun the final approach segment of an instrument approach procedure and after that receives a later weather report indicating below-minimum conditions, the pilot may continue the approach to DA/DH or MDA.

48. If the pilot-in-command's flight time in a particular type airplane is less than 100 hours, what effect will that have on landing minimums? (14 CFR 121.652)

The minimums for the destination airport must be increased by 100 feet and one half statute mile.

49. What information must be contained in, or attached to, the dispatch release for a domestic air carrier flight? (14 CFR 121.687)

It must contain at least the following information concerning each flight:

a. Aircraft identification number.

b. Trip number.

c. Departure airport, intermediate stops, destination airports, and alternate airports.

d. A statement of the type of operation.

e. Minimum fuel supply.

f. Current weather information.

g. ETOPS diversion time, if flight is dispatched as an ETOPS.

50. Each Part 121 certificate holder must prepare a load manifest prior to each flight. What Information should that manifest contain? (14 CFR 121.693)

a. Weight of the aircraft, fuel and oil, cargo, baggage, passengers, and crewmembers.

b. Maximum allowable weight at which the flight can comply with the requirements of §121.693.

c. Actual weight at takeoff.

d. Evidence that the aircraft is loaded within weight and balance limitations.

e. Passenger names (unless this information is maintained by other means).

51. **What documents are required to be carried on board a domestic air carrier flight?** (14 CFR 121.695)

The PIC of an airplane shall carry in the airplane, to its destination, a copy of the completed load manifest (or information from it, except information concerning cargo and passenger distribution), a copy of the dispatch release, and a copy of the flight plan.

G. 14 CFR Part 135

1. **What type of manual is a Part 135 certificate holder required to provide and maintain?** (14 CFR 135.21)

Each certificate holder shall prepare and keep current, a manual setting forth the procedures and policies acceptable to the administrator. The manual must be used by the certificate holder's maintenance, flight, and ground personnel in conducting operations. The certificate holder shall maintain at least one copy of the manual at its principal base of operations. A copy of the manual, or appropriate portions of the manual (and changes and additions) shall be made available to maintenance and ground operations personnel as well as a copy to its flight crewmembers and representatives of the administrator assigned to the certificate holder.

2. **How should a certificate holder prepare and store load manifests?** (14 CFR 135.63)

Each certificate holder for multi-engine aircraft is responsible for preparing and ensuring the accuracy of a load manifest containing information on the loading of the aircraft. The load manifest must include the number of passengers, total weight of the loaded aircraft, maximum allowable takeoff weight, center of gravity limits, center of gravity of the loaded aircraft, registration number or flight number, origin and destination, and crew member identification and crew position assignments. The completed load manifest must be carried by the pilot-in-command of the aircraft to its destination, and the certificate holder must keep copies of completed load manifests for at least 30 days at its principal operations base or another location approved by the FAA Administrator.

3. What are the regulations concerning reporting mechanical irregularities? (14 CFR 135.65)

a. Each certificate holder shall provide an aircraft maintenance log to be carried on board each aircraft for recording or deferring mechanical irregularities and their correction.

b. The pilot-in-command shall enter or have entered in the aircraft maintenance log each mechanical irregularity that comes to the pilot's attention during flight time. Before each flight, the pilot-in-command shall determine the status of each irregularity entered in the maintenance log at the end of the preceding flight (if such information is not already known).

c. Each person who takes corrective action or defers action concerning a reported or observed failure or malfunction, shall record the action taken in the aircraft maintenance log.

d. Copies of the aircraft maintenance log will be maintained in the aircraft for access by appropriate personnel.

4. Which persons may be carried aboard an aircraft without complying with the passenger carrying requirements of 14 CFR Part 135? (14 CFR 135.85)

a. A crewmember or other employee of the certificate holder.

b. A person necessary for the safe handling of animals on the aircraft.

c. A person necessary for the safe handling of hazardous materials.

d. A person performing duty as a security or honor guard accompanying a shipment made by or under the authority of the U.S. government.

e. A military courier or a military route supervisor carried by a military cargo contract air carrier or commercial operator in operations under a military cargo contract, if that carriage is specifically authorized by the appropriate military service.

f. An authorized representative of the Administrator conducting an enroute inspection.

g. A person, authorized by the Administrator, who is performing a duty connected with a cargo operation of the certificate holder.

h. A DOD commercial air carrier evaluator conducting an enroute evaluation.

5. What are the regulations concerning carriage of cargo (including carry-on baggage) in or on the aircraft? (14 CFR 135.87)

No person may carry cargo, including carry-on baggage, in or on any aircraft unless:

a. Cargo is carried in an approved cargo rack, bin, or compartment, and is secured by an approved means.

b. Carry-on baggage is restrained to prevent movement during air turbulence.

c. Cargo is properly secured, packaged, or covered and does not exceed seat or floor load limitations.

d. Cargo does not obstruct access to exits or the view of any required signs.

e. The baggage under each passenger seat is prevented from sliding under crash impacts.

f. The cargo carried in compartments requiring entry for fire extinguishing must be loaded so a crewmember can reach all parts of the compartment with a hand fire extinguisher.

6. What are the pilot oxygen requirements? (14 CFR 135.89)

Unpressurized aircraft—At altitudes above 10,000 feet through 12,000 feet MSL for that part of the flight at those altitudes that is of more than 30 minutes duration and at altitudes above 12,000 feet MSL, each pilot must use oxygen continuously.

Pressurized aircraft—Use of supplemental oxygen as follows:

• Above 12,000 feet cabin pressure altitude—pilot at controls must use oxygen continuously.

• Above FL250—if one pilot leaves duty station, remaining pilot shall use oxygen.

• Through FL350—maximum altitude without one pilot wearing and using oxygen mask (if quick-donning oxygen mask available).

• Above FL350—at least one pilot shall wear a secured and sealed oxygen mask (quick-donning type).

7. **What is the minimum passenger-seating configuration that requires a second-in-command?** (14 CFR 135.99)

If the aircraft has a passenger-seating configuration of 10 seats or more (excluding any pilot seat), a SIC is required.

8. **Can a pilot log second-in-command flight time in a multi-engine airplane in a Part 135 operation that does not require a second-in-command?** (14 CFR 135.99)

Yes. A certificate holder authorized to conduct operations under instrument flight rules may receive authorization from the Administrator through its operations specifications to establish an SIC professional development program. As part of that program, a pilot employed by the certificate holder may log time as SIC in operations conducted under Part 135 and Part 91 that do not require a second pilot by type certification of the aircraft or the regulation under which the flight is being conducted, provided the flight operation is conducted in accordance with the certificate holder's operations specifications for SIC professional development program.

9. **What passenger-seating configuration (excluding any pilot seat) requires a flight attendant crewmember to be on board?** (14 CFR 135.107)

No certificate holder may operate an aircraft that has a passenger-seating configuration of more than 19 (excluding any pilot seat), unless there is a flight attendant crewmember on board the aircraft.

10. **Before each takeoff, the pilot-in-command of an aircraft carrying passengers shall ensure that all passengers have been orally briefed on what information?** (14 CFR 135.117)

The PIC shall ensure that all have been orally briefed on smoking, the use of safety belts, the placement of seat backs in an upright position before takeoff and landing, location and means for opening the passenger entry door and emergency exits, location of survival equipment, ditching procedures and the use of required flotation equipment (if the flight involves extended overwater operation), the normal and emergency use of oxygen (if the flight involves operations above 12,000 feet MSL), and the location and operation of fire extinguishers.

11. **What aircraft, operating under Part 135, are required to have a third gyroscopic bank and pitch indicator installed?** (14 CFR 135.149)

    Turbojet airplanes. In addition to two gyroscopic bank and pitch indicators (artificial horizons) for use at the pilot stations, a third artificial horizon indicator must also be installed. It must be powered from a source independent of the electrical generating system, be capable of reliable operation for a minimum of 30 minutes after total failure of the electrical generating system, and operate independently of any other attitude indicating system.

12. **Which aircraft must be equipped with an approved public address and crewmember interphone system?** (14 CFR 135.150)

    No person may operate an aircraft having a passenger-seating configuration of more than 19 (excluding any pilot seat), unless it is equipped with a public address system and a crewmember interphone system.

13. **What aircraft are required to have an approved cockpit voice recorder on board?** (14 CFR 135.151)

    A multi-engine, turbine-powered airplane or rotorcraft having a passenger-seating configuration of six or more and for which two pilots are required by certification or operating rules or that has a passenger seating configuration of 20 or more.

14. **In which airplanes are Class A TAWS required?** (14 CFR 135.154)

    No person may operate a turbine-powered U.S.-registered airplane configured with six to nine passenger seats, excluding any pilot seat, unless that airplane is equipped with an approved TAWS that meets the requirements of Class B equipment of TSO-C151a. It also states that no person may operate a turbine-powered U.S.-registered airplane configured with 10 or more passenger seats, excluding any pilot seat, unless that airplane is equipped with a TAWS that meets the provisions of Class A equipment of TSO-C151a.

15. What are the passenger oxygen requirements?
(14 CFR 135.157)

Unpressurized aircraft—Above 15,000 feet MSL, all passengers must be supplied with oxygen. Above 10,000 feet through 15,000 feet MSL, 10 percent of passengers must be supplied with oxygen for any part of flight of more than 30 minutes at those altitudes.

Pressurized aircraft—Above 15,000 feet MSL, the oxygen requirement depends on the aircraft's ability to descend safely to an altitude of 15,000 feet MSL in 4 minutes. If the aircraft can safely descend to 15,000 feet MSL within four minutes, only a 30-minute supply is required.

16. What is the required emergency equipment for extended overwater operations? (14 CFR 135.167)

For extended overwater operations (greater than 50 NM from nearest shoreline)—each seated occupant (not just passengers) must have:

a. Life preservers within easy reach and with approved survivor locator light.

b. Enough approved life rafts (to accommodate the occupants of the aircraft) which will include at least one approved survivor locator light, one approved pyrotechnic signaling device and additional equipment as specified in §135.167.

c. One raft must have a survival-type emergency locator transmitter.

17. In which aircraft, or under what conditions, is airborne thunderstorm detection equipment required? (14 CFR 135.173)

No person may operate an aircraft that has a passenger-seating configuration, of 10 seats or more (excluding any pilot seat) in passenger carrying operations, except a helicopter operating under day VFR conditions, unless the aircraft is equipped with either approved thunderstorm detection equipment or approved airborne weather radar equipment.

18. **What are the emergency equipment requirements for aircraft having a passenger-seating configuration of more than 19 passengers?** (14 CFR 135.177)

    No person may operate an aircraft having a passenger-seating configuration of more than 19 seats (excluding any pilot seat), unless it is equipped with the following emergency equipment:

    a. One approved first aid kit for treatment of injuries likely to occur in flight or in a minor accident.

    b. A crash axe carried so as to be accessible to the crew but inaccessible to passengers during normal operations.

    c. Signs that are visible to all occupants to notify them when smoking is prohibited and when safety belts must be fastened.

19. **To operate an aircraft with certain equipment inoperative under the provisions of a MEL, what document authorizing it must be issued to the certificate holder?** (14 CFR 135.179)

    No person may takeoff an aircraft with inoperable instruments or equipment installed unless an approved MEL exists for that aircraft and the certificate-holding district office has issued the certificate holder operations specifications authorizing operations in accordance with an approved MEL.

20. **A takeoff may not be made from an airport that is below the authorized IFR landing minimums unless what conditions are met?** (14 CFR 135.217)

    There must be an alternate airport with the required IFR landing minimums within 1 hour flying time, at normal cruising speed in still air.

21. **What weather must be forecast to exist at ETA for the destination airport, before a pilot may begin an IFR operation to that airport?** (14 CFR 135.219)

    No person may takeoff an aircraft under IFR or begin an IFR or over the top operation unless the latest weather reports or forecasts, or any combination of them, indicate that weather conditions at the estimated time of arrival at the next airport of intended landing will be at or above authorized IFR landing minimums.

22. When is an alternate for a destination airport not required for a Part 135 flight operating in IFR conditions? (14 CFR 135.223)

No alternate airport is required if a standard instrument approach procedure for the first airport of intended landing is provided and, for at least one hour before and after the estimated time of arrival, the appropriate weather reports or forecasts, or any combination of them, indicate that:

a. The ceiling will be at least 1,500 feet above the lowest circling approach MDA; or

b. If a circling instrument approach is not authorized for the airport, the ceiling will be at least 1,500 feet above the lowest published minimum or 2,000 feet above the airport elevation, whichever is higher; and

c. Visibility for that airport is forecast to be at least 3 miles, or 2 miles more than the lowest applicable visibility minimums, whichever is the greater, for the instrument approach procedure to be used at the destination airport.

23. An instrument approach procedure to an airport may not be initiated unless the latest weather report indicates what minimum weather conditions? (14 CFR 135.225)

The weather report issued by the weather reporting facility at that airport must indicate that weather conditions are at or above the authorized IFR landing minimums for that airport.

Note: A pilot may begin an IAP, or continue an approach, at an airport when the visibility is reported to be less than the visibility minimums prescribed for that procedure if the pilot uses an operable enhanced flight vision system (EFVS) in accordance with §91.176 and the certificate holder's operations specifications for EFVS operations.

24. **After beginning the final approach segment of an instrument approach procedure, a weather report is received indicating the visibility is below prescribed minimums. What action should be taken?** (14 CFR 135.225)

The pilot may continue the approach only if, on reaching the authorized MDA, the pilot finds that the actual weather conditions are at or above the minimums prescribed for the procedure being used.

Note: A pilot may begin an IAP, or continue an approach, at an airport when the visibility is reported to be less than the visibility minimums prescribed for that procedure if the pilot uses an operable EFVS in accordance with §91.176 and the certificate holder's operations specifications for EFVS operations.

25. **What are the operational requirements concerning frost, ice, and snow on aircraft surfaces during takeoff?** (14 CFR 135.227)

Except under certain conditions, no pilot may takeoff an aircraft that has frost, ice, or snow adhering to any rotor blade, propeller, windshield, stabilizing or control surface, to a powerplant installation, or to an airspeed, altimeter, rate-of-climb, flight attitude instrument system, or wing.

26. **To act as pilot-in-command of an aircraft during IFR operations under Part 135, what minimum experience is required?** (14 CFR 135.243)

a. The PIC must hold at least a Commercial Pilot Certificate with appropriate category and class ratings and, if required, an appropriate type rating for that aircraft.

b. The PIC must also have 1,200 hours flight time as a pilot including:
   - 500 hours of cross-country flight time;
   - 100 hours of night time; and
   - 75 hours of actual or simulated instrument time, at least 50 hours of which were in actual flight.

c. The PIC must hold an Instrument Rating or an Airline Transport Pilot Certificate with an Airplane category rating.

27. What are the operating experience requirements that must be met before a pilot may act as PIC of an aircraft operated by a commuter air carrier in passenger-carrying operations? (14 CFR 135.244)

The PIC must have completed the following operating experience in each make and basic model of aircraft to be flown:

- *Single-engine*—10 hours.
- *Multi-engine, reciprocating*—15 hours.
- *Multi-engine, turbine-powered*—20 hours.
- *Turbojet-powered*—25 hours.

Note: Hours of operating experience may be reduced to not less than 50 percent of hours required by the substitution of one additional takeoff and landing for each hour of flight.

28. What are the flight time limitation and rest requirements for Part 135 scheduled operations? (14 CFR 135.265)

No certificate holder may schedule any flight crewmember, and no flight crewmember may accept an assignment, for flight time in scheduled operations or in other commercial flying if that crewmember's total flight time in all commercial flying will exceed:

a. 1,200 hours in any calendar year.

b. 120 hours in any calendar month.

c. 34 hours in any 7 consecutive days.

d. 8 hours during any 24 consecutive hours for a flight crew consisting of one pilot.

e. 8 hours between required rest periods for a flight crew consisting of two pilots qualified under Part 135 for the operation being conducted.

29. What are the instrument proficiency check requirements to act as pilot-in-command under IFR? (14 CFR 135.297)

No certificate holder may use a pilot, nor may any person serve as a PIC of an aircraft under IFR unless, since the beginning of the sixth calendar month before that service, that pilot has passed an instrument proficiency check under this section administered by the Administrator or an authorized check pilot.

30. To serve as pilot-in-command in a Part 135 IFR operation, a person must have passed a line check. How often are line checks required? (14 CFR 135.299)

No certificate holder may use a pilot, nor may any person serve as a PIC of a flight unless, since the beginning of the twelfth calendar month before that service, that pilot has passed a flight check in one of the types of aircraft which that pilot is to fly.

31. What type of emergency training must a certificate holder provide to flight crews operating above FL250? (14 CFR 135.331)

Emergency training in such subjects as:

a. Respiration.

b. Hypoxia.

c. Duration of consciousness without supplemental oxygen at altitudes.

d. Gas expansion.

e. Gas bubble formation.

f. Physical phenomena and incidents of decompression.

32. What are the training requirements for persons involved in the handling or carriage of hazardous materials? (14 CFR 135.505)

No certificate holder may use any crewmember or person to perform any of the job functions or direct supervisory responsibilities, and no person may perform any of the job functions or direct supervisory responsibilities, unless that person has satisfactorily completed the certificate holder's FAA-approved initial or recurrent hazardous materials training program within the past 24 months.

H. 49 CFR Part 830 (NTSB)

1. When is immediate notification to the NTSB required?
(NTSB Part 830)

The operator of an aircraft shall immediately, and by the most expeditious means available, notify the nearest NTSB field office when an aircraft accident or any of the following listed incidents occur:

a. Flight control system malfunction or failure.

b. Crewmember unable to perform normal duties as a result of injury or illness.

c. Turbine engine failure of structural components.

d. In-flight fire.

e. Aircraft collision in flight.

f. Property damage, other than aircraft, estimated to exceed $25,000.

g. An aircraft is overdue and is believed to have been involved in an accident.

h. Release of all or a portion of a propeller blade from an aircraft.

i. Complete loss of information (excluding flickering) from more than 50 percent of an aircraft's EFIS cockpit displays.

j. ACAS resolution advisories issued to IFR aircraft and compliance with is necessary to avert a collision.

k. Helicopter tail or main rotor blade damage that requires major repair or replacement of blades.

l. Air carrier aircraft lands or departs on taxiway, incorrect runway, or area not designated a runway.

m. A runway incursion that requires operator or crew of another aircraft or vehicle to take immediate corrective action to avoid a collision.

2. **In addition to the accident and incident reports required for all aircraft, what additional reports are required for large multi-engine aircraft (more than 12,500 pounds maximum certificated takeoff weight)?** (NTSB Part 830)

   a. In-flight failure of electrical systems that requires the sustained use of an emergency bus powered by a back-up source such as a battery, auxiliary power unit, or air-driven generator to retain flight control or essential instruments;

   b. In-flight failure of hydraulic systems that results in sustained reliance on the sole remaining hydraulic or mechanical system for movement of flight control surfaces;

   c. Sustained loss of the power or thrust produced by two or more engines; and

   d. An evacuation of an aircraft in which an emergency egress system is utilized.

3. **After an accident or incident has occurred, how soon must a report be filed with the NTSB?** (NTSB Part 830)

   The operator shall file a report on NTSB Form 6120.1 or 6120.2, available from NTSB field offices or from the NTSB, Washington D.C., 20594:

   a. Within 10 days after an accident;

   b. When, after 7 days, an overdue aircraft is still missing.

   A report on an incident for which notification is required as described shall be filed only as requested by an authorized representative of the NTSB.

4. **Define the term *aircraft accident*.** (NTSB Part 830.2)

   An aircraft accident means an occurrence associated with the operation of an aircraft which takes place between the time any person boards the aircraft with the intention of flight and all such persons have disembarked, and in which any person suffers death or serious injury, or in which the aircraft receives substantial damage. For purposes of this Part, the definition of aircraft accident includes unmanned aircraft accident, as defined herein.

5. Define the term *aircraft incident.* (NTSB Part 830.2)

An aircraft incident means an occurrence other than an accident associated with the operation of an aircraft, which affects or could affect the safety of operations.

6. Define the term *serious injury.* (NTSB Part 830.2)

Serious injury means any injury which:

a. Requires hospitalization for more than 48 hours, commencing within 7 days from the date the injury was received;

b. Results in a fracture of any bone (except simple fractures of fingers, toes, or nose);

c. Causes severe hemorrhages, nerve, muscle, or tendon damage;

d. Involves any internal organ; or

e. Involves second- or third-degree burns affecting more than 5 percent of the body surface.

7. Define the term *substantial damage.* (NTSB Part 830.2)

Substantial damage means damage or failure which adversely affects structural strength, performance or flight characteristics of the aircraft and which normally requires major repair or replacement of the affected component.

8. Will notification to the NTSB always be necessary in any aircraft accident even if there were no injuries? (NTSB Part 830)

Refer to the definition of accident. An aircraft accident can be substantial damage and/or injuries, and the NTSB always requires a report if this is the case.

9. Where are accident or incident reports filed? (NTSB Part 830)

The operator of an aircraft shall file any report with the field office of the Board nearest the accident or incident. NTSB contact information can be found at **ntsb.gov**.

FAA ATP
Qualifications
Job Aid

Appendix 1

Airline Transport Pilot (ATP)—Airplane Multiengine
Applicant Qualifications Job Aid
For Applicants Engaged in Operations Under 14 CFR Part 61 or 141

APPLICANT NAME:	DATE:

I. General Eligibility

A. Applicant Age § 61.153(a)(1) and (2)

1. At least 23 years old for an Airline Transport Pilot (ATP) Certificate (II.A. below)	
2. At least 21 years old for a restricted privileges ATP Certificate (II.B. below)	

B. English Language Requirement

C. Good Moral Character

D. Pilot Qualifications

1. FAA Commercial Pilot Certificate and an instrument rating **OR** FAA ATP Certificate with restricted privileges	
2. Official U.S. military records as prescribed in § 61.73	
3. A foreign commercial pilot license (CPL) with an instrument rating or a foreign ATP license with instrument privileges issued by an International Civil Aviation Organization (ICAO) country and contains no limitations and a valid verification letter obtained from AFB-720 (§ 61.71(c))	

E. Valid Certified Knowledge Test Report

F. Valid Graduation Certificate From an ATP Certification Training Program (CTP)

G. Current FAA Medical Certificate (at least Third Class) (not required if the test is completed entirely in a flight simulation training device (FSTD))

H. Part 135 Training and Qualification Records § 61.39(a) If using second in command (SIC) time logged in accordance with § 61.159(c)

II. Aeronautical Experience (Complete A or B)

A. ATP Certificate § 61.159

1. 1,500 hours of total flight time	
2. 250 hours as pilot in command (PIC) or as a required SIC performing the duties of PIC while under the supervision of a PIC, or any combination thereof (reference § 61.51 on logging time)	

3. 500 hours of cross-country flight time; 100 hours PIC cross-country flight time	
4. 100 hours of night flight time; 25 hours PIC night (may substitute landings)	
5. 75 hours of instrument flight time	
6. 50 hours of flight time in class (Up to 25 hours may be in a full flight simulator (FFS) representing a multiengine airplane may be credited toward the flight time requirement of § 61.159(a)(3) if the training was accomplished as part of an approved training course in part 121, 135, 141, or 142.)	
B. Restricted Privileges ATP certificate § 61.160 Applicants for a restricted privileges ATP Certificate must meet the requirements in 1, 2, 3, **OR** 4 below, **AND** the following:	
• 250 hours as PIC, or as a required SIC performing the duties of PIC while under the supervision of a PIC, or any combination thereof (reference § 61.51 on logging time)	
• 200 hours of cross-country flight time; 100 hours PIC cross-country flight time	
• 100 hours of night flight time, 25 hours PIC night flight time (may substitute landings)	
• 75 hours of instrument flight time	
• 50 hours of flight time in class (Up to 25 hours may be in a FFS representing a multiengine airplane may be credited toward the flight time requirement of this paragraph if the training was accomplished as part of an approved training course in part 121, 135, 141, or 142.)	
1. U.S. Military Pilot or Former U.S. Military Pilot	
• 750 hours of total time as a pilot	
• Required documentation per § 61.160(a)	
2. Graduate of a Bachelor's Degree Program with an Aviation Major	
• **1,000 hours of total time as a pilot** (students who have completed at least 60 credit hours in accordance with § 61.160(b)) **OR** • **1,250 hours of total time as pilot** (students who have completed at least 30, but less than 60 credit hours in accordance with § 61.160(d))	
• Certifying statement on official transcript or other acceptable document	

(continued)

3. Graduates of an Associate's Degree Program with an Aviation Major	
• **1,250 hours of total time as pilot** (students who have completed at least 30 credit hours in accordance with § 61.160(c))	
• Certifying statement on official transcript or other acceptable document	
4. 1,500 Hours Total Time as a Pilot	
• Meet the requirements of § 61.160(f)	

Source: FAA Order 8900.1, drs.faa.gov.

Applicant's Practical Test Checklist

Appendix 2

Applicant's Practical Test Checklist

Appointment with Examiner

Examiner's Name _____

Location _____

Date/Time _____

Note: Applicability of each item is contingent on the aircraft or flight simulation training device used.

Acceptable Aircraft

Aircraft Documents
___ Airworthiness certificate
___ Registration certificate
___ Operating limitations

Aircraft Maintenance Records
___ Logbook record of airworthiness inspections and AD compliance
___ Pilot's Operating Handbook, FAA-approved Airplane Flight Manual
___ Current weight and balance data

Personal Equipment

___ View-limiting device
___ Current aeronautical charts (printed or electronic)
___ Computer and plotter
___ Flight plan form
___ Flight logs (printed or electronic)
___ *Chart Supplements U.S.*, airport diagrams, and appropriate publications
___ Current FAR/AIM

Personal Records

___ Identification—photo/signature ID
___ Pilot certificate
___ Current medical certificate
___ Completed FAA Form 8710-1, Airman Certificate and/or Rating Application, with instructor's signature (or IACRA equivalent with applicant's FTN and application ID)

___ Original Knowledge Test Report
___ Pilot logbook with appropriate instructor endorsements
___ FAA Form 8060-5, Notice of Disapproval of Application
(if applicable)
___ Letter of Discontinuance (if applicable)
___ Approved school graduation certificate (if applicable)
___ Original ATP CTP graduation certificate (if applicable)
___ Evaluator's fee (if applicable)